The Credit Crunch

The Credit Crunch

Housing Bubbles, Globalisation
and the Worldwide Economic Crisis

GRAHAM TURNER

Pluto  Press

LONDON • ANN ARBOR, MI

in association with

GFC Economics

First published 2008 by Pluto Press
345 Archway Road, London N6 5AA
and 839 Greene Street, Ann Arbor, MI 48106

www.plutobooks.com

British Library Cataloguing in Publication Data
A catalogue record for this book is available from the British Library

ISBN   978 0 7453 2811 9   hardback
ISBN   978 0 7453 2810 2   paperback

Library of Congress Cataloging in Publication Data applied for

This book is printed on paper suitable for recycling and made from fully
managed and sustained forest sources. Logging, pulping and manufacturing
processes are expected to conform to the environmental standards of the
country of origin.

10   9   8   7   6   5   4   3   2   1

Designed and produced for Pluto Press by
Chase Publishing Services Ltd, Fortescue, Sidmouth, EX10 9QG, England
Typeset from disk by Stanford DTP Services, Northampton
Printed and bound in the European Union by
CPI Antony Rowe, Chippenham and Eastbourne

CONTENTS

List of Tables and Figures   vi
Preface   ix
Glossary   xiii
GFC Economics   xvi
Acknowledgements   xvii

1   Introduction   1
2   Global Contagion   14
3   Addicted to Debt   26
4   'Free Trade' and Asset Bubbles   48
5   Dealing With the Fallout   84
6   A Global Credit Bubble   109
7   Japan's Bear Market   135
8   Policy Failures in a Liquidity Trap   159
9   Where Are We Heading?   188

Notes   194
Index   222

LIST OF TABLES AND FIGURES

Tables

4.1	Manufacturing job losses under New Labour	70
6.1	South East Asia, balance of payments 1996	112
6.2	Foreign exchange reserves, various countries, December 2007	116
6.3	Turkey and South Africa, balance of payments 2006	119
6.4	Capital flight, South East Asia	124
6.5	Capital flight, various countries	125
6.6	Import cover ratios, various countries	126
6.7	Balance of payments, year before crisis	127
7.1	Japan property prices – the turning point	144

Figures

1.1	US house prices	2
2.1	US business investment/GDP, real terms	21
2.2	US consumption deflator, durables	22
2.3	US current account/GDP	24
3.1	US homeownership	31
3.2	US residential mortgages, foreclosures started	32
3.3	US residential mortgages, delinquencies	33
3.4	US household debt payments	34
3.5	US personal sector debt/disposable income	36
3.6	UK personal sector debt/disposable income	37
3.7	UK inflation	39
3.8	US inflation	39
3.9	UK average earnings	40
3.10	US average earnings	41
3.11	US trade balance	42
3.12	UK trade balance	42

3.13	US house prices	43
3.14	UK house prices	43
3.15	UK retail sales and mortgage approvals	46
4.1	US wages and salaries/GDP	49
4.2	UK real average earnings	49
4.3	China trade balance	52
4.4	US personal savings ratio	56
4.5	US home equity loans	58
4.6	China direct investment inflows/GDP	61
4.7	US trade balance with China	62
4.8	US trade balance with Mexico	63
4.9	UK trade balance	64
4.10	UK trade balance with China	65
4.11	UK trade balance with Poland	65
4.12	UK trade balance with Hungary	66
4.13	UK trade balance with Czech Republic	66
4.14	UK trade balance with India	67
4.15	UK trade balance with Turkey	67
4.16	UK manufacturing employment	68
4.17	UK business and financial services jobs	71
4.18	UK current account excluding financial services	72
4.19	UK net external assets/GDP	72
4.20	US manufacturing employment	74
4.21	Developing country imports	75
4.22	China imports from US/China imports	76
4.23	China imports from UK/China imports	77
4.24	China trade balance	78
5.1	US asset-backed securities, mortgages	91
5.2	US durables 'inflation', consumer price index and import price index	93
5.3	UK retail sales deflator, non-food stores	94
5.4	UK retail sales deflator, household goods	95
5.5	OECD consumer prices 1971–79	104
5.6	OECD consumer prices 2000–08	105
6.1	Foreign exchange reserves	115
6.2	Eastern Europe and UK, private domestic debt	118
6.3	Baltic Three and UK, private domestic debt	119

6.4	CIS, private domestic debt	121
7.1	Japan land prices, nationwide	143
7.2	Japan land prices, six largest cities	145
7.3	Japan money supply, M2+CDs	145
7.4	Discount rate and yen/$	147
7.5	Japan domestic wholesale prices	148
7.6	Japan velocity of circulation, M1	153
8.1	Japan nationwide land prices	160
8.2	Japan savings, worker households	161
8.3	Japan corporate bankruptcies and bond yields	163
8.4	Japan yield curve	166
8.5	Japan government debt	167
8.6	US Fed funds target adjusted by core consumption deflator	171
8.7	Japan compensation of employees	173
8.8	Japan banks assets, JGBs	176
8.9	Japan bank lending and deposits	177
8.10	Japan, BoJ assets/GDP	179
8.11	Japan consumption deflator	184

PREFACE

'Save Burberry jobs, save Burberry jobs', they chanted. Around 60 angry residents had travelled from the former mining town of Treorchy in South Wales, to protest outside Burberry's flagship stores in London's expensive New Bond Street and Regent Street.

On 6 September 2006, 300 workers at the Burberry factory in the Rhondda Valley had fallen victims to 'commercial logic'. The factory at Treorchy had been producing clothes since 1939 and had been taken over by Burberry in 1989. Now the jobs were heading to China. Treorchy was no longer financially 'viable' the company claimed.[1] It cost £11 to make one of its popular polo shirts in South Wales, but in China, it would cost £4. With the power of the Burberry brand, they would sell for £60.[2]

Burberry had underestimated the backlash. Devastated by the closure of so many coal mines, Wales had also lost more than 46,000 manufacturing jobs since the mid 1990s.[3] The workers of Treorchy vowed to fight the closure, and enlisted the backing of local hero Tom Jones, Manchester United manager Sir Alex Ferguson, and actors Ioan Gruffudd, Rhys Ifans and Emma Thompson. Defiant to the last, the residents campaigned hard to keep the factory open.

They failed, and on 30 March 2007, the workers marched from the factory gates through the streets of Treorchy, joined by a male voice choir, for their final rally in the town.

And for what? Like so many others, the luxury retailer had concluded that it could raise its profits by relocating somewhere cheaper. The annual cost savings of £1.5 million were less than 1 per cent of the company's operating profits.[4] But any boost to the bottom line, however small, would in theory boost the company's share price. And it did, for a short while.

Less than a year after the factory closed, Burberry was forced to issue a profit warning. Its share price fell more than 16 per cent in one day. From the high of 725.5 pence reached a month after the factory's demise, Burberry's share price had slumped to 406.5 pence. As the credit crunch intensified, it carried on sliding, hitting a low of 364 pence.[5] The share price had fallen 49.9 per cent in less than a year. Free trade based around the simple premise of cost cutting was not working, and not just for the people of the Rhondda Valley.

It was a stunning reversal, and one small example of what has gone wrong in the world economy. The credit bubble is the direct result of numerous companies across the West abusing free trade, moving jobs offshore simply to boost profit margins. It has not worked for Burberry, because companies need consumers to buy. Consumers need jobs to be able to buy their goods and services. And they cannot do that indefinitely by getting deeper into debt.

As more and more companies fled the West in search of cheaper production bases, the central banks were obliged to keep interest rates low, to stimulate economic growth. The rise in debt was the flipside of jobs being lost to the East. Eventually, the credit bubble burst. As an economic strategy, it made little sense, even for the Burberrys of this world. After seven years of debt-fuelled growth, stock markets are now lower than they were in 2000.[6] Free trade driven by cost cutting feeds and nourishes credit bubbles. It does not benefit the workers, but it has failed corporations too.

This book is not an attack on free trade. It merely seeks to unravel the causes of the credit bubble and the inevitable implosion of housing markets. Free trade is a good thing, but not when it is used by companies simply as a ruse to cut costs. The West has seen a build-up in debt levels that will take years to unwind. And the risks of serious policy mistakes aggravating the fallout are high. This book also draws a number of parallels with Japan's experience of *debt deflation*, which the authorities are ignoring. Debt deflation occurs when falling prices push up the real burden of debts, precipitating more defaults, triggering bigger price declines thus perpetuating a vicious cycle. The Federal

Reserve left it too late to start cutting interest rates. And it was too slow in stemming the tidal wave of foreclosures.

This book suggests the blame should not be laid exclusively at the doors of financial institutions, central banks or regulatory authorities – though much of the criticism now aimed in their direction is unequivocally justified. The reckless lending policies fuelled the bubble and will aggravate the long downturn.

But if we limit our focus, we shall fail to understand the real cause of the credit bubble. The politicians who stood by and let debt levels rise remorselessly, accepting the plaudits while the economies ostensibly boomed, are the real culprits. The subprime lenders were given a green light by the Federal Reserve, because the US politicians wanted economic growth, at any cost. Democrats and Republicans signed up to the free trade agreements that drained jobs from the heart of industrial America, caused the real median wage to fall and led to an inexorable rise in debt.

Northern Rock was a bank out of control because it was not supervised. The Financial Services Authority and Bank of England failed because they ignored the warning signs. But New Labour was the architect of an economic policy that created the monster of Northern Rock. Gordon Brown boasted repeatedly that the economy was enjoying the best performance for three centuries, even though it was built on nothing more than debt.

If the West is sinking in a sea of red ink, supporters of free trade will argue that many developing countries have at least benefited. But we shall show that this is a fallacy too. They have also become subsumed by grotesque credit bubbles. In a large number of cases, their borrowing has risen faster than that of even the UK or US. And they are also heading for trouble. The great unwind began with the US, but will end with many of the emerging market economies.

The damage inflicted by these credit bubbles will depend on how the authorities respond. If they make the same mistakes as the Bank of Japan in the 1990s, we are all in trouble. There will be a backlash against free trade, and the recessions will be steep and prolonged. If we learn the lessons quickly, the world economy may bounce back in short order. But time is running out. As the world's largest consumer, the US is key. A deep recession here seems inevitable. The US housing market has imploded, and the authorities have vastly underestimated the scale of the problem. The US threatens to drag the rest of the Industrialised West into the mire. The UK, weighed down by an even bigger debt burden than the US, is acutely exposed to a prolonged unravelling of the credit bubble.

The roots of this crisis must be understood to ensure there is no repeat of the flawed economic policies that have created the biggest credit bust since the 1930s. If we understand the causes, the damage can be mitigated. It may seem perverse, but deep interest rate cuts are mandatory irrespective of the rise in oil prices, to stem the risks of a debt trap taking hold. Extreme monetary policy responses including quantitative easing will be necessary. Public bailouts and nationalisation of banks that run into trouble will become more frequent.

But governments will have to realign their policy away from the exclusive promotion of 'big business' that lies at the heart of the recent credit bubbles. Fostering free trade with the 'benefits' too heavily skewed in favour of companies has created the pretext for asset deflation. The bubble will take years to unwind. In that time, a new economic agenda will arise, one that balances the interests of companies and workers more evenly, and promotes a free trade that does not fuel the boom and bust seen today.

GLOSSARY

Asset Inflation – A continuous rise in either property prices or the stock market.

Average Earnings – Monthly average wages or salaries, per person.

Balance of Payments – A broader term for a country's external transactions, including the current account and capital flows (see below).

Bank of England – Central bank of the United Kingdom.

Bank of Japan – Central bank of Japan.

Capital Account – The net inflows and outflows of all capital, financial and real, i.e., bonds, equities, loans and direct investment (see below).

Capital Inflows/Outflows/flows – Measure of external transactions in assets, including equities, bonds and direct investment.

Credit Crunch – A sudden downturn in lending precipitated by distress at financial institutions.

Current Account – Measure of a country's net transactions in goods, services, income and transfers.

Debt Deflation – High levels of debt leading to falling asset prices.

Debt Trap – Attempts to pay off outstanding loans lead to a higher debt burden, as a result of the negative impact on prices.

Deflation – The opposite of inflation, whereby prices are falling.

Delinquencies – Borrowers missing repayments on debt.

Direct Investment – Investment into another country, into real estate or fixed assets, such as factories.

European Central Bank – Central bank of the 27 countries in the Eurozone.

External Assets/Debt – Assets or debt held by the citizens, companies or the government in another country.

Federal Reserve – Central bank of the US.

Financial Balance – The International Monetary Fund's broadest measure of capital flows, including direct investment.

Foreclosure – Properties foreclose when borrowers default and banks repossess the asset.

Foreign Exchange Reserves – Central banks hold reserves, either in gold or a foreign currency, notably dollars, but also sterling, euros and yen, to help provide a buffer against foreign sellers of their domestic currency.

Gross Domestic Product (GDP) – A broad indicator reflecting the size of an economy, usually in terms of output, but also in terms of spending and income.

Intervention – Central banks intervene when they try to influence the direction of a currency or exchange rate, usually when attempting to provide support.

Keynesian Liquidity Trap – Keynes identified a liquidity trap would occur when long term bond yields could no longer fall by natural means, and had reached a point of resistance. Liquidity traps usually occur after interest rates have been cut to their lowest point.

Money illusion – Investors or consumers suffer from money illusion when they overemphasise the nominal return on assets, nominal interest rate or nominal wages, by failing to take into account sufficiently either inflation or deflation.

Overinvestment – Usually refers to an economy where the proportion diverted to capital spending in real terms has reached a high and unsustainable proportion of the economy.

Peak Oil – Peak in the production of oil, by one or more countries.

Private Domestic Debt – Reflects borrowing by individuals and companies within an economy.

Private Sector Credit – Reflects borrowing by individuals and companies within an economy.

Sterilised Intervention – Central banks sterilise their intervention when they buy or sell domestic debt or securities, to absorb the impact of intervention on money supply. For example, intervention to stop a currency or exchange rate appreciating necessarily leads to an increase in domestic money supply. Sterilised intervention aims to reduce the money supply. The opposite applies when central banks intervene to support the domestic exchange rate.

Supply Side – Usually refers to economic policies that emphasise tax cuts or cuts in costs, possibly through reform of the labour market, to try and make an economy grow faster.

Trade Balance – A narrower measure than the current account. This reflects the net flow of a country's trade in just goods. The current account includes goods, as well as services, income and transfers. Transfers are not capital flows, but may typically include government aid abroad, or aid received.

Unit Labour Costs – A measure of total wage costs per unit of output produced by workers/employees.

Unsterilised Intervention – Intervention where the central bank does not seek to offset the impact on money supply.

GFC ECONOMICS

GFC Economics is an independent economic consultancy based in London. Founded in 1999, it services more than sixty major financial institutions across the world, providing in depth analysis of economic developments as they impact on financial markets.

For more information, please email Pat Sharp at Pat.Sharp@gfceconomics.com or Graham Turner at Graham.Turner@gfceconomics.com, or visit www.gfceconomics.com

ACKNOWLEDGEMENTS

All Charts are provided courtesy of Datastream.

Retrospective simulations were carried out by Oxford Economic Forecasting.

Graham Turner would like to thank Pat Sharp of GFC Economics for her unstinting support and assistance in helping to produce this book. Thanks also to Vanessa Rossi at Oxford Economic Forecasting, for important insights and expertise in the realm of econometrics. Thanks also to Hayley Male for valuable editing during her two weeks at GFC Economics. Thanks to Roger van Zwanenberg of Pluto Press for giving GFC Economics the chance to state its case, and for his patience. Thanks also to Ray Addicott and Oliver Howard of Chase Publishing Services for their expertise. Finally, a big thanks to Jackie for providing the time and space to complete the book.

Solutions to a Liquidity Trap: Japan's Bear Market and What it Means for the West

Published by GFC Economics (June 2003)

Solutions to a Liquidity Trap is an in depth analysis of Japan's long bear market and examines in detail the policy mistakes made by the Japanese authorities as they battled against more than a decade of deflation. It contains a strong historical narrative of all the financial crises that erupted from 1990 onwards, in chronological order, including a detailed record of all the key bankruptcies that wreaked so much havoc.

It also contains the retrospective simulations referred to in *The Credit Crunch*, carried out with Oxford Economic Forecasting, which show how different policy outcomes from the Bank of Japan may have averted deflation.

To order a copy of *Solutions to a Liquidity Trap* please send a cheque for £25 (includes postage and packaging) to GFC Economics, Suite 220, 3 Coborn Road, Bow, London E3 2DA.

1

INTRODUCTION

The US is embroiled in economic crisis. The housing market is suffering its biggest slump since the 1930s. Across the US, house prices were falling by an annualised rate of 17.5 per cent in the final three months of 2007 (see Figure 1.1). Distressed sellers have seen property prices tumble by up to 50 per cent in some areas of the US.[1] Record defaults and the prospect that more than 2 million families may lose their home in 2008 alone, signals capitalism's biggest test in the post-war era. The credit shock is reverberating across the Industrialised World. Ten years of growth financed by record borrowing are starting to unravel in the UK. Property markets are imploding in Spain, Ireland and across Euroland. And the world's third largest economy, Japan, shows no sign of winning its long, tortuous 18-year battle with deflation.

Globalisation predicated on unfettered markets is going awry. The housing bubbles were not an accident, spawned simply by careless regulatory oversight. They were a necessary component of the incessant drive to expand free trade at all costs. Dominant corporate power became the primary driving force for economic expansion. Profits were allowed to soar. A growing share of the national income was absorbed by companies at the expense of workers. And the record borrowing provided a short term panacea, to bridge the yawning wage gap that ineluctably followed. Governments fostered housing bubbles to stay in power. Consumers were encouraged to borrow, to ensure there would be enough economic growth.

With the US housing market in freefall and the UK suffering its first bank run since 1878, the mainstream financial press has been turning in on itself, searching for scapegoats.[2] Regulators,

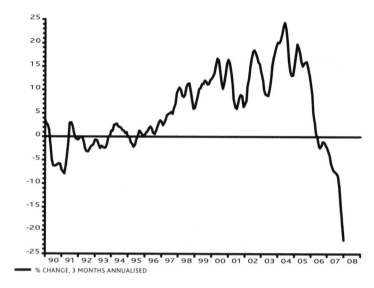

Figure 1.1 US House Prices

Source: S&P/Case-Shiller, Home Price Index, 10-City Composite.

central banks and management at the more reckless banks have been selectively targeted and criticised for their lack of due diligence. The opprobrium heaped on chosen culprits sanctifies and provides redemption for those that failed to spot the inherent dangers in allowing economic growth to be financed by untrammelled borrowing.

But there is no mention of the underlying causes of this explosion in debt. These commentators dare not venture there, out of fear that the contradictions and flaws with the economic philosophy they have espoused will be exposed. Greed is good, but some just got a little carried away. Rap a few knuckles, offer a few sacrificial lambs and let the party recommence.

Financial markets have been bailed out before, there is no reason to stop and take a hard look at how we arrived here. That would be too painful and would force recognition of the brutal truth: such an uneven society breeds asset bubbles. Rising inequality explicitly leads to extreme house price cycles. If we want to get off this destructive rollercoaster, the limits to unbridled trade need to be acknowledged. The case for a more even distribution of income has to be accepted too.

In a bid to preserve a status quo, few meaningful policy changes of substance have been mooted or advocated, far less promoted. The collapse of the dotcom bubble saw a mere tweaking of regulation, a few token limited fines, and the next wave of speculation was fermented to drive economic growth. Under government sanction, central banks stepped back from the plate and facilitated a cataclysmic accumulation of debt.

With companies given such free rein to drive wage costs down, creating property inflation became a necessary stimulus for economic growth in the Industrialised West. After the precipitous meltdown in high-tech share prices during the early part of this decade, few governments complained when strong consumer borrowing and a proliferation of debt provided the fuel for economic recovery. And few objected as an explosion in credit trading buried in a blizzard of abbreviations – MBS (mortgage-backed securities), CDOs (collateralised debt obligations), CDS (credit default swaps) or SIVs (structured investment vehicles) – allowed banks to conceal the inevitable risks from an unsuspecting and pliant public.

Money Illusion

Indeed, rising house prices became symbolic, a modern era indicator of wealth and success. House prices were soaring, we must all be better off. Never mind that debt was rising too. Never mind that house price inflation is a zero sum game. Society as a whole does not benefit from a rise in house prices. Those already on the ladder can only gain at the expense of a growing number unable to reach the first rung.

In the short run, housing bubbles can provide a stimulus to economic growth if they hoodwink people into believing they are wealthier. And governments that have been promoting the free trade and profits first agenda are content to foster the delusion. Indeed, governments rely upon *money illusion*, hoping homeowners will take a myopic view of their record debts. Witness New Labour's boast – 'ten years of GDP growth, the longest for 300 years'.[3] Growth was everything, it told the electorate. Runaway house prices were a function of the strong economy and a shortage of properties. A similar refrain was widely uttered in Japan during the late 1980s. Record debt levels did not matter, it was claimed, because property prices were soaring. Just focus on the asset side of the balance sheet. Eighteen years on, Japan is still suffering from that disastrous miscalculation.

Therein lie the dangers facing governments today. Japan struggled to defy the march of asset deflation, slashing interest rates to zero, pushing all the fiscal levers available and running up record budget deficits. For more than a decade, it did not work. Finally, the Bank of Japan resorted to extreme measures, printing money and buying government debt in one last desperate bid to reflate. It succeeded for a short while, but only because Japan was able to ride the crest of a boom in China and other emerging market economies.

But the curse of deflation soon returned, led by another onslaught on the incomes of Japanese workers. Wages started to contract again – in both nominal and real terms – even as company profits soared to record highs. Japan had tried to model itself on the Anglo-Saxon way of doing business, restructuring, rationalising and putting the pursuit of profits first. However, that simply pushed the economy back into the deflation quagmire, which first snared Japan following the stock market peak on 31 December 1989. Even the Bank of Japan now admits globalisation and competition from low-cost foreign producers has broken the transmission mechanism, with profits rising but wages falling.[4]

Growing income inequalities are an affliction for all of the Industrialised World, not just Japan. But Japan's experience should be salutary. Successive Japanese governments have responded to deflation by introducing aggressive pro-market policies, and the country has become more competitive. Labour costs have now fallen for eight consecutive years and its exports have soared.[5] But it has still failed to shake off deflation as consumer confidence plummeted again in 2007, threatening to send the economy back into recession.

US – Heading into a Debt Trap?

For the US, the stakes are already high. A two-and-a-half year downturn in the housing market is in danger of spiralling out of control despite the Federal Reserve's belated decision to cut interest rates in the autumn of 2007. The US authorities lost valuable time. Federal Reserve officials were sidetracked by numerous voices claiming inflation would continue to accelerate.

Inflation is not the primary issue, precisely because of the free market policies that feed and nourish property bubbles in the first place. Just as Japan overestimated inflation pressures at the top of its housing boom in the late 1980s, the US and UK are also exaggerating the risks. The same downward pressure on wages, the income inequalities and the rise in profit ratios that have driven asset prices, will ensure that any pick-up in inflation will be constrained.[6]

Oil and food are a problem. Climate change and Peak Oil constitute fundamental costs that will have to be borne by producers and consumers alike. Nevertheless, a closer examination of the consumer prices indices suggests that by the beginning of 2008, the underlying inflation rate was running at little more than 2 per cent in the US and 1 per cent in the UK. In Euroland, it was just over 1.5 per cent.[7] The bigger secular threat for all these industrialised nations imitating Japan may well prove to be one of falling asset prices leading to a debt trap – or debt deflation.

And the theory of debt deflation, first put forward by US economist Irving Fisher in response to the depression of the 1930s, now provides a key template for the risks facing all industrialised economies. An aggressive free market response to a debt crisis could easily serve to make the problem worse and any collapse in asset prices more entrenched. Many of the same commentators who underestimated the debt risks now claim 'markets will have to clear'. This, they argue, can only happen by allowing lenders to fail. Miscreants have to go under, to teach others a lesson. Capitalism purges itself by the economic equivalent of natural selection.

But a policy of tough love only works if central banks are alert to the dangers. Too often these voices drown out the counter arguments predicated on historical experience. And they illustrate the folly of allowing the market to operate unchecked. Attempts to dispose of bad debts and repossess properties may lead to more deflation and push more lenders into trouble. The debt burden may go up in real terms, not down. And the cycle may just repeat itself until such point that a systemic financial crisis signals the need for a change of policy. Even then critics will claim there is no other way, arguing that one more round of bank failures will soon bring the debt trap to a close. Instead, it may simply prolong the fallout.[8]

Japan's experience also highlights the dangers that many economies in the Industrialised West may yet slip into a Keynesian liquidity trap. The attempts to reflate may not succeed if investors take fright at a perceived inflation threat. The economist John Maynard Keynes was quite clear in his prognosis: interest rates had to come down quickly in a housing bust. If that did not work then there would be a clear case for government intervention to correct the market's failings.

If the authorities bail out lenders too early, mistakes will be repeated. It is a fine line between going too early and leaving it too late – the moral hazard argument. In the UK, the housing market started slowing sharply from the summer of 2004 onwards.[9] At the turn of 2005, fears of a property crash were widespread. But just one rate cut by the Monetary Policy Committee in August of that year was enough to convince legions of buy-to-let 'investors' and other speculators that property remained a one-way bet to riches. A new wave of landlords succeeded in crowding out first-time buyers and driving homeownership down.

In a similar vein, cutting interest rates to 1.0 per cent in 2003 has widely been cited as the primary cause of the US housing bubble. But the Federal Reserve had little choice. Recent housing bubbles have not been the fault of central banks *per se*, but of governments allowing corporate power to exploit wage differentials in the pursuit of higher profit margins. As a result, overinvestment in high technology during the dotcom boom was quickly followed by a precipitous decline in pricing power that threatened deflation and a steep recession. Unemployment was heading up, and as it was, the jobless total still climbed by nearly 4 million even with the deep rate cuts.[10]

Free and easy credit was widely held responsible for Japan's property bubble and subsequent collapse. Frustrated by the rising trade imbalance between the two countries and a subsequent slide in the dollar, the US administration put pressure on the Japanese Ministry of Finance and Bank of Japan to slash borrowing costs. During the summer of 1987, interest rates fell to an unthinkable 2.5 per cent.[11] But at this early stage, Japan was already gripped by endemic overinvestment and a squeeze on wages that would consume the rest of the West two decades later. That was the fundamental imbalance which led inexorably to Japan's housing bubble.

Unbalanced Globalisation

Cutting interest rates aggressively during an economic downturn triggered by a housing collapse is never a complete solution. An easier monetary policy does not cure the roots of a speculative mania. That way lies a revaluation of the political economy that begets asset inflation in the first place. Indeed, should central banks get their timing right and succeed in reflating the economy, that may simply allow governments to deflect any searching examination of the inequities that presaged overinvestment and excessive borrowing in the first place.

And one of the key inequities that must be addressed is the galloping pace of globalisation with inadequate checks and balances to corporate power. The rapid growth in world trade has been trumpeted as one of the key economic triumphs of a free market. It seems churlish to quibble when world GDP growth has been unrelentingly strong over the past four years.[12]

But dig a little below the surface and the picture is not quite so benign. The systematic tearing down of trade barriers in the absence of appropriate protection and rights for ordinary workers accelerated a two-decade trend towards higher profit ratios in the West. That was unsustainable. Profit ratios can only continue to rise at the expense of a further decline in the share of national income taken by labour income, or wages. And such a divergence will increase the tendency and political pressure for consumer borrowing and house price inflation to fill the gap, between over-investment and inadequate demand.

And this dichotomy will ultimately trigger a financial crisis that will lead to a sudden reversal in profit margins. Ironically, and perhaps unwittingly, the point was made eloquently by the current Federal Reserve chairman, Ben Bernanke, in January 2004. He endorsed a key tenet from overinvestment theories, the 'tendency of the rate of profit to fall', which explains much of the lurch from boom to bust in today's deregulated markets.[13] By deduction, profit ratios can only increase *ad infinitum* by heightening the long term threat of debt deflation.

We should draw a distinction between rising profit *ratios* and high profit *levels*. The latter may occur in a more sustainable direction if free trade is matched by appropriate labour rights, so that consumption can rise without governments having to foster asset inflation as a substitute for economic growth. Hence, it is in the long term interests of free trade advocates to allow a greater share of the spoils to accrue to workers. It is also in their interest to permit a more even distribution of wages given the clear differences in marginal propensity to consume between income groups.

Relocation, Relocation

But emboldened by their success in pushing profit ratios up to a four-decade high, they remain unwilling to temper their unquenchable enthusiasm for raw, free trade. Each and every company has the incentive to push the boundary of globalisation to its limit. If my competitor can relocate from low-cost China to an even cheaper Vietnam, so should I. Indeed, if I do not, my competitor will drive me out of business. Out of a naked self-interest, companies will never voluntarily agree to partake in a less uneven and destabilising mode of globalisation.

Similarly, left to their own devices, multinational corporations will have little incentive to prevent global warming, inflicting irreparable damage upon the climate. Food shortages are already appearing and prices are climbing. Climate change may ostensibly appear to heighten the risks of inflation.[14] But instead, it will aggravate the threat of debt deflation in the West due to the very dominance companies enjoy over workers. Debt deflation – a cycle of falling asset prices pushing up the real debt burden and defaults – can and will coexist with persistently high headline inflation. Indeed, the inability of workers to match rising food prices with higher wages implies climate change will simply squeeze real incomes, making it harder for consumers to spend on other goods and services. But that is not for companies to fret over. If they pay any more than lip service to the damage their trading practices inflict on the environment, in today's global economy they will suffer a competitive disadvantage.

The only resolution can come from governments acting in unity to ensure an orderly rebalancing of worker and environmental rights vis-à-vis the all pervading dominance of corporations. It can not happen in isolation. France has tried it with attempts to limit the working week, but its efforts were undercut by European neighbours and other competitors, who remained engaged in a race to drive down labour costs. Real wage rates in Germany have experienced their longest period of contraction in modern times, and they are still going down.[15] Their export industries may have outperformed their French counterparts. But wage growth across Euroland has been too weak in the past five years to sustain domestic growth. And consumer spending has slumped, both in Germany and countries that had ridden high on housing bubbles.[16] The collapse of the property market was hitting the once high-flying Spanish economy hard, with a vicious downturn in consumption.[17]

Here again, governments have thus resorted to house price bubbles to drive economic recovery and bring unemployment down. The strategy has not worked in the US, and it is coming unhinged in Euroland as well as the UK. Indeed, governments today behave no differently from the typical self-interested multinational corporation, vying for the most competitive edge – not just on labour rights but also on taxes and the environment

– in a short term bid for growth. But they have only secured growth by deliberately creating credit booms.

Cross border labour unions are an obvious riposte to overarching corporations. But here again, the real impact of globalisation is thrown into stark relief. Even if unions in the steel sector, for example, were to unite across a hundred countries – a tall order indeed – there would still be many more countries where producers could choose to relocate. Companies that are now bigger than many small and medium countries can play one off against the other. Wal-Mart is now China's eighth biggest trading partner.[18]

And it is the threat of relocation that proves just as powerful as the reality of a transfer somewhere cheaper. Accept more flexible terms, or we will walk. This is arguably the overriding and most significant point of globalisation that led to rising profit ratios and housing bubbles. It is the stick for companies to beat workers into accepting a smaller share of the national income pie.

Proponents of free trade claim the growth of emerging markets and the rise in demand for 'high value exports' from the Industrialised West will more than compensate for the loss of lower skilled jobs. However, the argument is falling short on two counts. For the two-way transfer to succeed, exchange rates have to be allowed to reflect the new equilibrium offered by reduced barriers and increased trade flows. A failure of this rebalancing to occur anywhere near enough has accentuated the risks of debt deflation in the West.

China is a key example. Chinese workers are not necessarily more productive than their Western counterparts. They are just cheaper, more abundant and receive fewer labour rights. Their average incomes may have risen over the past decade, but not enough to compensate for the loss of earnings in the West. As a result, China over-invests and under-consumes, and at current exchange rates, there can be no realignment of supply and demand. Chinese import demand will remain woefully inadequate, precisely because the economy is deliberately structured to underpin the corporate-led model driving the Industrialised West.[19] Exchange rates will have to adjust sharply, but in the short run, that may aggravate the fallout.

The accumulation of trade surpluses in emerging markets and huge foreign exchange reserves mirrored the explosion of consumer debt in the West. Governments in industrialised economies have appeased the process, because it fits neatly with their avowed strategy of promoting free trade irrespective of the costs. And the asset bubbles that fill the gap in demand allow them to deceive their citizens into believing that globalisation in its current format works. Developing countries hardly dare challenge the rules of the game, lest it should jeopardise their place at the world trading table.

Western companies are not in a rush to challenge the status quo either. They benefit from the increased leverage over workers in their domestic markets, but profit from their overseas operations too. Hence, China is now a major profit source for many Western companies.[20] A growing share of UK and US companies' profits are derived from abroad. As these returns flow to shareholders, that further exacerbates income inequalities at home.

This is only one part of the story. The free trade argument falls down in its current guise because it makes no allowance for the increased income inequality that it drives intra-country, i.e., between a nation's citizens. Trade flows may have flourished since the creation of the World Trade Organisation in 1995. That is not in dispute. The argument is not about reactivating trade barriers *per se*, but creating a more even balance of power between omnipotent capital and weak labour, and not just in the Industrialised West.

China is growing rapidly, not through its own innovation, but simply because it provides multinationals with the opportunity to cut costs, and with huge consequences for the environment and income distribution. Even supporters of free trade have looked on in horror, as the growth of multi-billionaires in developing economies and plutocracy endangers the legitimacy of globalisation.[21] There are other ways to foster free trade that do not depend simply upon driving profit ratios up and labour incomes down, with the attendant fallout for debt and inequality.

But a rebalancing of corporate versus labour rights can also be achieved by reversing policies that have allowed companies to become dominant. The easy lending fostered by Western governments has fuelled mergers, takeovers and acquisitions by private equity funds that concentrates corporate power, underpinning the fundamental forces that create asset bubbles. Tighter lending restrictions are critical to restoring the imbalance between corporate and labour power. Mergers that create corporate monoliths and increase market dominance need to be resisted. More appropriate tariffs and constraints need to be applied to trade in goods and services where the price mechanism fails to reflect the environmental costs. And such a tariff may be necessary where increased trade is no longer a reflection of any comparative advantage, but simply a means to exploit wage differentials.

Only time will tell whether governments and central banks can prevent the inherent flaws of rising profit ratios and over accumulation of capital tipping countries into debt deflation. The omens are not encouraging. The US is certainly the major, pivotal risk in the decade-long experiment with corporate-led globalisation. The US authorities are running out of time. A backlash against the shortcomings of today's unregulated free trade model is gathering momentum. And the country is sinking deeper into a Japanese-style debt trap that could take years to unwind.

Japan's experience remains invaluable for central banks in the West today as they grapple with record personal sector debt burdens. In Chapters 7 and 8, we look at how Japan's bubble deflated, and the key mistakes made by the Bank of Japan and successive governments, recounting some of the country's major financial crises. The credit bubbles that have swept emerging market economies are discussed in some detail in Chapter 6. The extreme levels of borrowing were not an accident. They followed ineluctably from the free trade policies pursued by the West. In Chapter 5, we address the policy issues that follow from today's housing market collapse and the lessons that need to be drawn for politicians today. In Chapter 4, we examine the issues and arguments around globalisation in the context of housing bubbles. The Industrialised West is not alone in suffering from excessive borrowing over recent years. In Chapter 3, we show just how important it was for governments to create housing bubbles, to mask shortcomings in their promotion of free trade. But we start, in Chapter 2, by examining the historical context of today's financial turmoil.

2

GLOBAL CONTAGION

The recent turmoil in financial markets has a familiar ring. Whether it is the crash of 1987, the housing slumps of the early 1990s, South East Asia in 1997, hedge fund Long Term Capital Management in 1998 or the unravelling of dotcom mania, the world economy has grappled with a succession of financial crises over the past two decades. And yet, each time the global financial apparatus withstood the onslaught and, it would appear, came back stronger and more robust than before. Every blow seemed to only make the economic polity more resilient. Encouraged, the major actors in this evolution of a new era in unfettered markets took on bigger, bolder and more aggressive bets in the pursuit of relentlessly higher profits.

But there is a distinction that needs to be drawn between these numerous crises. The first two were remnants of the battle against inflation and were characterised by *overconsumption*. In the classic monetarist phase, there was too much demand chasing not enough supply. However, from 1997 onwards, the financial panics were disinflationary or deflation shocks, driven by the increasing dominance of big business and its ultimate manifestation – overproduction and *overinvestment*.[1] Financial crises are as old as capitalism. But in recent years, they have evolved in response to a shift in the balance of power between corporations and workers. A pronounced swing in the relative strength of capital versus labour lies at the heart of today's financial turbulence.

The ability of companies to invest and expand aggressively has waxed and waned over the decades. During the 1920s, a proliferation of investment opportunities in the US, triggered by a boom in autos and the introduction of mass production techniques, saw capital spending rise sharply. New consumer goods such as radios, refrigerators and vacuum cleaners were unknown at the start of the 1920s, but were ubiquitous by 1929.

The crisis of overinvestment was only possible because workers were marginalised and union power was weak – in many cases non-existent. Overinvestment triggered a financial crisis because wages did not rise enough to allow workers to absorb the increased output of goods. They were encouraged to borrow instead, and between 1925 and 1929, US consumer debt more than doubled.[2]

The Wall Street crash of October 1929 was a response to this critical imbalance between supply and demand, between capital and labour. There was little inflation, and prices for many goods had been under concerted downward pressure. Prices for furniture and household durables fell by 5.6 per cent between 1926 and 1929. Many other goods and commodities were suffering from deflation.[3] Speculators had misread the potential return from such heady investments, because they failed to recognise the importance of higher wages in driving a balanced and sustainable economy.

The subsequent depression of the 1930s was aggravated by a series of policy mistakes, including the reluctance of the Federal Reserve to cut interest rates quickly. A failure to intervene and prevent the collapse of so many financial institutions also led to a steep contraction in the availability of credit, exacerbating the downturn. The rise of trade barriers as governments sought to protect their own industries from the logic of overinvestment, compounded the fallout.[4] But they could not prevent the decline in prices from accelerating. Within four years of the crash, prices for furniture and household durables had plunged a further 20.3 per cent. Motor vehicle prices had dropped 12.9 per cent. The rate of deflation intensified sharply for a wide range of goods.[5]

The ensuing economic strife provided fertile breeding ground for the extremism that led ineluctably to the Second World War. The prescient warning of economist John Maynard Keynes at the end of the First World War was disregarded by the politicians signing the Versailles Peace Treaty. Instead, they seized the opportunity to expropriate some of Germany's assets, enlarging a capital base that would merely accelerate the pace of overinvestment for the winners, and fuel hyperinflation for the losers.[6]

Attempts to penalise Germany with untenable demands for reparations compounded the folly. They would, Keynes argued, precipitate such economic and political difficulties that all of Europe 'would ultimately lose the peace'.[7] In this sense, the over-investment crisis of the late 1920s proved even more cataclysmic, propelling a downward spiral of the German economy, and the arrival of Adolf Hitler onto the world stage.[8]

The Pendulum Swings

The 1930s depression left a deep political scar, and after the Second World War a strong consensus emerged for a more equitable distribution of income, replete with greater rights for workers. There was a marked shift from the laissez faire *modus operandi* of the 1920s. Over the next two decades, enhanced labour protection seemed to offer little barrier to sustained economic growth. Indeed, they went hand in hand with a prolonged rise in living standards for many.

By the early 1970s, however, inflation had started to accelerate, and within a decade that had ushered in the arrival of Thatcherism and Reaganomics. Under the guise of monetarism, both leaders ostensibly sought to curb union rights in a bid to tame inflation. Indeed, high inflation itself became a political weapon to attack the labour movement. Year-long battles against the miners' union and printworkers were the defining moments of a shift in the economic landscape in the UK. President Reagan's showdown with air traffic controllers marked a similar sea-change in the balance of power between unions and employers in the US.

The net result was a series of steep recessions as governments sought to bring down inflation through a mix of high interest rates and rising unemployment. Set in this context, the first two of these financial crises – the stock market crash of 1987 and the housing slumps of the early 1990s – were essentially hangovers from the battle to tame inflation. Central banks were still engaged in a war of attrition, to drive inflation expectations down.

In mitigation, the 22.6 per cent or 508 points decline in the Dow Jones Industrials recorded on 27 October 1987 was preceded by only a modest rise in short term interest rates. Borrowing costs had risen by just 1 per cent during the year beforehand. At face value, the plunge in share prices would appear to have been a correction to a rather dizzying rise in share prices. The Dow Jones Industrials had jumped 44 per cent in less than ten months.

However, there had been a steep climb in long term rates driven by the fear of inflation – which at the time was well founded. The dollar was falling in response to a rising trade deficit. Rapid growth in demand from the US consumer and a Reagan Administration engaged in an arms race with the Soviet Union, was met by a sharp rise in imports. The underlying inflation rate would eventually rise to a peak of 5.6 per cent in early 1991.[9] The need for a more aggressive tightening of policy, as evident by the flight from the US dollar over the summer of 1987, led to the panic selling in the stock market during October of that year.

The First Housing Recession

The crash did not produce the desired cooling or rebalancing of the economy away from overconsumption. The cost of borrowing was forced up again. Between October 1987 and the spring of 1989, interest rates went up a further 2 per cent.

That eventually triggered a major downturn in the US housing market through the early 1990s, and the now infamous rout of the so-called junk bond market. Large numbers of US companies had borrowed heavily to finance mergers or acquisitions. In many cases, the companies either had poor quality balance sheets, or were borrowing over-optimistically in pursuit of their takeover target. The housing crisis was exacerbated by the role of so-called Savings and Loan Institutions (S&Ls). These banks had lent heavily to many homeowners. Spurred on by deregulation, many had been engaged in systematic fraud too. More than a thousand S&Ls failed in 'the largest and costliest venture in public misfeasance, malfeasance and larceny of all time', with estimated losses of $150 billion.[10]

The nature of this sudden reversal contained many lessons for the financial crises that followed more than a decade later. Both the dotcom boom/bust and the housing collapse from 2005 onwards had some similarities with the early 1990s recession. The dotcom bubble was accompanied by rapid growth in very poor quality borrowing by companies similar to that witnessed in the late 1980s. And endemic, institutional fraud became a hallmark of the housing boom engineered after the dotcom recession.

The 1987 crash and the 1989/90 recession were still fundamentally different from the more recent financial turbulence. Inflation was the core threat that forced the authorities to tighten monetary policy in the late 1980s. A decade later, the dynamics had changed. The systematic dismantling of the protection previously enjoyed by workers saw the balance of power swing decisively in favour of corporations. Globalisation and the removal of trade barriers accelerated the shift. Overinvestment and overproduction became the key threats, not inflation.

This realignment did not materialise over one short decade. The full effects of this seismic shift would take more than two decades to emerge. Nevertheless, even by the recession of 1991, the forces of change were apparent. Although core inflation had accelerated in the US, it peaked at much lower levels compared to the high of 13.6 per cent reached in June 1980. And it required a smaller rise in unemployment to secure that shift in the balance of power, to beat organised labour into submission. The peak in US unemployment during the early 1990s was 3 per cent below that seen a decade before.[11] Slowly but surely, inflation pressures were being ground out of the system, albeit at a very high cost.

And the Asian crisis of 1997 was a warning that the pendulum was swinging further away from inflation towards a potential new world of debt deflation. The run on the baht in July that year had been preceded by mounting anxiety over Thailand's trade deficit. The shortfall in the current account (the widest measure of any country's trade deficit, including goods, services, income and other transfers) had been running at uncomfortable levels for some time. Indeed, while it reached a hefty 8.1 per cent of GDP in 1996, it had been even higher in 1990. Investors had been happy to fund Thailand's high trade deficit for some years, as it was regarded as a strong emerging market with sound long term development prospects.

But during the early months of 1997, concern over the durability of Thailand's export earnings intensified. Quite simply, Thailand got caught in a classic overinvestment squeeze, with overproduction in a number of its key exports leading to a significant loss of earnings. Thailand had become a major centre for electronics, with multinationals using it as a low cost base to export a range of high-tech products. However, it was not the only recipient of these direct investment inflows. The rush of large manufacturers to open up production facilities across a range of developing countries was fuelling a glut of output and pushing prices down.[12]

Investors had been happy to fund such extreme current account deficits on the premise that strong export earnings would pay for a rising import bill. And imports were being driven higher by the need for machinery and capital goods to expand Thailand's nascent industrial base.

However, the hit to export earnings undermined investors' assumptions. As in 1929, they had misread the fundamental problem starting to appear worldwide, that too much investment was chasing insufficient consumer demand. It might work for an individual firm to cut labour costs and aggressively expand capacity in developing economies. But collectively, their actions would lead to periodical bursts of downward pressure on pricing power for goods in excess supply.

The Asian crisis was a difficult pill for the Japanese to swallow, as Japan had been suffering from an overinvestment crisis of its own since the early 1990s, and was now battling with the subsequent fallout. The collapse of the Thai baht ricocheted through Malaysia, Indonesia, South Korea and other Asian countries, depressing demand for Japanese goods. Four months after the run on the Thai baht, Japan's seven-year crisis would reach a calamitous milestone, with the bankruptcy of leading stockbroker Yamaichi Securities.[13]

A New Paradigm

The impact on the Industrialised West was short-lived. The US was in the early stages of its own overinvestment boom and Europe was following on its coat tails. The spread of the internet coincided with a sharp rise in capital spending in the US that was remarkably similar in scale to the investment surge of the late 1920s.[14] The Federal Reserve chairman, Alan Greenspan, initially tried to dampen the euphoria that saw share prices rise swiftly from early 1995 onwards. He soon gave up trying to stand in the markets' way, partly under political pressure, but he was swayed by the hype of speculators too. Increasingly they argued that the business cycle had been consigned to history by the internet.

Mr Greenspan also backed down because he reasoned there was not that much of an inflation threat. And there was little risk of a sustained build-up in prices precisely because the economic landscape had changed dramatically since the 1970s and 1980s. Companies were able to hold down wages even as the economy boomed. A growing share of GDP was diverted towards the sharp growth in investment, notably in high-tech capital goods (see Figure 2.1). That in turn allowed companies to invest in labour-saving techniques, to keep wage costs down, *and in theory*, drive profits up. The stock market soared, as investors saw only a virtuous cycle of higher profits, rising investment, leading to greater productivity gains and thus improved profitability. The economy had reached nirvana.[15]

The flaw was self-evident to those who chose to look a little more closely at the profit numbers being published by US companies. Many companies were manipulating their earnings to bolster their share prices. Enron was perhaps the most notorious example, but it was hardly alone.[16] According to the more reliable government data, aggregate profits had not risen during the last three years of the dotcom bubble.[17] When the crash arrived, many companies would be forced to restate their earnings, hitting confidence again and sending stock market prices even lower.

The stock market was brought tumbling down by a fundamental lack of pricing power for many high-tech goods. Indeed, the first

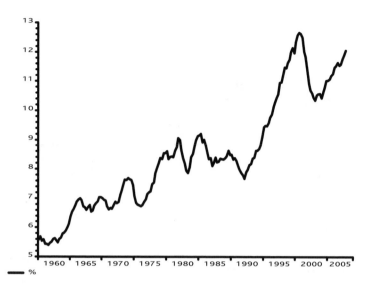

Figure 2.1   US Business Investment/GDP, Real Terms

Source: Bureau of Economic Analysis.

signs of overinvestment and falling prices had appeared way back in the autumn of 1995. Investors and economists tended to use the widely followed Consumer Price Index (CPI) as the main indicator for measuring inflation. But there was another index lesser used at the time but now followed closely by the Federal Reserve. The *consumption deflator* was better at capturing the discounts retailers and producers were being forced to offer, to sustain sales. And for consumer durables – cars, appliances, electronics, etc – this measure of inflation turned negative in September 1995 (see Figure 2.2).[18]

The US was starting to experience deflation for a wide range of consumer goods less than a year into the dotcom boom, and long before Asia ran into trouble in 1997. It was not the Asian crisis or the run on the Thai baht that triggered the long period of falling goods prices, and helped underpin low inflation over the next decade or so. It was the tendency to overinvest and overproduce triggered by the arrival of Reaganomics and Thatcherism. Asia

Figure 2.2   US Consumption Deflator, Durables

Source: Bureau of Economic Analysis.

was merely caught out by the secular forces unleashed by the political shift towards free markets.

By the time the US stock market had reached a peak in the spring of 2000, prices for consumer durables had been falling for four and a half years without interruption. Consumer durable prices had dropped by a cumulative 9.5 per cent.[19] So long as the stock market was going up, the wealth effects were generating just enough demand to convince investors that deflation was not an issue. But as the first doubts started to surface, the whole pack of cards came tumbling down.[20] The fall in equity prices wiped out the share options of many high earners, immediately hitting consumer demand. With far too much capacity, high-tech manufacturers were forced to slash payrolls.[21] The loss of disposable income fed into even weaker demand, triggering more job losses.

The impact on inflation was swift. Core inflation peaked at a modest 2.7 per cent in 2001, just half the high point witnessed a decade earlier. It began to tumble, led by an even sharper decline in the prices for consumer durables.[22] And the Federal Reserve began to panic, fretting that the spectre of deflation bedevilling Japan would become a reality in the US. The current chair, Ben Bernanke, declared in November 2002 that the authorities would 'take whatever means necessary to prevent significant deflation in the United States'.[23]

And that was the starting point of the US housing bubble. The US authorities had little choice but to reflate aggressively. The US was heading for steep recession, and there was a palpable fear the scourge of deflation, not dissimilar to that seen in Japan, would take root.

The Dollar Standard

The threat of deflation was ultimately a response to shifting, secular political forces. But it was exacerbated by one other fault-line that stemmed back to the Vietnam War. The pressures to pay for the long military campaign ultimately precipitated the collapse of the international monetary system that had underpinned the world economy since 1945.

During the final months of the Second World War, the US and its allies created a fixed exchange rate system based around the US dollar to replace the discredited gold standard. The US dollar was fixed to gold at $35 per ounce. Other major currencies were pegged to the US dollar, and by extension, to gold too. This Bretton Woods system was designed to ensure countries did not manipulate their exchange rates. And there were inherent adjustments within the system, to prevent countries running large and persistent trade deficits and surpluses. Critically, the system was symmetrical. The pressure to take corrective action applied equally to countries, whether they were in deficit or surplus.

The new architecture functioned well for two decades or so. But during the second half of the 1960s, the US started to run sizeable trade deficits. The Vietnam War was proving unwinnable, and heavy defence spending was pushing imports up and contributing to a worsening of the trade balance. In comparison with recent years, the deficits were still modest.[24] But under the Bretton Woods system, the US was obliged to take corrective measures.

The authorities needed to cool the economy. At a time when the war was causing support for President Nixon to haemorrhage, a recession would have made the US administration even more unpopular. It capitulated and suspended the convertibility of dollars into gold, and Bretton Woods collapsed.

From then on, countries were free to borrow and run persistent trade deficits, subject to the willingness of international creditors. But the US enjoyed a unique privilege. As a result of its pivotal role at the apex of Bretton Woods, many central banks were happy to hold US dollars in their reserves. The US was under even less pressure to curb its trade deficits. The current account deficit rose during the late 1970s, and then took off following the arrival of Reaganomics (see Figure 2.3). It reached an unthinkable 3.4 per cent of GDP in 1987, nearly seven times the deficit that had brought about the demise of Bretton Woods – triggering a dollar rout and stock market collapse.

Just over a third of that deficit was with one country, Japan. US auto manufacturers were reeling from the onslaught of Nissan,

Figure 2.3   US Current Account/GDP

Source: Bureau of Economic Analysis.

Toyota, Honda and Mazda. The Japanese authorities came under acute pressure to reflate their economy, and buy more US exports. But the US dollar was falling, and the Bank of Japan was frantically buying US dollars to prevent a more crippling rise in the yen too. Inflation had already turned negative in Japan. The Bank of Japan's foreign exchange reserves ballooned, and with interest rates at historic lows, the two combined to set the stage for a credit boom that engulfed the country during the late 1980s.

But this chain of events is instructive. A similar build-up in central bank reserves contributed to the Asian boom of the mid 1990s, although in this case, the countries were running trade deficits. Instead, countries at the heart of the Asian crisis were engulfed by huge capital inflows that fuelled rapid credit growth and fed asset bubbles across the region. When the currency pegs broke in the summer of 1997, the implosion of these asset markets amplified the economic crisis. As we shall see in Chapter 3, the subsequent fallout in turn played a part in fuelling the housing bubbles of the US less than a decade later.

3
ADDICTED TO DEBT

It is not difficult to see how important debt has been for the UK and US. Borrowing has soared in both countries over the past decade. When New Labour came to power in the summer of 1997, total debt held by individuals was £570.0 billion.[1] Just over ten years later, it had risen to £1,511.7 billion, a leap of 165.2 per cent. That was equivalent to an average annualised increase of 10.0 per cent. The personal sector debt to disposable income ratio had jumped from 101.6 per cent to a record 173.1 per cent, higher than any other major industrialised economy.[2] Once the increase in borrowing by companies was taken into account, the rise in the UK's debt was even more onerous. Total private sector debt had gone up from 133.5 per cent of GDP to 227.4 per cent.[3]

The increase dwarfed the run-up in debt witnessed during the much maligned 'Lawson Boom'.[4] Gordon Brown's original pledge to the electorate in 1997 for 'no more boom and bust' was a direct attack on the profligate policies of the Thatcher era. The debt to disposable income ratio had climbed steadily under successive Conservative governments. It had reached a peak of 112.4 per cent in early 1991, triggering a deep recession, more than a quarter of a million home repossessions and the misery of negative equity for millions.[5] But the increase in the debt burden was still less than under New Labour. Under 18 years of Conservative rule, the debt ratio had gone up by 49.8 per cent. Under ten years of Mr Brown's tenure, it had risen by 71.5 per cent.[6]

The acceleration in borrowing has been no less startling in the US. Personal sector debt has risen by 159.1 per cent since the summer of 1997 – just before the Asian crisis struck – jumping from $5,547.1 billion to $14,374.5 billion.[7] The debt to disposable income ratio went up from 93.4 per cent to a post-1945 record of 139.0 per cent.[8] Once again, the increase was far greater than in the boom of the late 1980s.[9]

The dynamics of the rise in debt burdens have been essentially the same in both countries, with one caveat. The increase in borrowing was somewhat faster in the UK, while disposable incomes grew less.[10] Wages have been under pressure across the Industrialised West in recent years. But a more pronounced squeeze in the UK left many consumers struggling with a far bigger jump in debt relative to income.

And the increase in corporate sector borrowing has also been more extreme in the UK, leaving it even more exposed to an unravelling of the credit bubble. Indeed, compared with the US, private sector debt rose two and a half times as quickly in the UK.[11]

Debt and Rising House Prices

For some, these increases have been viewed as simply the mirror image of rising house prices and no reason to fret. In both countries, the property market has soared over the past decade or so. According to the Office of Federal Housing Enterprise Oversight, house prices in the US had climbed by 104.5 per cent since the summer of 1997, before the slump began.[12] In the UK, the increase was even more stunning. Based on the Halifax index, property prices had jumped by 189.6 per cent, before they started to slide in the autumn of 2007.[13] The Nationwide index posted a bigger gain, a spectacular 211.9 per cent before it too turned down in the final months of 2007.[14]

These astonishing gains ensured that net wealth still went up despite the higher debt burden. In the UK, net wealth or total assets minus debt rose from 633.0 per cent of disposable income in 1997 to 824.3 per cent nine years later.[15] Hence, for policymakers, the heavy borrowing was never deemed a major concern. The personal sector's balance sheet was ostensibly strong. Higher debt was offset by an even faster rise in the value of housing and other financial assets. More than three months after the credit squeeze erupted, one member of the Bank of England's Monetary Policy

Committee was still claiming the balance sheets of individuals were in a 'relatively strong position'.[16]

The same argument was widely heard throughout Japan during the late 1980s. On the back of soaring share prices and a property boom, the net wealth ratio had climbed to a peak of 947.6 per cent by 1990, up from 789.7 per cent three years earlier.[17] Rising net wealth would provide a cushion against record debt, it was claimed. But it proved to be a fallacy. When the crunch inevitably arrives, the asset side of the equation, propped up by sky-high property values, invariably falls more quickly than the flipside – borrowing. That is true because of the very nature of debt-fuelled increases in house prices. When the bubble bursts, it becomes impossible for the personal sector to reduce its overall debt levels without triggering even bigger falls in house prices and further declines in aggregate net wealth.

If the monetary policy response is inadequate and interest rates do not come down quickly enough, all of the gains in net wealth witnessed during the boom can easily be lost during the crash. That happened in Japan. Net wealth fell sharply during the early years of the bear market, and because the authorities misjudged their policy response, it never recovered. Seventeen years later, net wealth had dropped to 748.7 per cent of disposable income, lower than in 1987, when the Japanese property market took off.[18]

In the US, the increase in net wealth during the recent housing bubble did not even replace all of the losses inflicted by the collapse of high-tech share prices. At the top of the dotcom boom, rising share prices had pushed the net wealth ratio up to a post-war high of 628.6 per cent.[19] The value of shares held by individuals had nearly quadrupled during the 1990s.[20] The dotcom bubble had drawn a huge swathe of new investors into the stock market, with nearly 50 per cent of the US population owning shares prior to the crash.[21]

As the dotcom boom unravelled, the losses snowballed and within three years, the net wealth to disposable income ratio had fallen to just 495.5 per cent.[22] The bear market destroyed paper wealth equivalent to more than the annual disposable income of the US.[23] It was partly the sheer magnitude of these losses that forced the Federal Reserve to slash interest rates to 1.0 per cent by the summer of 2003, thus setting the stage for the frenzied run-up in house prices. Consumer demand turned down very sharply during 2001. Many of the largest shareholders were wealthier individuals absorbing a disproportionately higher share of consumption.[24] Spending would have been even weaker without the rapid fall in borrowing costs.

Critics of the Federal Reserve policy in 2003 – and there have been many – failed to explain what else the US central bank could have done faced with such a predicament. Even with house prices accelerating it was not possible for the Federal Reserve to replace all of the net wealth destroyed by the dotcom crash. The over-investment 'bubble' that gripped the Industrialised West in the late 1990s forced the Federal Reserve to loosen monetary policy. It was the logical outcome of the free trade agenda pursued by Western governments through the 1990s.

Property Shortage?

The UK government sought to deflect criticism of its loose monetary policy by citing a lack of building and a shortage of properties as the reasons for sky-high house prices. As Chancellor of the Exchequer, Gordon Brown had in 2006 instructed one of his external appointees to the Monetary Policy Committee to 'Conduct a review of issues underlying the lack of supply and responsiveness of housing in the UK'.[25] With such a tight remit, there was never any doubt that the report would conclude a lack of building was the culprit for high prices, and the key to making housing more affordable. Nowhere in Ms Barker's report were record debt levels or the pressure from buy-to-let investors mentioned as contributors to runaway house prices. It was all the fault of planners, builders and the countryside lobby for refusing to allow more development on greenfield sites.

Again, it was an argument familiar to Japanese historians. A shortage of supply and the lack of land available for development had also been cited in the late 1980s as an explanation for soaring property prices. When the cycle turned, this spurious notion of a lack of supply was exposed, as the so-called shortage was suddenly replaced by a glut that helped to drive prices down for more than a decade. In some areas of Japan, they are still going down. More recently, other countries gripped by property mania have also seen a huge increase in the construction of new homes, including Spain, Ireland and the US. House building leapt well above the increase needed to meet population growth in the US, and yet prices still soared.[26] This suggested the UK boom was unlikely to be just a supply constraint.

Rising and Falling Homeownership

Some economists argued that the record debt levels were simply a reflection of rising homeownership. With more people buying and fewer renting, it was logical that the debt burden should rise in aggregate, it was claimed. But the increase in homeownership during the property booms was modest. And it started to trend down again long before house prices reached their peak. The property bubbles were increasingly driven by forces that were undermining homeownership in both countries.

In the UK, the rapid growth in buy-to-let investors was playing a key role in preventing individuals trying to get on the first rung of the property ladder. A proliferation of mortgage products geared specifically towards landlords saw the number of buy-to-let mortgages soar from 58,500 in 1998 to more than a million by 2007. Total buy-to-let lending had climbed to £122.1 billion, or 10.3 per cent of all mortgages outstanding.[27] Capital-rich landlords were scooping up houses, fuelling a virtuous cycle of rising prices, falling supply and inevitably a plentiful supply of tenants, from those forced by a rising market to rent. And because many were sitting on large capital gains, buy-to-let lending carried on rising even as the housing market started to turn down in the final months of 2007. As a result, the number of people living in their own home has been falling since 2005. Homeownership rose during the early years of this decade, stalled in 2005, and has since been dropping.[28] Repossessions have thus far been limited, but the risks of an extended rise pulling homeownership down more quickly, are real.

In the US, the proportion living in their home also climbed during the early part of this decade, rising from 66.9 per cent at the end of 1999 to a peak of 69.2 per cent.[29] Homeownership was initially given a boost by the explosion in subprime lending. It was a point highlighted by the former Federal Reserve chairman, Alan Greenspan, to justify the wilful neglect of so many lenders operating outside the central bank's regulatory orbit. Even in the early weeks of 2008, he was still claiming the surge in subprime mortgages had been worth the risk, helping to broaden home ownership, particularly among minorities.[30]

However, homeownership started to turn down in the US in the autumn of 2004, a full year before the housing bubble had even reached its climax. And with so many individuals and families defaulting, the numbers living in their own house started to fall sharply in 2007. By the end of the year, homeownership was sliding at its fastest rate in decades.[31] It had fallen to its lowest level since the second quarter of 2002 (see Figure 3.1). All the gains from the expansion of subprime lending touted by Alan

Figure 3.1   US Homeownership

Source: Department of Commerce.

Greenspan had been wiped out within two years of a bear market. With house prices a long way from hitting bottom and defaults climbing, there is every chance homeownership will fall back to levels not seen since the 1980s.

The widely respected Center for Responsible Lending (CRL) based in Durham, North Carolina had been quite strident on this point. In a highly critical and prescient report released in December 2006, the CRL warned that 2 million borrowers, many of them subprime, were likely to be made homeless by the housing crisis.[32] At the time, the prediction was dismissed for being alarmist. But a year later, another prominent forecaster suggested the number of families that could lose their homes might climb above 3 million.[33] And by early 2008, US Treasury Secretary Henry Paulson was forced to admit that the CRL estimate would be realised in 2008 alone. The final tally of foreclosures was likely to be several times higher.[34] Indeed, by the end of 2007, the number of homes in foreclosure had soared (see Figure 3.2). Delinquencies, or the

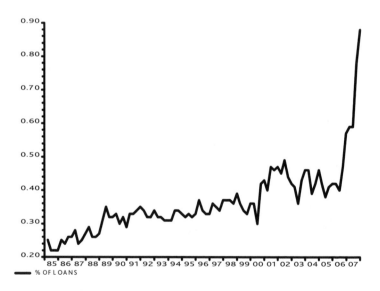

Figure 3.2   US Residential Mortgages, Foreclosures Started

Source: Mortgage Bankers Association.

number of borrowers falling behind on repayments, were rising fast too (see Figure 3.3).

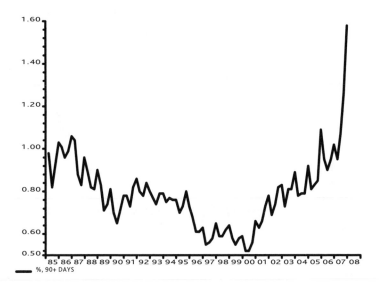

Figure 3.3   US Residential Mortgages, Delinquencies

Source: Mortgage Bankers Association.

Low Inflation, Easy Lending

It was the persistence of low inflation and profligate lending that allowed individuals to take on higher debt. As interest rates fell sharply during the dotcom recession, debt burdens started to rise quickly. Ordinarily, they should have fallen, as they did after the early 1990s recession. On that occasion, the economic downturn persuaded many individuals to reduce their debt commitments.

Not this time. As the cost of borrowing fell, house price inflation was embraced as a substitute for the deflation threatened by the dotcom recession. By the end of 2000, mortgage lending in the US was already responding to the policy stimulus. Over the next two years it accelerated sharply, with the annual growth rate eventually hitting a peak of 14.8 per cent in the third quarter of

2003, just after the final rate cut to 1.0 per cent.[35] It slowed a touch thereafter, but remained comfortably above 10.0 per cent until the end of 2006, when the pace of lending finally turned down. By then, aggregate debt servicing costs (i.e. interest and repayments) for homeowners had climbed to a record 18.2 per cent of disposable income (see Figure 3.4).[36]

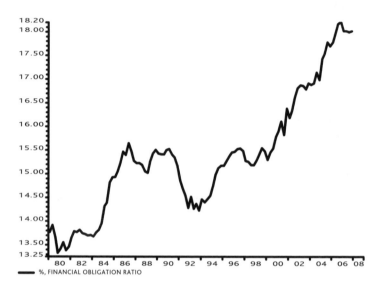

Figure 3.4   US Household Debt Payments

Source: Federal Reserve.

In the UK, debt servicing costs rose sharply too, although they did not surpass the peak of the Lawson Boom. According to the Council of Mortgage Lenders, interest payments as a percentage of incomes rose to 18.9 per cent in December 2007, compared with a 1989 peak of 26.7 per cent.[37] The increase for first-time buyers was more pronounced. Interest payments had climbed to 20.7 per cent of income by the end of 2007, compared with the 1989 high of 27.3 per cent.[38]

None of these figures include repayments of the outstanding loan, however. And higher house prices were forcing borrowers to take out loans on far bigger income multiples.[39] Stretched by rising valuations, many buyers had opted for interest-only loans.[40] However, for the remaining two-thirds, total debt servicing costs were unlikely to have been that far short of the 1989 peak.

Winding the Clock Back

It is instructive, therefore, to wind the clock back and consider what might have happened if borrowing had not been allowed to rise so sharply in the UK and US. To carry out such an exercise, we can examine retrospective simulations on the econometric models run by Oxford Economic Forecasting.

In essence, we have imagined an alternative world, not so very different from the 1960s when lending was controlled. In these simulations, we have assumed the rise in personal sector debt as a percentage of disposable income was constrained from 1997 onwards. The controls were not deemed that aggressive. The ratio of debt to disposable income was still allowed to rise. But the increases were assumed to be more modest. In the UK it rose to 120 per cent by 2007, up from the 102 per cent level of ten years earlier. In the US, the debt to disposable income ratio was allowed to climb to 107 per cent, up from the 93 per cent level recorded a decade earlier (see Figures 3.5 and 3.6). In the case of the UK, that was just over a quarter of the rise actually seen. And in the US, it was just under a third.

There are legitimate questions over how this might have been achieved. For the purpose of this exercise, we have assumed the slower borrowing was secured by direct controls on bank lending. Quantitative restrictions on lending were a regular feature of monetary policy throughout the 1950s and 1960s. After a brief hiatus, quantitative controls were reintroduced in the UK in 1973 in the shape of the Supplementary Special Deposit Scheme, also known as the Corset. And in the late 1970s, central banks set monetary targets to limit the growth in consumer credit and lending. Targets were eventually abandoned in the UK in 1986. Money supply targets were used in the US from April 1975 until 1986.

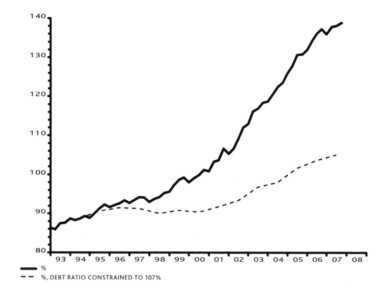

Figure 3.5   US Personal Sector Debt/Disposable Income

Sources: Federal Reserve, Bureau of Economic Analysis, Oxford Economic Forecasting and GFC Economics .

Such controls would have been less effective in the 1990s, for a number of reasons. Deregulation and the ability of consumers to borrow outside their domestic market would have undoubtedly hindered any direct attempt to slow the growth in borrowing. In the UK, consumers now have increased access to loans in an enlarged European Union. Foreign currency mortgages have gained in popularity.

That underlines the very flaw with the current economic strategy, which has extended to the supervision of banks. Lending controls might have been a useful policy tool, but they were eschewed because they did not fit with the prevailing dogma. Individuals were free to get into debt, because it suited policy.

Either way, we have assumed in these simulations that central banks succeeded in restraining the pace of borrowing by the use of lending controls, and not through higher interest rates. And it was assumed the banks did not offset slower personal sector

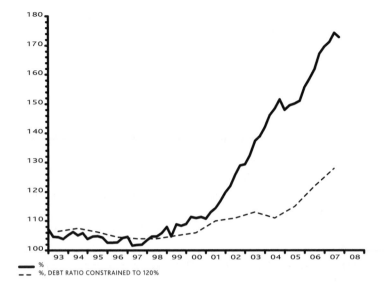

Figure 3.6   UK Personal Sector Debt/Disposable Income

Sources: Office for National Statistics, Oxford Economic Forecasting and GFC Economics.

borrowing by lending elsewhere, either to companies, or overseas for example.

And we have assumed some counter-cyclical tightening of fiscal policy. Slower personal sector borrowing would inevitably mean fewer tax receipts, and that would have given governments less room to increase public spending. In this case, we assumed that governments were forced by the shortfall in tax receipts that came from slower growth, to limit the rise in the deficit, to around half that would have occurred otherwise. This triggers a further shortfall in demand, which adds to the deflationary pressure.

How Would the Economies Have Fared?

First and foremost, without the sharp run-up in borrowing there would have been a significant shortfall in consumer demand. Critically, there would have been a more pronounced squeeze on wages too.

In both the US and UK, *nominal* consumption would have been 20 per cent lower at the end of the ten-year period, compared to that seen under the policy of uncontrolled lending pursued by the Federal Reserve and Bank of England. These are compelling demand gaps. Note, we have *not* allowed interest rates to decline in response to this demand shortfall: we are deliberately trying to isolate the impact of debt on the economy.

The drop in *real* spending would have been less. In the UK, real consumption would have been reduced by 8.9 per cent over this ten-year period, while in the US it would have been lowered by 6.2 per cent. That is because inflation would have been much weaker. Consumer prices would have been 12.5 per cent lower at the end of this ten-year period in the UK, and 17.1 per cent lower in the US.

Inflation would have averaged 0.2 per cent in the UK, compared with the actual outcome of 1.5 per cent. There would have been significant periods in which there was outright deflation, including four consecutive years from 2000 through to 2003. Throughout the entire period, inflation would never have got above the target set by the Labour government, 2.0 per cent (see Figure 3.7).[41]

In the US, inflation would have averaged 0.7 per cent compared with the 2.6 per cent seen over the past ten years. Indeed, the US would have been stuck with deflation for six consecutive years, from 2002 to 2007 (see Figure 3.8). After turning negative in response to the bursting of the dotcom bubble, it would have been impossible to get inflation back above the zero threshold. The Federal Reserve was worried about the spectre of deflation when it slashed interest rates, and it was right to have been.

Furthermore, there is no telling how consumers would have responded to a prolonged period of falling prices. Deflation in Japan has proved difficult to eradicate, partly because consumers have got used to falling prices, creating a 'wait and see' mentality. There is less reason for consumers to buy today if prices are expected to fall.

The significant drops in consumer prices underline the impossible task central banks faced in fulfilling their mandates.

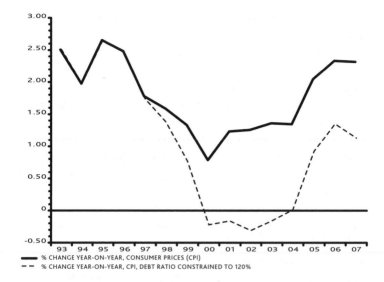

Figure 3.7   UK Inflation

Sources: Office for National Statistics, Oxford Economic Forecasting and GFC Economics.

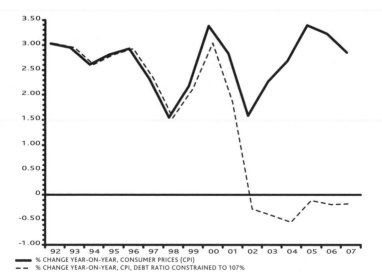

Figure 3.8   US Inflation

Sources: Bureau of Labor Statistics, Oxford Economic Forecasting and GFC Economics.

The excessive run-up in borrowing was needed to stop inflation falling below target.

Globalisation was giving the world a much cheaper pool of labour and exerting persistent downward pressure on prices. If central banks had not tried to counter that, consumers would have benefited from lower prices, which would have limited the fall in real consumption. But unemployment would have been higher too.[42] Debt was allowed to soar, to stop deflation taking root.

And it is instructive to see how far wages would have suffered. On these simulations, average earnings in nominal terms would have been 12.5 per cent lower in the UK after ten years. In the US, there would have been a drop of 21.4 per cent compared to that actually seen. The shortfall in wages on this scale underlines the problem with the way globalisation has been allowed to squeeze labour costs. Without the huge increase in borrowing, wages would have shown very little increase (see Figures 3.9 and 3.10).

Strikingly, both the US and UK would still have been running substantial trade deficits even with this much reduced rise in

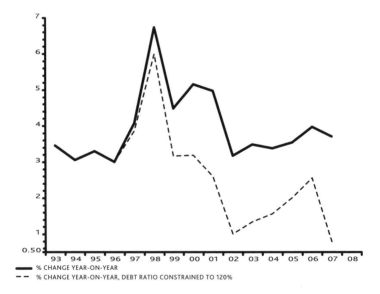

Figure 3.9 UK Average Earnings

Sources: Office for National Statistics, Oxford Economic Forecasting and GFC Economics.

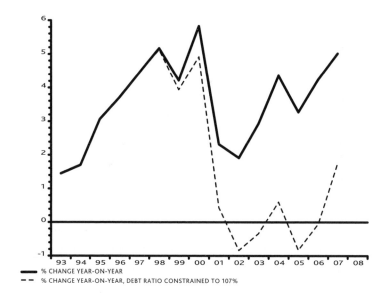

% CHANGE YEAR-ON-YEAR
% CHANGE YEAR-ON-YEAR, DEBT RATIO CONSTRAINED TO 107%

Figure 3.10   US Average Earnings

Sources: Bureau of Labor Statistics, Oxford Economic Forecasting and GFC Economics.

borrowing (see Figures 3.11 and 3.12). This is an important point that we shall revisit in Chapter 4. As we shall see, it goes to the heart of the credit bubble, as so many manufacturing jobs in the Industrialised West were lost to cheaper, low-cost countries.

Last but not least, it is interesting to see how far house prices would have risen under a more controlled increase in debt. In the UK, property prices would have risen by a third of the increase seen, while in the US, house values would have climbed just over a quarter of the run-up witnessed since 1997 (see Figures 3.13 and 3.14). These numbers show quite conclusively that debt was a major factor in driving the property market, not a lack of supply, or strong economic growth *per se*.

What Should They Have Done?

Faced with such a large demand shortfall from the squeeze on wages, it is easy to view the monetary response as an unfortunate

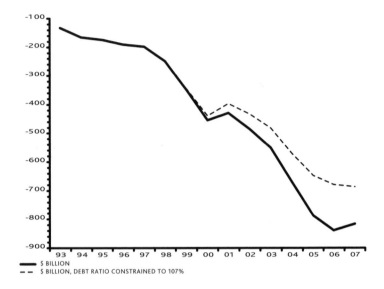

Figure 3.11   US Trade Balance

Sources: Department of Commerce, Oxford Economic Forecasting and GFC Economics.

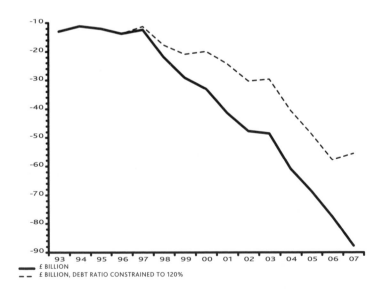

Figure 3.12   UK Trade Balance

Sources: Office for National Statistics, Oxford Economic Forecasting and GFC Economics.

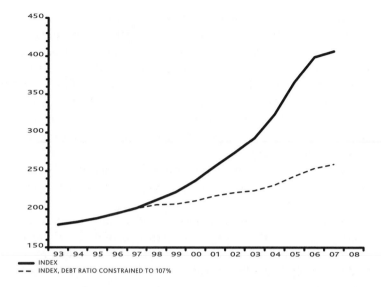

Figure 3.13   US House Prices

Sources: Oxford Economic Forecasting and GFC Economics.

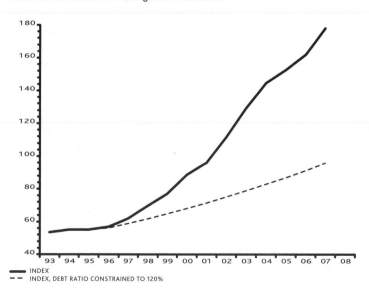

Figure 3.14   UK House Prices

Sources: Oxford Economic Forecasting and GFC Economics.

and unintended by-product of globalisation. It is all too easy to claim that nobody could have forecast that Asia would have driven so much deflation for goods in the West. That is a debatable point in itself. The imbalances that precipitated the Asian crisis were quite evident before the run on the Thai baht in July 1997. Japan was already immersed deep in a prolonged battle against debt deflation. If it was not obvious then that the predominant threat was overinvestment, it certainly became clear during the dotcom boom. Indeed, the CPI for core goods started to fall before New Labour came to power in the summer of 1997, and the decline accelerated thereafter, reaching a peak of 4.0 per cent year-on-year in July 2000.[43]

By the time the bubble had burst in 2000, China was moving centre stage too with the help of Western industrialists seeking to cut costs, pushing its share of world exports up at a rapid pace, and triggering huge downward pressure on wages and prices. The determination of so many emerging economies to export aggressively to the West, build strong current account surpluses and accumulate huge foreign exchange reserves, was starting to create serious imbalances. If Gordon Brown did not recognise the threat in 1997, it was glaringly evident by the time Labour had secured its second term in June 2001.

At that point, the personal sector debt burden had been rising steadily under New Labour, but the really significant increases still lay ahead. There might still have been time to change tack. But the Bank of England was operating under a very narrow remit, to ensure inflation remained between 1 and 3 per cent. Nothing else mattered. As inflation fell to the lower end of this target in 2001, it had carte blanche to let borrowing spiral upwards.[44] Indeed, it had to cut interest rates and fuel a rise in debt, to stay within target. There was no mention of debt or financial stability in the Bank of England's very short and ill-defined mandate, drawn up by the Treasury in 1997. Interest rates were to be set according to one criterion only – inflation. So long as inflation stayed low, then according to the chancellor, Gordon Brown, nothing else mattered.

If there is one very clear criticism of the Bank of England, it should be here. The Monetary Policy Committee ought to have challenged the government over its mandate and warned that financial stability was being imperilled by attempts to ensure inflation did not fall below target. But supervision of the banks had long been passed to the Financial Services Authority, to the dismay of the Bank of England, and officials did not want to rock the boat. They meekly acquiesced, with disastrous consequences for financial stability and debt levels.

The Bank of England in time began to accept inflation targeting was all that mattered. It effectively colluded with an economic policy that was destined to end in financial chaos. It went out of its way to claim that the housing market was not an important factor driving the economy. Numerous articles were published by in-house economists and members of the Monetary Policy Committee suggesting that there was a tenuous link between rising property prices and consumer spending.[45] But, if anything, the link was getting tighter. The correlation between various indicators of the housing market and consumer spending grew closer as debt levels climbed. There was compelling evidence to show that the economy was supported by record borrowing. Mortgage approvals developed into one of the most closely followed indicators, precisely because it provided an increasingly reliable lead on consumer spending (see Figure 3.15). But the evidence was deliberately ignored by the Bank of England and, of course, the government.

Easy Al

In the US, the policy mandate was not set so tightly. The Federal Reserve had dual targets – stable inflation and the promotion of growth. It had more direct responsibility for financial stability too. But the outcome was still the same. The Japanese debacle of the 1990s was casting a long shadow over the Federal Reserve. Officials were paranoid that the US would slip into a debt trap similar to Japan's. As the economy turned down in 2001 following the collapse of the dotcom bubble, the Federal Reserve decided to slash interest rates. The US administration was cutting taxes aggressively too.[46]

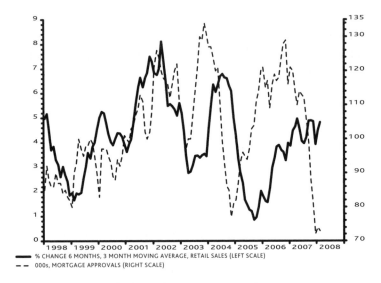

Figure 3.15   UK Retail Sales and Mortgage Approvals

Source: Office for National Statistics.

Some economists now argue that the Federal Reserve was wrong to cut the cost of borrowing quite so far. The 13 rate cuts down to a low of 1.0 per cent in June 2003 unequivocally set the stage for the housing bubble. Indeed, the super-low interest rates encouraged a proliferation of the very mortgage products that would prove so destructive in later years, propelling a downward spiral of house prices.

But critics of the Fed's response to the dotcom recession never explain how the authorities would have filled the shortfall in demand evident from the simulations outlined in this chapter. By deduction, and by their failure to put forward any coherent alternatives, one is left to conclude that the Federal Reserve should have simply allowed the economy to stagnate and deflation to prevail.

Some might argue that would have been a better outcome in the long run. By reflating so aggressively, the economy may have ostensibly benefited in the short run, but only by hiking the personal sector debt burden to record levels. The boost to growth may prove ephemeral, if the housing boom is followed by a prolonged stagnation. Cutting interest rates was the easy short term solution to the dotcom crash. If the Federal Reserve had not cut interest rates to 1 per cent, perhaps the US authorities might not be facing the fallout from a prolonged housing bubble today. It is easy to criticise the Federal Reserve, and it made many mistakes in its handling of the banks that aggressively promoted toxic mortgages. But blaming the Federal Reserve alone ignores the far more important issue of why the credit bubble was deliberately created.

4

'FREE TRADE' AND ASSET BUBBLES

As we saw in Chapter 3, wages would have fallen a long way in the US and UK without an explosion of borrowing. Debt was a panacea for the 'flattening of wage compensation', described by Alan Greenspan as a key economic feature of the West in recent years.[1] Remarkably, even with a huge run-up in debt driving an economic boom, the US real median wage has still fallen since 2001.[2] Wages and salaries have slipped to their lowest proportion of GDP in decades (see Figure 4.1).

In the UK, the compression of wages has been striking too. Despite a 'strong' upturn in the economy following the dotcom recession, real average earnings still contracted in 2007, the final year of the housing boom (see Figure 4.2).[3] Aggregate wage compensation was up, but it rose just 1.8 per cent in real terms. At the top of the last bubble in 2000, the increase was more than three times as fast, with wage compensation climbing 6.0 per cent.[4] In the absence of record consumer borrowing, the downward pressure on wages would have been even more severe.

The precise cause of this squeeze on labour costs has been hotly debated. It can be viewed as an extension of the anti-inflation policies adopted in the late 1970s and early 1980s. As we have already seen, clamping down on wages was central to Reaganomics and Thatcherism. During the 1990s, the minimum wage was back in vogue. The British prime minister Tony Blair introduced one, and President Clinton boosted basic pay rates.[5] But they failed to reverse the squeeze on organised labour that underpinned the low inflation strategy.

Some economists routinely claimed that 'policy credibility' played a critical role in keeping inflation expectations and thus

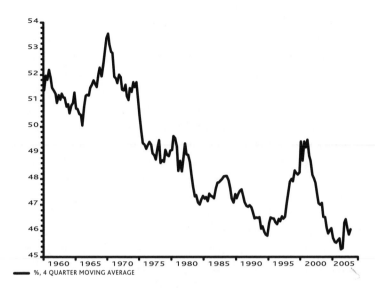

Figure 4.1   US Wages and Salaries/GDP

Source: Bureau of Economic Analysis.

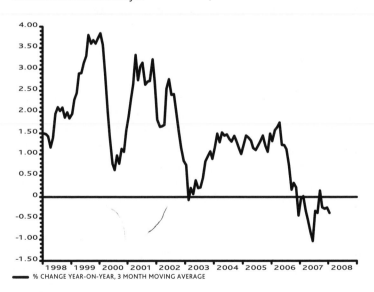

Figure 4.2   UK Real Average Earnings

Source: Office for National Statistics.

wages in check. 'Independent' central banks were also cited as critical to achieving low inflation or 'price stability'. Free from political interference, the public came to accept that central banks would not take risks with monetary policy. The success in securing low inflation since the early 1990s created a virtuous cycle. Wage bargainers came to expect low inflation, and that was just as important in ensuring inflation would not spiral upwards again.

These arguments are misconceived. Inflation initially fell in response to two deep recessions during the early 1980s and 1990s. It remained low because of a fundamental shift in the balance of power between capital and labour, or companies and workers. Central banks acted aggressively to tame inflation in the Industrialised West with high interest rates. And government policies sought to strengthen the corporate hand over employees. Thereafter, there was little they needed to do to achieve low inflation. Policy credibility was largely irrelevant.

And 2007 underlined the point. Higher oil and food prices pushed inflation up in both the US and UK, but wages barely responded. Workers had precious little bargaining power, and real incomes were hit hard.

Technology or Free Trade?

The pressure on wages might not have been an extension of the anti-inflation policies adopted in the early 1980s. Alternatively, it may have been 'globalisation' that squeezed labour costs and led central banks to drive borrowing up to record levels. And within that rather loose term, there may have been two different forces playing a part – rapid technological change, or lower trade barriers underpinning the dominance of corporations.

Federal Reserve chair Ben Bernanke was quite clear. In his view, the high-tech revolution was chiefly responsible for the downward pressure on wages for some workers, not the growth in trade with low-cost countries.[6] Mr Bernanke's conclusion was warmly embraced by supporters of free trade. Politically, it was a far more appealing explanation than acknowledging the perils posed by a rising tide of cheap imports.

And if technological change has depressed the demand for low-skilled workers, the prescription seems quite straightforward. Displaced workers need to retrain. For that reason, governments in the West have buttressed their support for free trade with a call for improved education standards. It is a line that has been pursued with some enthusiasm by Mr Bernanke too. It neatly complemented his support for unalloyed free trade.[7]

However, that does not explain why debt has been allowed to rise so sharply. Historically, there have been countless technological revolutions that have triggered steep declines in consumer prices that were not destructive, notably in the late 1800s.[8] Periods of concerted downward pressure on the wages for workers made redundant by innovations are nothing new. Within any economy undergoing rapid change, there will be winners and losers. But that does not justify central banks allowing debt levels to soar in recent years. Prices for consumer goods should fall leading to a boost in real standards of living, once displaced workers regain employment. Technological revolutions do not have to result in extreme asset price cycles.

Excess Savings?

Focusing on technology provided a convenient distraction from a more pernicious issue. The arrival of China and so many other low-cost countries as major trading partners has also been a key force behind the 'flattening of wage compensation'. China was a huge competitive shock for many manufacturing industries in the West. It provided such a deep pool of cheap labour that its emergence as a major exporter was bound to be deflationary.

Rather than acknowledge this obvious point, the Federal Reserve turned the argument round. Having blamed technology for the compression of wages, the housing bubble was then deemed to be the fault of foreign investors. A number of countries had 'excess savings' which were being lent to the West.[9]

Keynesian tautology implies that a country with a large trade or current account surplus must by definition have an excess of savings over investment. From this perspective, it was not the

West's fault that it was mired in record debt levels. Asia, oil exporters and developing countries were running inordinately large trade surpluses and not doing enough to stimulate demand at home. Stronger consumption across these countries would have allowed the Industrialised West to export more, it was argued. And that would have obviated the need for central banks in the West to reflate quite so aggressively, creating housing bubbles.

It is certainly true that a number of countries have been running huge trade surpluses, some since the onset of the Asian crisis, others more recently. The four countries most closely associated with the financial tumult of 1997 – Thailand, South Korea, Malaysia and Indonesia – all saw their current account deficits suddenly move into surplus within a year. The first three notched up enormous surpluses averaging 12.5 per cent of GDP in 1998.[10] And that set a pattern for the next decade. Across South East Asia, strong trade surpluses became the norm, culminating in China's rise as an exporting powerhouse (see Figure 4.3).[11]

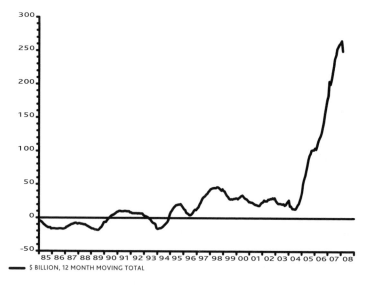

■ $ BILLION, 12 MONTH MOVING TOTAL

Figure 4.3   China Trade Balance

Source: General Administration of Customs.

The Asian crisis taught many governments in so-called developing economies a brutal lesson. In today's globalised economy where investors are able to move large sums around effortlessly, governments could be punished savagely for running trade deficits. The dollar standard, outlined in Chapter 2, made it much easier to incur deficits in the first place. The funding could also evaporate suddenly, without warning it seemed.

The turmoil of 1997 precipitated deep recessions across South East Asia, pushing Japan further into trouble too. Exchange rate implosions were also responsible for severe economic downturns in Latin America and Russia. Thereafter, Brazil and Argentina began to run persistent current account surpluses.[12] Mexico dramatically reduced its deficit, and Russia amassed enormous surpluses from 1999 onwards after it had been hit by a savage currency devaluation.[13]

Not all countries were scarred. And despite the painful losses sustained from numerous currency panics and the dotcom crash, there was never a shortage of funds seeking out the next great 'emerging market miracle'. Eastern Europe, Turkey and South Africa became notable hotspots where investors turned a blind eye to soaring current account deficits reminiscent of South East Asia in the mid 1990s.[14] Investors were lending to a number of industrialised economies, including Iceland and New Zealand, to fund deficits bigger than Thailand's before it ran into trouble.[15]

Within Euroland, investors were seemingly oblivious to the massive trade imbalances that emerged in Greece, Portugal, Spain and Ireland. All of these countries had seen an explosion in house prices, leading to a sharp rise in imports.[16] Without the protection of the euro, their housing markets would have collapsed long before the bubble finally burst in 2007. Prior to the single currency, countries routinely came under attack from speculators for running far smaller deficits.

In this respect, the creation of the euro and the single market facilitated the creation of housing bubbles even bigger than in the UK.[17] By the early months of 2008, the strains were beginning to show, with bond markets across Euroland diverging sharply, as investors fretted over the credit rating of countries with huge housing debt.[18]

Oil Exporters

There was another group of countries eager to accumulate large trade surpluses that also understood the vicissitude of financial markets – oil exporters. During the 1970s, they had seen a dramatic transformation in their economic fortunes as oil prices soared. But the good times did not last, and through the 1980s many oil exporters ran into acute financial difficulty. As prices plunged, the heady surpluses of the 1970s were replaced by massive deficits, and retrenchment followed.[19]

Faced with their own experience of boom and bust, the oil-rich nations were not going to fritter away a second opportunity to secure a durable buffer against inherently volatile markets, particularly with Peak Oil looming (see Chapter 5). Even before oil prices started to take off during 2004, Saudi Arabia's current account surplus had already risen to a hefty 13.1 per cent of GDP.[20] Kuwait, United Arab Emirates and Qatar were all running huge trade surpluses before the surge in spot crude towards $100 per barrel began.[21] Across the Middle East, only war-torn Iraq and Lebanon were running deficits.[22]

As oil prices soared, so did the trade surpluses. By 2007, Saudi Arabia was running a current account surplus equal to 25.5 per cent of GDP. Kuwait was even further in front, with a truly astonishing surplus reaching 47.9 per cent of GDP.[23] The pattern was repeated outside of the Middle East. Other oil exporters, including Venezuela, Nigeria, Russia, Uzbekistan and Azerbaijan also accumulated large surpluses.[24]

A Tautology

Flushed with excess savings, these countries have been forced to invest abroad, with a significant proportion of these funds flowing into financial markets in the Industrialised West. This, the Federal Reserve claimed, reduced borrowing costs, fuelling not only housing booms in the West, but also making it easier for companies to fund takeovers, mergers and acquisitions, and helping to sustain the private equity boom. The US was merely a passive victim, it was claimed. The countries running large trade surpluses or excess savings were the culprits.

It is unsurprising that Alan Greenspan and Ben Bernanke were vocal supporters of this theory. It was an audacious attempt to deflect mounting criticism over the reckless lending driving the housing bubble. It was not 'our fault'. Asia and the oil exporters drove the record capital inflows, helped finance the huge trade deficits in the US and the UK, funded runaway mortgage lending and greased the wheels of corporate finance. The Federal Reserve – if one believes Mr Greenspan's explanations for the housing bubble – was powerless to intercede.

But one country's surplus is another's deficit. The excess savings of Asia, oil exporters and developing countries were matched by inadequate savings in the Industrialised West. That is a tautology too. The argument could just as easily be turned on its head. There might instead be a savings shortfall in the US.

Mr Bernanke didn't see it that way. When the current Federal Reserve chairman elaborated upon his theory of 'excess savings', he claimed 'there is no obvious reason why the desired saving rate in the United States should have fallen precipitously' since 1996.[25] Instead, because of population ageing, the West was probably trying 'to save more, not less', but they were supposedly thwarted by cash-rich investors from abroad.[26] From this one-sided perspective, the fall in the savings ratio to a record low was not because of runaway house prices (see Figure 4.4).[27]

The high-tech bubble itself also coincided with a sharp downturn in the savings ratio during the late 1990s. Flush with capital gains from rising share prices, consumers were spending heavily over and above their incomes, pushing the trade deficit up and their savings ratio down.[28] But on the basis of the Federal Reserve's view of the world, that was not the fault of US policy either. It was foreign investors force-feeding US consumers.

Ironically, this was not a view shared by Mervyn King, the Bank of England governor. Mr King was clear that the low savings ratio

Figure 4.4   US Personal Savings Ratio

Source: Bureau of Economic Analysis.

in the UK was not anybody else's fault. The large trade deficit run by the UK was simply the result of a poor savings ratio, which had fallen to a record low of 2.4 per cent.[29] That needed to rise, Mr King warned. This still begs the question of why the housing market was allowed to spin out of control, driving the savings ratio down in the first place. However, like the Federal Reserve, the Bank of England's Monetary Policy Committee had a mandate that forced it to offset the deflation being driven by globalisation by creating asset bubbles.

A Conundrum

Both Ben Bernanke and Alan Greenspan buttressed their claims by suggesting overseas investors were suppressing market interest rates in the US during the property bubble. As the Federal Reserve started to hike rates from June 2004 onwards, it was a surprise to some, including Alan Greenspan, that government bond yields did not rise more sharply.[30] Foreign investors were also enthusiastic buyers of the mortgage bonds that drove the housing boom. The US was awash with record capital inflows that seemed to be fuelling the housing bubble.

But there was one good reason why government bond yields did not rise. It was clear that the housing market would eventually run into trouble. The economy was being driven by a debt binge that was patently unsustainable. Any rational investor could see that, eventually, short term interest rates would have to fall again. When interest rates drop, government bonds become more valuable because they promise to pay a fixed coupon. There was a natural ceiling to bond yields precisely because of the debt-driven economic policies pursued by the US authorities.

Subsequent events have proved the point. The Federal Reserve has since been forced to slash interest rates. It was not just the 'excess savings' that were suppressing borrowing costs and fuelling the debt binge. It was also a realisation that the US would eventually head back into recession. The reprieve from the dotcom crash would prove short-lived.

Subprime Trouble

As the housing market took off, the Federal Reserve sought to cool the pace of borrowing. But it was never that troubled by the dramatic rise in mortgage lending. It was puzzled that foreign investors were willing to keep buying government bonds, and Mr Greenspan discussed the so-called bond market conundrum at length. He sounded few alarm bells during the early stages of the bubble, and played down the rise in debt levels, claiming it was not a problem, since the value of assets had risen too. House prices had gone up, so record levels of borrowing were not an issue. That was a common refrain in Japan during the late 1980s. He eulogised the 'the improvements in lending practices driven by information technology' that allowed 'lenders to reach out to households with previously unrecognised borrowing capacities'.[31] Mr Greenspan had become a cheerleader for the banks aggressively promoting loans to those who had previously been on the margins – subprime borrowers.

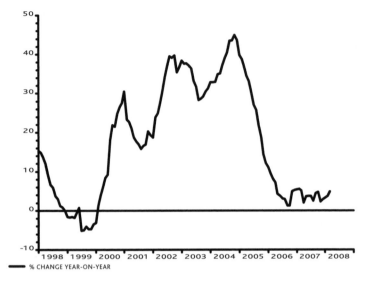

Figure 4.5 US Home Equity Loans

Source: Federal Reserve.

And he never fretted over the sharp rise in the number of people using their homes as a cash machine, tapping into rising equity as house prices soared. The 'surge in cash-out mortgage refinancings (*equity release*) likely improved rather than worsened the financial condition of the average homeowner', Mr Greenspan ventured. Home equity loans soared (see Figure 4.5). But according to the Federal Reserve, getting deeper into debt was good for you. It improved one's 'financial condition'.[32]

In reality, many homeowners were running into trouble long before interest rates started to rise. But the evidence was ignored. Large numbers of subprime borrowers were experiencing acute difficulty in keeping up with their interest payments, even before interest rates started to climb again in June 2004. Based on an in-depth analysis of 1998 to 2004, the Center for Responsible Lending (CRL) found that as many as one in eight subprime loans had either ended or would end in foreclosure within five years.[33]

And the true level of distress was even higher. The strong housing market had allowed borrowers who fell behind on their payments to exit their mortgages under duress without being foreclosed. During this six-year period, house prices had gone up 60.5 per cent.[34] Once these 'forced prepayments' were taken into account, the CRL found that 'the *composite* subprime failure rate was approaching 25 per cent within five years'.[35]

The seeds for the subprime crisis were sewn. Borrowers slipped into even more trouble as interest rates began to climb. Many of the subprime loans that proved so toxic during 2007 were variable mortgages based on short term interest rates, that were highly responsive to Federal Reserve policy. Fixed rate mortgages were influenced by the low Treasury yields and the strong capital inflows. But this was not where the explosive growth in mortgage lending occurred. The subprime crisis was created by the Federal Reserve standing idly by as lenders promoted mortgages that benefited from a loose US monetary policy, not the net excess savings of Asia and others.

And if monetary policy was being distorted by China and others recycling their savings or foreign exchange reserves into the US, the Federal Reserve could have pushed their lending rates up more quickly. Given the importance of variable mortgages in fuelling the housing boom, a more aggressive hiking of rates would have cooled the housing market sooner, preventing some of the worst excesses. But the Federal Reserve was in no rush to raise interest rates, hiking 0.25 per cent at a time. Globalisation was keeping inflation under control and the Fed saw no reason to act. It was happy to let the party roll.

Ignore the Bigger Picture

Ultimately, the excess savings theory was a smokescreen to shield the Federal Reserve from critics. It was wrong to blame foreign investors for the housing bubble without reference to the bigger picture. The capital flows into the US were a response to the forces of globalisation and the drive by US companies to cut labour costs in the first place. We have to go back to the starting point, namely the overinvestment that triggered the Asian debacle and the dotcom recession, which presaged the housing bubbles.

As we saw in Chapter 2, it is also impossible to divorce these events from the wider forces that precipitated the shift to floating exchange rates in 1973. Aside from the costly Vietnam War, the dollar also came under heavy pressure during the late 1960s from US companies expanding aggressively overseas. From late 1961 to 1966, the US economy boomed. Profits soared and, flush with excess funds, US companies began to expand abroad.[36] The resulting capital outflows were far larger than the trade deficits credited with causing the dollar crisis.[37] They played a critical role in persuading the US administration to let the US dollar float.

Spurred on by a dramatic improvement in company profits during the 1990s, overseas investment accelerated again, fuelling South East Asia's boom.[38] Japan was a big contributor to the capital flooding into the region too.[39]

These destabilising capital flows should be seen in the context of the secular forces outlined in Chapter 2. Overinvestment has not been limited to the West. It has been a global phenomenon. The succession of free trade pacts signed during the 1990s spawned enormous opportunities for companies seeking to cut costs, stimulating large capital flows that central banks have failed to control. But it is instructive to see the global ambitions of US corporations stretch back four decades. They helped to break Bretton Woods, and in turn provide further impetus to the boom and bust cycles so prevalent in recent years.

It was the culmination of all these events that left the Federal Reserve desperately trying to stimulate demand with low interest rates between 2001 and 2003, fearful that deflation would take root. As we saw in Chapter 3, their fears were valid. Without the record borrowing, prices and wages would have fallen. But this chronology of events is overlooked by revisionists who seek to blame Asia and oil exporters for the US housing bubble. And it is also ignored by those who argue that the housing bubbles are solely the fault of central banks. The roots go much deeper.

Trade Deficits and Cutting Labour Costs

Based on the assertions of Mr Bernanke and Mr Greenspan, the US housing bubble was driven by the unwillingness of competitors to buy enough US goods. That created a demand shortfall that led ineluctably to a housing bubble, which foreign investors were eager to finance. In reality, the sharp rise in house prices was the logical outcome of Western companies aggressively cutting labour costs by shifting jobs abroad.

China's economic boom was spurred in no small measure by companies taking advantage of a large pool of cheap labour, to boost profit margins. For more than a decade, the road to China has been a well trodden one for Western company executives, setting up factories to import cheap goods to the West. Direct investment flows into China accelerated in the early 1990s. In anticipation of China's acceptance into the World Trade Organisation in 2001, capital poured into the country (see Figure 4.6). It was these inflows that provided the funding and catalyst for an explosion in Chinese export growth to the US, UK and other countries, where workers could not hope to compete at prevailing exchange rates. By the end of 2007, the US trade deficit with China had risen to a record $256.3 billion (see Figure 4.7).

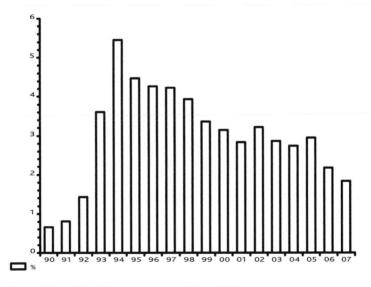

Figure 4.6   China Direct Investment Inflows/GDP

Source: Economic Intelligence Unit.

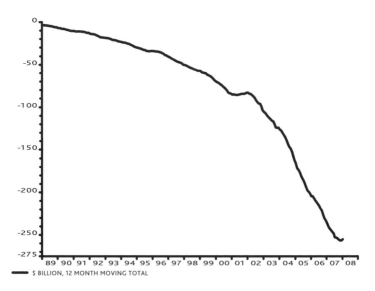

Figure 4.7   US Trade Balance With China

Source: Department of Commerce.

China was hardly alone in benefiting from the opportunities to export cheap goods to the West. Mexico became a major destination for US companies seeking to cut labour costs. When the North American Free Trade Agreement was signed in 1993, direct investment flows into Mexico were $4.4 billion. The US enjoyed a small trade surplus of $1.7 billion with its southern neighbour. Eight years later, US companies were investing heavily in Mexico. The direct investment inflows had more than quadrupled to $25.0 billion. And the US trade deficit with Mexico had swollen to $74.3 billion (see Figure 4.8).[40] The two trends were far from a coincidence. They were the direct result of 'free trade'.

Red Ink UK

After the fall of the Berlin Wall, Eastern Europe became a major recipient of direct investment inflows too. It soon overtook Asia as a magnet for capital, with a number of countries receiving a

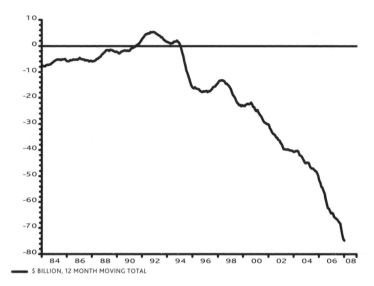

Figure 4.8 US Trade Balance With Mexico

Source: Department of Commerce.

huge influx of investment, notably Slovakia, the Czech Republic, Poland and Hungary. For the UK, Eastern Europe fulfilled the same role Mexico provided for US companies. Its close proximity, low labour costs and high unemployment rates provided compelling savings for companies looking to relocate.

The UK's trade deficit soared too. By the final quarter of 2007, the goods deficit had climbed to an annualised rate of £93.2 billion, equal to a record 6.6 per cent of GDP. That was even higher than the 5.5 per cent of GDP reached at the peak of the Lawson Boom, in 1988. The current account deficit had reached a new high too, hitting 5.4 per cent of GDP in Q3 2007, before falling back in the following quarter.[41]

There is nothing new about the long and steady decline in the UK's trade position. It has been going on for so long it rarely seems to trouble policymakers (see Figure 4.9). But it should. It lies at the heart of the UK housing bubble. Imports of cheap goods from low-cost countries have been fundamental to the downward pressure on wages for many workers.

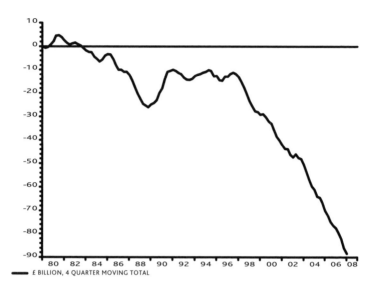

Figure 4.9   UK Trade Balance

Source: Office for National Statistics.

The UK has been running a trade deficit with China since 1988, and it has risen in every subsequent year, without exception. But it has accelerated sharply since the turn of this decade, hitting a hefty £14.7 billion in 2007 (see Figure 4.10).[42] And the deficit has climbed to record highs against a wide range of low-cost competitors, including Poland, Hungary, the Czech Republic, India and Turkey (see Figures 4.11–4.15).

And the growth rate in imports has been startling. In four years, total imports into the UK have risen 30.0 per cent. From China, however, they have jumped 121.9 per cent. The rise in imports from Eastern Europe has been astonishing. Imports have climbed 106.1 per cent from the Czech Republic, 113.0 per cent from Hungary, 132.8 per cent from Poland and a remarkable 389.6 per cent from Slovakia. Imports from India and Turkey were up 77.5 per cent and 76.8 per cent respectively, less rapid than Eastern Europe, but still double the overall increase.[43]

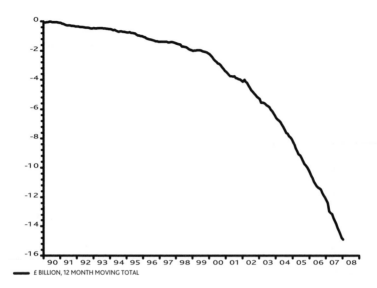

Figure 4.10   UK Trade Balance With China

Source: Office for National Statistics.

Figure 4.11   UK Trade Balance With Poland

Source: Office for National Statistics.

Figure 4.12   UK Trade Balance With Hungary

Source: Office for National Statistics.

Figure 4.13   UK Trade Balance With Czech Republic

Source: Office for National Statistics.

Figure 4.14   UK Trade Balance With India

Source: Office for National Statistics.

Figure 4.15   UK Trade Balance With Turkey

Source: Office for National Statistics.

Manufacturing Job Losses

The UK runs trade deficits with other countries that are hardly low cost. The biggest bi-lateral imbalance is with Germany. But it is the sheer pace of change that demonstrates the profound impact of corporate cost-cutting, which has resulted in just under a third or 1.3 million of manufacturing job cuts in the UK since the end of 1997 (see Figure 4.16).[44]

This is hardly new. The disappearance of manufacturing jobs has been unrelenting since the early 1980s. Over a million jobs vanished in the recession of the early 1980s, and a further million were shed following the Lawson Boom.

There is a crucial distinction, however. These losses occurred as a result of recession. The jobs lost since New Labour came to power have been the result of free trade and cost-cutting. There has been no recession to explain the contraction of manufacturing employment over the past decade, although one is now looming.

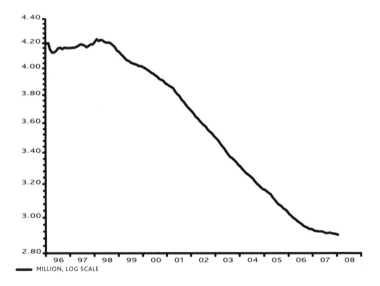

Figure 4.16   UK Manufacturing Employment

Source: Office for National Statistics.

And the losses overlap with the areas where the UK trade balance has deteriorated so far. Unsurprisingly, the biggest job cuts have been in clothing and footwear, where the trade deficit has climbed from £4.7 billion in 1997 to £11.3 billion a decade later. But there have been big declines in areas which are hardly 'low value'. In ten years, a surplus of £3.8 billion in machinery has turned into a deficit of £17.4 billion, and more than 30 per cent of the jobs have disappeared in this sector. A deficit of £6.9 billion in road vehicles has grown into a shortfall of £15.2 billion, despite the success of Japanese manufacturers moving in to the country. There is precious little left of Britain's indigenous car industry. 'Scientific and photographic' has swung from a surplus of £0.9 billion to a record deficit of £0.5 billion.[45] Once again, high-value manufacturing is disappearing from Britain. Every single category of manufacturing employment has fallen since 1997, with many industries shedding a fifth of their workforce and more (see Table 4.1).

Despite these losses, total employment has gone up, hitting new highs at the end of 2007. Nearly 30 million have jobs, a record.[46] For New Labour, this is proof that unmitigated free trade works. There is nothing politicians or policymakers can do to stem the job losses to cheap countries, they claim. But so long as service employment continues to absorb the slack, there is no reason to fret. An economy can thrive without manufacturing, so the argument goes.

Bubble Jobs

Theoretically that is true. London is a service economy, and has ostensibly boomed. What is true for a large city can apply nationwide. But the flaw in this argument can be seen in the sheer scale of the rise in consumer debt needed to counter the deflationary impact of shipping so many goods east.

The downward pressure on prices of consumer goods that results from globalisation allowed central banks to keep interest rates low, driving debt levels up. The housing bubble in turn provided alternative jobs in the service sector. Britain has created

Table 4.1 Manufacturing Job Losses Under New Labour

	Jan 1997 (000s)	Sept 2007 (000s)	Change (000s)	Change (%)
Manufacturing industries	4,043	2,870	–1,173	–29.01
Food products, beverages and tobacco	459	398	–61	–13.29
Manufacture of clothing, textiles and leather	370	114	–256	–69.19
Wood and wood products	86	79	–7	–8.14
Paper, pulp, printing, and recording	460	362	–98	–21.30
Chemicals. Chemical products, manmade fibres	243	184	–59	–24.28
Rubber and plastic products	239	180	–59	–24.69
Non-metal, mineral products, metal and metal products	705	480	–225	–31.91
Machinery and equipment	386	269	–117	–30.31
Electrical and optical equipment	493	300	–193	–39.15
Transport equipment	379	310	–69	–18.21
Coke, nuclear and other manufacturing	223	195	–28	–12.56

Source: Office for National Statistics.

large numbers of service sector jobs. But they have in many cases been contingent on the credit bubble that the authorities had to create, to fill the void generated by the loss of manufacturing jobs (see Figure 4.17).

For a while, 'globalisation' worked for the UK, as it benefited not just from the surge in house prices at home, but also the credit bubbles that have emerged across the world too. As we shall see in Chapter 6, there have been many, and the financial sector in the UK has boomed on the back of a global credit bubble. Now of course, it is starting to unravel. As an economic strategy, it was never sustainable. If the housing bubbles deflate aggressively across the West triggering problems in emerging market economies, it

Figure 4.17   UK Business and Financial Services Jobs

Source: Office for National Statistics.

will have inflicted immense damage to the longer term growth
prospects of the UK economy.

The flaw can also be seen in the trade numbers. The service
sector has been unable to replace the loss of export earnings as
manufacturers closed down, despite record profits in the financial
sector during 2007. Net income on financial services soared to
a record £27.5 billion in the year to Q3 2007, accounting for
the lion's share of the total surplus on services of £36.0 billion.[47]
However, this covered only a small proportion of the deficit in
goods. Indeed, without the contribution from the financial sector,
the UK's current account deficit would have been 7.8 per cent of
GDP, nearly as big as Thailand's when the Asian crisis struck in
1997 (see Figure 4.18).[48]

Years of running large trade deficits also turned the UK into a
large debtor with the rest of the world. When New Labour came
to power, the UK had net external debts of £33.8 billion. A decade
later, that had risen nine-fold to a record £318.9 billion, or 22.5 per
cent of GDP (see Figure 4.19). This was even bigger than that of

Figure 4.18   UK Current Account Excluding Financial Services

Source: Office for National Statistics.

Figure 4.19   UK Net External Assets/GDP

Source: Office for National Statistics.

the US.[49] The high level of external borrowing meant the UK was now running a deficit on its investment income balance too.[50] And that was feeding into an even bigger current account deficit.

These numbers underline the futility of relocating abroad simply to cut costs. UK companies had accumulated substantial external assets worth £796.9 billion by Q3 2007. This helped to generate a net profit of £28.6 billion in the year to Q3 2007. That sounds impressive, but it was overwhelmed by interest payments on external debt incurred to pay for the persistent trade deficits.[51] UK companies were making a profit from outsourcing. But for the UK economy, the 'benefits' had been wiped out by the borrowing needed to finance record imports. Once again, it was hard to see how shedding over a million manufacturing jobs had strengthened the UK economy. It had merely undermined the country's external accounts, and saddled future generations with huge debts.

New Labour had promised an end to the profligate policies of the 1980s. But the external deficit was now bigger than at the worst point of the Lawson Boom. It is small wonder sterling began to slide towards the end of 2007, as investors concluded that without the global credit bubble, there would be little to drive the economy.

Wal-Mart

The story is no different for the US, which has lost more than a fifth of its manufacturing workforce since 1997 (see Figure 4.20).[52] The US has arguably been less exposed to the full blast of free trade, as imports are a lower share of GDP.[53] But that has not stopped US retailers from leading the wholesale transfer of jobs to low-cost countries, providing cheaper imports, but ultimately a record debt burden for US consumers too. Wal-Mart is routinely cited as a key force 'that propelled global outstourcing', precisely because 'it controls so much purchasing power of the US economy'.[54]

The story of Wal-Mart and other retailers such as Target, Kmart, Toys 'R' Us and Home Depot shows once again that the housing bubble cannot be blamed solely on Asia, oil exporters or emerging market economies manipulating their currencies.

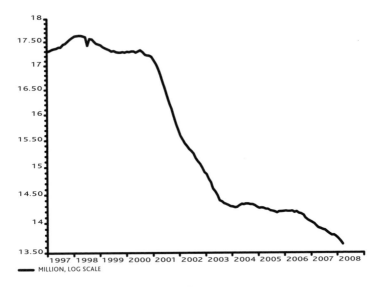

Figure 4.20   US Manufacturing Employment

Source: Bureau of Labor Statistics.

US retailers led the off-shoring of US jobs, not Asian companies. They ruthlessly exploited the lower wages available in China and elsewhere. An estimated 1.8 million jobs have been lost due to cheap imports between 2001 and 2006. And Wal-Mart was responsible for nearly 200,000.[55]

Buying From Each Other

It is unsurprising that emerging market countries receiving massive investment inflows from Western companies have enjoyed strong economic growth. What is surprising – to some – is that this did not always benefit the Industrialised West. Emerging market countries were importing heavily, but more often than not from each other.

Developing countries have boomed and their imports have soared. According to the International Monetary Fund (IMF), developing countries have increased their imports from industrialised countries by 162.2 per cent between the beginning of 2002 and August 2007, when the credit crunch erupted. By contrast – and this is a crucial point – they have increased their imports from each other by 301.8 per cent (see Figure 4.21).[56] The industrialised economies have been unable to compete.

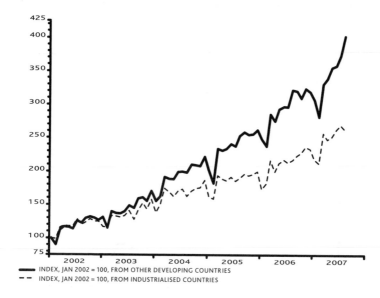

INDEX, JAN 2002 = 100, FROM OTHER DEVELOPING COUNTRIES
INDEX, JAN 2002 = 100, FROM INDUSTRIALISED COUNTRIES

Figure 4.21   Developing Country Imports

Source: International Financial Statistics.

China is a case in point. As growth accelerated, imports rose sharply. Its share of world imports climbed from 4.0 per cent to 6.8 per cent since the start of 2002. But within that, there has been a sharp drop in imports from industrialised countries. In 2002, 48.2 per cent of China's imports came from the industrialised 'bloc'. That has since fallen to 36.9 per cent. By contrast, developing countries for the first time now account for more than half of China's imports. The proportion has risen from 48.0 per cent to 55.8 per cent.[57]

And the US has been losing out since the early 1980s. In 1982, 23.4 per cent of China's imports came from the US. By the early months of 2006, that had dropped to just 7.3 per cent, and the share has remained static since. China wants to import, but not from the US it seems. The UK has fared little better. Back in 2004, China took 2.4 per cent of its imports from the UK. That has since dropped to a desultory 0.8 per cent.[58] In both cases, the declines since China joined the World Trade Organisation have been notably steep (see Figures 4.22 and 4.23)

Figure 4.22   China Imports from US/China Imports

Source: International Financial Statistics.

The point is corroborated by the detailed breakdown of the UK trade data. According to HM Revenue and Customs, manufacturing accounted for virtually all of the UK's deficit with China in 2007. One of the three components is 'miscellaneous manufacturing', which includes clothing and electrical goods among others. Imports of miscellaneous manufacturing from China reached £7.2 billion in 2007. In return, UK exports to China were just £271 million. Imports dwarfed exports by a factor of 27. No wonder so many of the ships return home to China empty.

As economies industrialise, these imbalances are supposed to be self-correcting. Demand for goods made in the West should

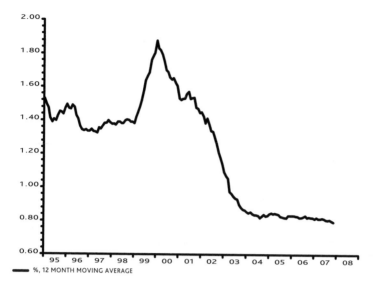

Figure 4.23   China Imports from UK/China Imports

Source: International Financial Statistics.

rise. In reality, China and others are simply moving up the value chain, exploiting their competitive edge in industries that have traditionally been dominated by the West. For years China's biggest trade surplus used to be in textiles and clothing. Not anymore. By the end of 2007, that had been overtaken by machinery and electronic equipment (see Figure 4.24).[59] China is no longer just a competitor in cheap goods. It is expanding in cars, railways, computer chips and even aircraft.

In this respect, proponents of free trade who argue that China's arrival onto the world stage would only bring a one-off deflation hit for the West are wrong. The price index for US imports from China was starting to rise during 2007, reflecting the weaker US dollar. But the range of goods being imported from China will continue to expand until labour costs are equalised. The renminbi is now appreciating more quickly, but full equalisation of labour costs will not happen for years. In the meantime, workers in the West will continue to be undercut by companies exploiting cheap labour in China.

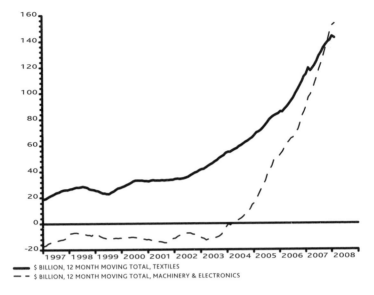

Figure 4.24   China Trade Balance

Source: General Administration of Customs.

Clearly a recession in the US will cap China's enormous trade surplus. After soaring in the first half of 2007, exports to the US started to slow. However, Chinese exports to the US were still registering double-digit gains.[60] Even in recession, Chinese imports into the US might continue to rise, because the misalignment of labour costs is so great. And that should concern policymakers. This will not be an orderly correction of global imbalances.

Indeed, it is by no means certain the US trade deficit will shrink by much even as the housing downturn intensifies. As we shall see in Chapter 6, attempts by many emerging market economies to secure a competitive advantage have spawned asset bubbles that are unlikely to prove sustainable. As the economic downturn in the West intensifies, asset bubbles will be punctured around the globe, hitting demand for US goods. US exporters will be vulnerable to a global recession, since many of the country's strengths lie in highly cyclical industries – technology, aircraft and construction equipment.

Reflate or Revalue

At this juncture, it is tempting to suggest the fault still lies with countries running large trade surpluses, for not doing more to stimulate their economies. But they could hardly reflate any faster. The huge capital inflows into these countries and persistent intervention by central banks to hold down their currencies were fuelling asset bubbles. Credit growth was soaring across the developing world. Emerging stock markets had tripled in value in just four years.[61]

The Chinese government has routinely been stamping down on the frenetic pace of economic growth since 2004. The threats of climate change and Peak Oil have been putting severe upward pressure on headline inflation (see Chapter 5). Endemic pollution and the environmental consequences of such rapid growth have been taking their toll. The government started shutting factories across a huge swathe of northern China early in 2008, to reduce the smog in Beijing ahead of the Olympic Games.[62]

If emerging market governments were unwilling to ramp up domestic demand to bail out the Industrialised West, it is argued, they could have still let their currencies appreciate more quickly. That would have stimulated demand for goods produced in the West, and produced a more balanced world economy that would not be facing a widespread implosion of asset bubbles. By intervening so extensively, Asia and other developing economies have clearly gained a significant competitive edge, exacerbating the demand shortfall in the West.

From 2002, the US dollar did start to fall in response to the burgeoning current account deficit in the US. By the end of 2007, it had fallen to its lowest level in eleven years against a weighted average of other currencies. It was back down to levels last seen prior to the Asian crisis.

But the dollar had fallen more against other industrialised economies. It was depreciating against developing countries, but nowhere near as quickly. Many of the central banks in these countries were still intervening to slow the appreciation of their currencies. Exporting to the US had become a major prop for these economies, and they were reluctant to concede their competitive advantage, and allow their exchange rates to rise too rapidly.

It is not unreasonable to wonder whether the outcome might have been different if developing countries had not been manipulating their exchange rates. Countries that have prevented their currencies from appreciating are abusing the notion of free trade too. But their unwillingness to 'play by the rules' has to be seen in context. As we saw in Chapter 2, Asia's boom and bust of the 1990s was in part a response to the persistent trade deficits incurred by the US through the 1980s. It was a point conveniently overlooked by Mr Bernanke when he expounded upon his excess savings theory, as he tried to shift the blame for the US housing bubble.

And it was telling that there had been only a limited improvement in the trade deficit by the end of 2007, even after such a hefty fall in the US dollar. Exchange rates are only part of the story. The trade deficits have been driven in the main by corporations exploiting huge wage differentials between the industrialised and industrialising worlds. A realignment of exchange rates may not do much to eliminate trade imbalances in the short run. Furthermore, as we shall see in Chapter 5, the long slide in the dollar was compromising the ability of the Federal Reserve to contain the fallout from the housing market crash. The Bank of England was getting hemmed in by a falling pound too.

And it was instructive to see in Chapter 3 how the trade imbalances would still have been substantial even if both central banks had chosen to dampen credit growth aggressively. The misalignment of labour costs was so great that even if central banks had chosen not to reflate through housing bubbles, the US and UK would still have lost large numbers of manufacturing jobs, squeezing wages.

Reversing the Tide

Free trade will continue to provide opportunities for large companies to move production across the world, exploiting labour cost differentials to improve profit margins. But the cost of this economic strategy, endorsed by Western governments and embraced by developing economies, has been higher debt levels in the West, as central banks seek to offset the downward pressure on wages at home.

A backlash against free trade is now gathering momentum in the US, and protectionism has become a key battleground for the 2008 presidential election. 'China's steel comes here, our jobs go there' was Hillary Clinton's blunt assertion to a gathering in Ohio ahead of the primary on 4 March 2008. Ohio has suffered more than most states from the loss of manufacturing jobs, and property foreclosures were rising here long before they hit the more speculative southern states. 'We play by the rules, they manipulate their currency. And we get tainted fish, lead-laced toys and poisoned pet food in return', lambasted the presidential hopeful.[63]

Writing in the *Journal of Economic Perspectives* in 2004, Nobel Laureate Paul Samuelson caused a stir too by suggesting that the arrival of India and China onto the world stage might inflict more harm than good on US workers.[64] Credited with developing the comparative theory of trade in 1964, Mr Samuelson has provided much intellectual justification for the explosive growth in international trade. Mr Samuelson's most recent intervention on the subject was inevitably met by fierce rebuttals from supporters of free trade.

Few economists would dispute the original premise of the theory of trade. It makes sense for a country with a comparative advantage to trade with another where it suffers a relative disadvantage. If Norway enjoys a comparative advantage in logging timber for example, it makes sense for it to buy wine from France.

But free trade today is no longer driven by comparative advantage, rather the ability to maximise profits by cutting costs. And the cost advantage enjoyed by so many developing economies is so great, that it has been impossible for many manufacturing industries in the Industrialised West to compete.

The debate over globalisation has become increasingly polarised. Its detractors have exploited the recent financial turmoil to call for limits on free trade. Its supporters urge governments to respond by exposing companies in the West even further to the full blast of competition from low-cost countries, accelerating free trade agreements. The Doha round of negotiations are seen as critical to the future health of the world economy by many who fail to see how previous trade agreements, with few checks and balances to excessive corporate power, have laid the foundations for the credit bubble that is now unravelling so fast.

Many aspects of globalisation should be embraced, not rejected. Technology has brought countries and their citizens closer together. There is no turning the clock back. The internet is here to stay. The ability to outsource has manifestly been transformed by the dotcom revolution. To pretend otherwise would be foolish and deny the potential benefits – both economic and political – that may come from an integrated world economy.

Equally, ardent supporters of free trade have to concede ground, otherwise the protectionists who want to retreat into isolationism will win the argument. We will return to the 'beggar thy neighbour' policies of the 1930s. The benefits of free trade have to be kept in perspective, set against the costs of allowing huge asset bubbles to emerge, not just in the West, but also in emerging market economies. The two are indelibly linked. Those railing against protectionism never acknowledge this fundamental point. The concerted downward pressure on wages created the pretext for asset bubbles which are now bursting all across the Industrialised West.

Advocates of unlimited free trade will claim that central banks should have still prevented asset inflation by running tighter monetary policies. In their assessment, the run-up in house prices and reckless lending is divorced from the issue of free trade. But it was the same laissez-faire policies that drove the free trade agenda which also led the central banks to back off, ignoring the surge in lending. Mr Greenspan and Mr Bernanke were tireless promoters of free trade. It is unsurprising that they were disinclined to intervene when the pace of lending spun out of control from 2004 onwards. It reflected their ideology.[65]

If the Federal Reserve and Bank of England had decided financial stability mattered and tried to dampen the housing markets early on, growth would have been very anaemic as jobs disappeared to low-cost countries. The current ructions over free trade would have occurred much sooner. They might have dominated the US presidential campaign of 2004, not 2008. And governments might have been forced to acknowledge their economic strategy was flawed.

Free trade is a positive, but not when companies abuse it and use it as an excuse to cut costs and boost profit margins. When two countries engage in trade because each has a comparative advantage, free trade works. When 'free trade agreements' simply provide the green light for companies to shunt jobs around in search of short term cost savings, then it is destined to fail. There will be a backlash, because the politicians have promoted a free trade that creates asset bubbles that inevitably rupture with debilitating consequences.

5

DEALING WITH THE FALLOUT

The drive by transnational corporations to cut costs has spawned asset bubbles not just in the West, but across the globe. Masquerading under the banner of free trade, companies have been free to relocate, squeezing wages in the West, fuelling credit bubbles and threatening to destabilise the world economy. Central banks and governments now have to deal with the consequences.

Ironically, the most pressing policy prescription is arguably the one weapon that got so many industrialised economies into such difficulty in the first place – slashing interest rates. It was the failure of the Bank of Japan to lower borrowing costs quickly after the bubble burst in 1990 that led to such a prolonged struggle against debt deflation. The Bank of Japan and Ministry of Finance refused to acknowledge the enormous damage being inflicted from keeping interest rates too high in the early years of the property collapse. They were oblivious to the risks that Japan would become subsumed by a Fisher-style debt trap.[1]

By the end of February 2008, both the Federal Reserve and the Bank of England had responded by lowering interest rates. The US central bank had cut five times, reducing its key lending rate – the Fed funds target – from 5.25 per cent to 3.0 per cent. The Bank of England had cut twice by 0.5 per cent to 5.25 per cent.[2] It was a start. Before the summer of 2007, few economists were expecting interest rates to fall by the end of the year. Looking back, one might conclude the policy response had been swift.

That would be wrong. It took far too long for the Federal Reserve to swing into action. The first rate cut did not materialise until two years after the peak in the property market.[3] The Fed finally cut on 18 September 2007. House prices were already tumbling in every major city. By the end of 2007, prices had fallen 10–15 per cent in many cities. San Francisco, San Diego, Los Angeles, Las Vegas, Phoenix, Detroit, Tampa and Miami were all posting double-digit declines, with the latter down 17.5 per cent year-on-year.[4]

Foreclosure notices were running at record levels as banks sought to repossess properties from borrowers unable to keep up with soaring repayments.[5] Turnover in the property market had been sliding for more than two years.[6] Attempts to dispose of foreclosed homes were driving prices down even more quickly. Auctioneers were triggering a rout, with prices plunging 50 per cent or more.

With the stock market in turmoil, the Federal Reserve finally caved in and slashed interest rates on 22 January 2008. The 0.75 per cent cut in borrowing costs was the biggest since September 1982. The following week it had cut again by 0.5 per cent. Doubtless, there will be further falls as 2008 unfolds. Interest rates may well slide to 1.0 per cent or lower before the year is out. A return to the zero rates seen in Japan is not out of the question. Whether that stabilises the US economy remains to be seen.

The Early Mistakes

It is instructive to look back at Japan's disastrous property bubble to see the Federal Reserve has made many of the same mistakes. That should worry all of us. The first rate cut in Japan's long downturn was implemented in July 1991, 18 months after the top of the asset price cycle. Thereafter the Bank of Japan was very slow in cutting interest rates. After the first reduction, it sat on its hands for five months. Nevertheless, the early stages in the deflation of any asset bubble are always critical. In comparison with the much maligned Bank of Japan, the Federal Reserve was just as tardy, indeed more so.

The Federal Reserve was making the same mistake as the Bank of Japan. It was judging policy in the context of economic growth, instead of assessing the obvious dangers posed by a collapse of the housing market. Rather than look ahead, it was staring blankly into the rear view mirror. So long as the economy was not in recession, there was little urgency. The Federal Reserve seemed almost ambivalent about the downturn in the property market. Most economists agreed that the sheer speed of the run-up in house prices had been undesirable and unsustainable. Perhaps a modest correction was not such a bad thing.

It was only when the money markets froze on 9 August 2007 that the Federal Reserve acknowledged the housing crisis was serious, and might send the US into recession. Even then, it was slow to act, focusing on the distress facing banks in the money markets, rather than dealing with the core of the problem – falling house prices. It cut the discount rate, not the Fed funds target.[7] That benefited the banks, but did little for homeowners struggling with high debt burdens and caught with rising negative equity. In the Federal Reserve's view, the events of 2007 represented a crisis of confidence in banks, not the economy. The real economic data was holding up comparatively well, it claimed. It was hard to say that a recession was imminent.

That was precisely the mistake made by the Bank of Japan. It failed to recognise there might simply be a lag between the housing market turning, and the economy getting hit. After such a prolonged boom, it can take time for households to shift their behaviour, accepting their biggest asset is tumbling in value. Expectations are often adaptive or retrospective. It's not just central bankers that have a habit of looking backwards. Many households were in denial and clung in vain to a belief that house prices would carry on rising.

A report from the Boston Consulting Group in May 2007 – just before two hedge funds at US bank Bear Stearns went into meltdown – found that 85 per cent of homeowners still believed their house would be worth more in five years' time. The survey concluded 'Americans believe their homes are still the best investment. They're positive about their home values.'[8] In reality, house prices had already been falling in many areas for a year and a half. Record borrowing and runaway house prices had driven the economy on the way up. They would lead it into recession too, if the Federal Reserve did not act.

In Japan's case, the failure to accept that such a sharp decline in both property and share prices would hurt the economy was particularly baffling. In the US, optimists were at least able to point to a resilient stock market – for a short while. The same forces that drove the US housing boom also spurred a dramatic rise in company profits from early 2003 onwards. There was a genuine 'profits renaissance'. When the housing market started to slide, the stock market was not that overvalued compared to 2000, when the dotcom bubble burst.[9] It had risen a long way from the lows of 2003, but share prices were still below the 2000 peak. And during the first year of the housing slump, company profits continued to rise. The dollar was falling too, and that was giving an important boost to US companies operating overseas.[10]

But investors overlooked one very obvious point. As the housing market imploded, company profits would eventually fall. And margins would come under even more pressure than normal, because they were so high in the first place. Once the easy credit tap was turned off and consumers were forced to retrench, profits would crumble from price wars and intense discounting.

As we shall see in Chapter 7, there really were few excuses for the tardy response from the Bank of Japan during the early years of the bear market. The yen was strong on the foreign exchange market and it did not take long for inflation to start falling. But the Bank of Japan feared inflation and failed to respond, with catastrophic consequences. After more than a decade of endemic deflation these concerns now seem hopelessly misplaced.

The Federal Reserve fell into the same trap. It spent most of 2007 worrying about inflation, not the collapse of property prices. The Bank of England and European Central Bank were also allowing the fear of inflation to corrupt their policy response in the early months of 2008. Neither had learnt from the biggest housing boom and bust seen in modern times.

Policy Gridlock

There were a number of obstacles to rate cuts cited by economists in the US. None of them were valid, but they created policy gridlock.

Ironically, they also demonstrated a failure to comprehend how globalisation had distorted monetary policy in the first place. The central banks never acknowledged that they were inflating the housing markets to mask obvious shortcomings with the aggressive promotion of free trade. It is unsurprising, therefore, that they underestimated the potential for contagion when the bubble finally burst.

Both the US and UK were running high trade deficits. They were obvious counterparts to the housing booms, with strong consumer demand sucking in imports at a frenetic pace and driving the deficits up to record levels.

By the second quarter of 2005, the US current account deficit had reached an annualised equivalent of 6.5 per cent of GDP.[11] That was not far short of the massive deficit that precipitated the run on the Thai baht in July 1997.

The dollar had started to fall in response to the yawning trade gap from early 2002. And the long devaluation was seen as a major inflation threat. The slide was steady but unspectacular. Periodical declines were followed by modest recoveries. Considering the size of the current account deficit, the dollar's decline was remarkably orderly. There was rarely a sense of crisis. Compared to the turmoil that had accompanied the devaluation between early 1985 and 1987 and culminated in the stock market crash, the sell-off was less frenetic.

That in part reflected very strong demand for US assets and the persistent capital inflows the US was able to attract, even after house prices had peaked. There seemed to be no shortage of foreign investors willing to park their savings in the US. It was quite common to hear financial market commentators claim the capital inflows were a vote of confidence in the US economy.

That was akin to suggesting strong demand for high-tech shares justified the absurd valuations seen in the dotcom bubble. There was always a risk that the capital inflows would evaporate suddenly, causing the dollar to slide and creating a policy headache for the Federal Reserve. And that was likely to occur once the housing bubble had started to unravel.

The Asian crisis was triggered by such a *volte face* from foreign investors. Mexico (1983 and 1994), Russia (1998), Brazil (1999),

Argentina (2000) and Turkey (2000) were similar demonstrations of a brutal turnaround in foreign sentiment. There was no reason why it could not happen to the US. It was the world's largest economy and the dollar was still the principal reserve currency. But the dollar could not defy gravity.

And over the summer of 2007, the sheer depth of the housing crisis and the credit squeeze finally combined to leave the dollar acutely short of friends. Its long decline began to accelerate. One of the biggest sources of inflows had been into the asset-backed securities used to fund the property boom. Much of the rapid growth in mortgage lending had been financed by foreign investors. In pure accounting terms, it was the flipside of the current account deficit. When the money markets froze suddenly in August 2007, the issuance of these bonds ground to an abrupt halt, creating a huge funding gap for the dollar.

The US was also relying on strong inflows into two other classes of assets – corporate bonds and shares. They dried up dramatically over the summer of 2007 too. The housing crisis was making foreign investors wary of owning any US asset other than rock solid Treasuries, which stood to benefit as interest rates came down.

Ironically, the current account deficit was shrinking by this point, partly in response to a more competitive dollar, but also due to weaker US consumer demand as house prices fell. But the rate of improvement had been slow.[12] Getting the trade deficit down was not easy after so much of the manufacturing base had been shipped out to cheaper countries.

The US was also the world's largest external debtor, owing a mammoth $2.5 trillion to creditors overseas, equal to 19.2 per cent of GDP.[13] It managed to earn a higher rate of return on its assets than it paid out on its liabilities. As a result, its net investment income balance, which records the net cost of running such an onerous external debt burden, was still showing a surplus.[14] The US was able to borrow at comparatively low interest rates.

This in part reflected the dollar's role as a reserve currency. Many central banks held a significant proportion of their foreign exchange reserves in dollars. These reserves had risen spectacularly over recent years. This is a theme which we shall return to in Chapter 6. They provided a huge pool of funds looking for a home.

And the most natural home was the dollar. When the central banks intervened to keep their currency low on the foreign exchange market, they would often sell their own currency, and buy dollars. It was quite logical for the central banks to park their dollars in US assets. Indeed, if they did not, it would negate the whole point of intervention. If they wanted to hold their currency down against the dollar, central banks had to hold a large proportion of their reserves in US assets.

This ultimately created a major fault-line in the globalisation story which its proponents were slow to acknowledge. The US housing boom was a necessary response to the downward pressure on wages created by a competitive struggle the US could not win. The dollar needed to fall to allow US workers to compete with ultra cheap Chinese employees. But the Chinese central bank had been unwilling to allow the renminbi to appreciate quickly, until long after the housing market in the US had collapsed. Instead, it accumulated large reserves trying to underpin a massive competitive advantage. And these funds were lent back to the US, to fund its housing boom.

The story was repeated across the world. It was not just low-cost emerging market countries that were lending to the US. Euroland and Japan were also running large trade surpluses with the US. A large proportion of Japan's foreign exchange reserves was parked in US Treasuries too. Many Euroland investors had been sucked in to buying the mortgage-backed securities, which would default in such large numbers as the housing crisis intensified in 2007. It seemed like the perfect virtuous cycle.

Fleeing the Dollar

But foreign investors could not be fooled for ever. Even if central bankers were obliged to keep buying dollars, private investors turned against US assets with a vengeance. The collapse in capital flows to the US over the summer of 2007 was stunning, the biggest reversal of any major industrialised country in modern times. In

Q2 2007, net portfolio inflows into the US were running at an annualised rate of $823.4 billion, comfortably a record. In Q3, there was a net annualised outflow of $234.1 billion.[15] The $1.1 trillion reversal was three times bigger than any seen before.

The dam had burst. Private investors were no longer prepared to underwrite a US 'spending beyond its means', particularly after so many had suffered heavy losses buying mortgage bonds. There was considerable, understandable anger at the manner in which they had been duped, buying mortgage-backed bonds that suffered grievous downgrades, and should never have been rated Triple A in the first place. The issuance of mortgage-backed securities – the bonds that caused so much trouble in the subprime crisis – contracted by $234.6 billion (see Figure 5.1).[16] The sudden turnaround was testimony to the capricious nature of leveraged lending.

A number of economists were highlighting in no uncertain terms the dangers of lending to the US, particularly through mortgage-backed securities.[17] But many of these investors overlooked the

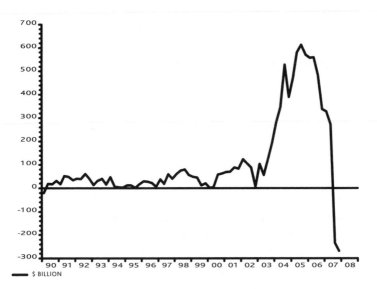

■ $ BILLION

Figure 5.1   US Asset-Backed Securities, Mortgages

Source: Federal Reserve.

risks precisely because they were awash with extraordinary sums they simply had to invest. Such aggressive intervention was creating huge excess domestic liquidity that needed to go somewhere. Globalisation had created a vast pool of funds simply looking for anywhere to call home.

During the autumn of 2007, the dollar started to slide more quickly. As it fell, governments and central banks in many countries began to acknowledge the futility of their strategy. Buying US assets might provide its manufacturers with a competitive short term boost, but it was a poor return on their funds. Private investors were driving the dollar down anyway, and central banks were now suffering from heavy capital losses too. More and more countries began to accept the inevitable, that their currencies would have to rise against the dollar.

The end result was a pick-up in import prices for the US that would ostensibly make it harder for the Federal Reserve to cut interest rates. By early 2008, import prices were rising at an annual rate of 13.6 per cent, the fastest increase for more than two decades.[18] Significantly, import prices for goods arriving from China were no longer falling and had started to climb.[19]

Globalisation Comes Full Circle

The great globalisation story had come full circle. Cheap imports had been a major selling point of the free trade agreements that had proliferated under the World Trade Organisation. They had been a key factor keeping inflation under control and allowing central banks to keep interest rates low, to fuel the housing bubbles. Import costs were now soaring, threatening to undermine the Federal Reserve's ability to cushion the fallout from runaway house prices. Outsourcing was not quite the free lunch its proponents had suggested.

In truth, the pick-up in import prices was less threatening than many economists claimed. The role of profit margins as a cushion against rising cost pressures – particularly in a world of low wages – was highlighted in Chapter 2. When profit margins are historically high, there is a greater tendency for rising costs to be absorbed. And when consumer demand slows, there is an increased potential for prices to fall quickly.

That had been evident since the peak of the housing market. Outside of food and energy, inflation fell swiftly in the US during the first two years of the housing slump, even as import prices rose. Many retailers had been outsourcing aggressively during the housing bubble, leading to a huge increase in their profits.[20] Retailers' profits rose from $66.7 billion in Q1 2001 to $140.2 billion Q3 2007, a remarkable rise of 110.2 per cent. That was far in excess of the 39.4 per cent rise in nominal GDP. Such was the power of outsourcing. Nearly 10 per cent of the goods sold by Wal-Mart were now purchased from Chinese suppliers.[21] This outsourcing was part of a wider trend that had made the housing bubbles necessary in the first place.

Price wars between stores intensified in the final months of 2006 in response to a slump in demand. Even as import costs carried on rising through 2007, prices for many consumer goods continued to fall (see Figure 5.2).[22]

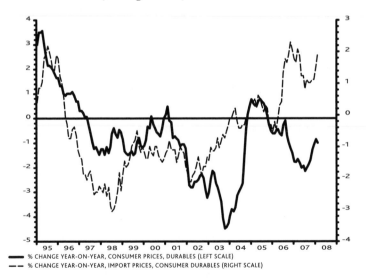

Figure 5.2   US Durables 'Inflation', Consumer Price Index and Import Price Index

Source: Bureau of Labor Statistics.

The evidence was even more startling in the UK. As the credit crunch hit consumer confidence, retailers came under intense pressure to cut prices. By the end of 2007, retail prices for all goods excluding food were falling 3.4 per cent year-on-year, the fastest decline since current records began in 1986 (see Figure 5.3).[23] For household goods, the discounting was extraordinary. Prices were falling at a record annual rate of 9.2 per cent (see Figure 5.4).[24]

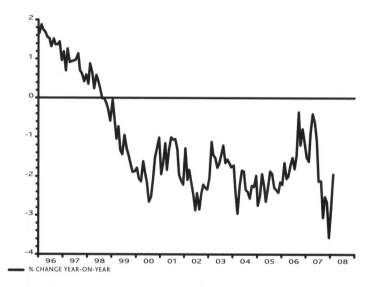

Figure 5.3   UK Retail Sales Deflator, Non-Food Stores

Source: Office for National Statistics.

Ignore Import Prices

The biggest risk posed by the falling dollar – and pound – was not the rise in import prices *per se*, but central banks balking at rate cuts as the housing market spiralled downwards. The Federal Reserve did cut interest rates three times during the final months of 2007 even though the dollar was sliding. But it was a *reluctant* rate cutter. It was reacting to events, failing to anticipate the inevitable fallout from an implosion of house prices. It fell

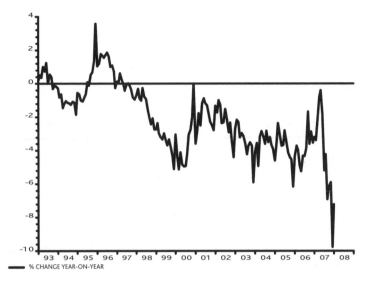

Figure 5.4   UK Retail Sales Deflator, Household Goods

Source: Office for National Statistics.

well behind the curve. It persisted in highlighting the threat of inflation, citing the dollar as a key risk. The Federal Reserve tried to stand its ground, ignoring the clamour for bigger rate cuts. But that just caused the stock market to panic, with investors fretting that without a much looser monetary policy, the risks of recession would rise sharply.

By early January 2008, the stock markets had started to tumble. The sudden loss of confidence eventually forced the Federal Reserve into an emergency rate cut. Borrowing costs were now starting to come down forcefully. But policy was never eased in the aggressive and proactive manner demanded by such a rapid deflation of the housing bubble. Critical time had been lost. And the delay will prove costly.

Peak Oil

The dollar's slump was not the only reason the Federal Reserve failed to act. Oil prices had been rising almost without interruption since the beginning of 2002. From a low of $18 per barrel, the benchmark West Texas Intermediate had soared to an unthinkable $99 by November 2007. House prices were tumbling, but the Federal Reserve fretted instead over a return to the runaway inflation of the 1970s.

Crude oil carried on rising even though more and more countries were slipping close to economic recession. Ordinarily, that should have cooled demand and capped prices. But on 20 February 2008, West Texas Intermediate finally closed above $100 per barrel.[25] By early March, it was racing up towards $110.

Something was amiss. The proponents of 'Peak Oil' had been proved right. The world was failing to produce enough oil. It was no longer possible to blame China, India or any other emerging market economy for pushing energy prices sky high, the popular explanation.

The concept of 'Peak Oil' sprung from pioneering research by geologist M. King Hubbert, who predicted in 1956 that oil production would peak in the US by the early 1970s.[26] His controversial analysis was rejected, notably by his employers. Mr Hubbert worked for Shell. But he was subsequently vindicated, as oil production in the US started to contract in the early 1970s.

His assessment was based on the notion that oil output depends linearly on the fraction that remains to be produced, or reserves. And that is contingent upon the rate of discovery. Oil discoveries peaked in the US in 1930 and production reached its zenith four decades later. Output has since fallen by nearly half, and the US has become increasingly dependent upon foreign oil. By 2007, net oil imports had reached a record $293.5 billion, accounting for more than a third of the US trade deficit.[27]

Around 1995, a number of analysts started to assess the outlook for world production applying Hubbert's method. And most concluded that the peak in output would occur some time between 2004 and 2008.[28] The forecasts were again ridiculed and dismissed, but the world has long since passed the peak in oil discoveries, widely cited to be 1965. Since the mid 1980s, oil production has exceeded the addition of reserves from fresh fields for every subsequent year.

A total of 865 new fields were found in the 1980s. That fell to 510 in the 1990s and has since plummeted. So far this decade, just 65 new fields have been found. Discoveries are poised to be the lowest this decade since the 1930s. Only 15 per cent of 2006's production came from fields found in the 1990s. Only 2 per cent came from fields tapped this millennium.[29] The world's 20 largest oil fields were all discovered between 1917 and 1979.[30]

The promise of new frontiers or 'technology' plugging this alarming gap is an illusion. Most of the easy, cheap oil has long since been 'discovered'. With little oil left to find, improved extraction techniques impact only at the margin. A Wood Mackenzie report released in early March 2008 revealed 'disappointing oil exploration results in the Gulf of Mexico'. New discoveries in 2007 were half of the levels a year before. The results were significant, since the Gulf represents 'what many companies believed was the safest, most prospective area open to them in the world', lamented one oil consultant.[31]

Predictions of a global peak have finally been borne out by the available data. One prominent US oil analyst, Matthew Simmons, believes the high-point in production for crude oil occurred in May 2005 at 74.3 million barrels per day. His assessment is based on 'raw numbers' from the US Department of Energy.[32]

Even the normally conservative International Energy Agency (IEA) is finding it hard to refute his claims. It estimates that total 'energy' production rose by 0.2 per cent in 2007 from a year earlier. When an allowance is made for the increased output from natural gas liquid and biofuels – included in this number – crude oil production fell.[33]

Saudi in Decline?

Critically, output in Saudi Arabia – until recently the world's largest producer – now looks to have peaked in 2005. The latest figures for 2007 show that output has dropped from a high of 9.06 million barrels per day to 8.47 million barrels per day.[34]

The decline of the giant Saudi fields and the huge difficulties in sustaining output has been well documented by Matthew Simmons. And his analysis should alarm central banks and governments, although it will reassure environmentalists. Much of Saudi's oil comes from seven giant fields and there are few comparable fields to be tapped. It is very unlikely that Saudi Arabia has the spare reserves it claims. These fields have all 'matured and grown old', but they continue to produce the lion's share of Saudi's output. The three biggest fields have 'been producing at very high rates for over 50 years'. And production has been 'maintained for decades by injecting massive amounts of water that serves to keep pressures high in the underground reservoirs. When these water injection programs end in each field, steep production declines are almost inevitable.'[35]

It is telling that Saudi has been unable to respond to the acceleration in prices by raising output. President Bush, in a candid moment, acknowledged the harsh reality in a visit to Riyadh in early 2008. When asked if he would be pressing Saudi officials to raise output to temper rising prices he replied, somewhat defensively, 'If they [Saudi Arabia] don't have a lot of additional oil to put on the market, it is hard to ask somebody to do something they may not be able to do' (15 January 2008, ABC Nightline).

Global output is now estimated to have dropped by nearly 2 million barrels per day in just over two years. Numerous other countries are experiencing significant declines in production that look set to accelerate. The US was the first major producer to peak, in 1970, followed by Kuwait (1973), Venezuela (1997), UK (1999), Norway (2000) and then Mexico (2004).

The decline in the giant Cantarell field in Mexico, the world's second largest, is a major concern. Production peaked in May 2005, and has already slumped by 41 per cent.[36] Mexico is expected to become a net importer by 2015. Other smaller producers have long since passed their Hubbert's Peak, including Egypt, Oman and Yemen. United Arab Emirates and China, both sizeable producers, may be passing their peak now.

Not OPEC's Fault

OPEC has been accused of operating a cartel and deliberately holding back supply, to drive prices up, curbing demand. But few OPEC countries have the spare production capacity to prevent prices climbing. Iraq has the reserves, but output remains constrained by a conflict that may be ignited if the Kurds succeed in securing independence. Angola has managed to buck the trend since 2005, along with Azerbaijan and Russia. But some analysts are even casting doubts over the ability of Russia – currently the world's biggest oil producer – to increase output. It may have reached a peak too.[37]

On current trends, world crude production could drop to around 69 million barrels per day by 2012.[38] In the absence of a major shift away from the 'carbon economy' – almost impossible in such a short time frame – prices will soar. At $110 per barrel, oil is still cheap. In a world of dwindling supplies, predictions of $200 per barrel are not so outlandish.

This is a very different oil shock from anything seen before. It is not one driven by geopolitics, OPEC cartels, strong emerging market demand, the speculative activities of hedge funds or even the oft-cited falling dollar. Oil prices have been climbing in euros, pounds, yen and nearly every other currency. The rise in prices has been caused by the failure to plan adequately for *viable* alternative sources of energy. The politicians paid no attention to followers of Hubbert's Peak, and critical time has been lost.

The rapid and sometimes pointless increase in shipment of goods from one country to another has hardly helped either. It has accelerated the depletion of oil reserves and the rise in carbon emissions. A leaked UN study underlines the folly. It found that the true scale of climate change emissions from shipping is 'almost three times higher than previously believed'.[39] Free trade that allows companies to relocate and exploit lower wages in developing countries depends upon cheap oil. There are many reasons to question whether such an economic strategy was wise. Peak Oil is one more.

The Madness of Biofuels

The failure to deal with the threat of Peak Oil has been compounded by the aggressive promotion of biofuels, which are not a viable alternative energy. An energy crunch has now metamorphosed into a food crisis. As oil stocks dwindle, biofuel production will soar, driving food prices even higher.

Rising oil prices have made biofuels more attractive. Unwilling to face up to some hard choices, governments have lavished generous subsidies on biofuels, sparking a boom in production. And that has triggered acute shortages of grains and many other crops, causing prices to rocket. Just five months after oil production reached its global peak, corn prices started to climb, and they have since tripled. From their low, wheat prices have quadrupled.

Rampant food inflation may deter central banks from cutting interest rates and increase the risks of housing slumps in the West. The impact on developing countries will be far greater. The growth of biofuels is already exacerbating world hunger. Filling a 25-gallon tank of an SUV with pure ethanol requires 450 pounds of corn, enough calories to feed one person for a year.[40] On present trends, the number of chronically hungry people could double by 2025 to 1.2 billion.[41]

Peak Oil and biofuels will squeeze the incomes of consumers hard. In poorer countries, 50–80 per cent of incomes are typically spent on food and energy. As prices soar, their ability to spend on other goods will slump. The miracle of strong emerging market economies will prove to be a mirage. Weighed down by a rapid rise in domestic debt, rampant food and energy inflation threatens hard landings across a wide swathe of the developing world (see Chapter 6 for more).

And it may not even reduce carbon emissions, one of the rationales for such generous subsidies. A growing body of scientists now claims biofuels will accelerate climate change. Studies that promoted the use of biofuels failed to take into account one rather obvious point. The decision by farmers across the world to clear forests and grasslands would increase emissions. The substitution of corn-based ethanol for conventional oil could double greenhouse-gas emissions.[42]

The Ethanol Craze

Ethanol accounts for over 90 per cent of biofuel production. And it is expanding fast. According to the Earth Policy Institute (EPI), there were 116 ethanol refineries in operation in the US at the end of 2006. A significant number of these were being expanded, and a further 79 were under construction.[43] By the end of 2008, ethanol production capacity is expected to have reached 11.4 billion gallons per year. Alarmingly President Bush has called on US producers to ramp this up to 35 billion gallons.[44]

According to the EPI, 28 per cent of the projected grain harvest in the US could be diverted to ethanol plants in 2008.[45] But even if the entire US grain harvest were converted to ethanol, it would only satisfy 16 per cent of the US auto fuel needs. Unless the US administration backs down, more than half of US grain supplies will soon be subsumed by biofuels.[46]

And the commercial viability of biofuels will keep on rising. Ethanol receives a subsidy of 51 cents per gallon, equal to $1.43 a bushel. According to the University of Illinois, when oil prices are $50 per barrel, it is profitable to convert corn into ethanol so long as the corn is below $4 per bushel. With oil prices at $100, however, the break-even point rises to over $7 per bushel. That compares with a 2007 close of $4.25 per bushel. If oil should rise to $140, distillers could afford to pay $10 for corn.[47]

The impact of biofuels is being felt far beyond grains. As farmers plant more acreage for corn, fewer acres are available for other important crops. Thus wheat prices are rocketing, alongside rice. Higher grain prices will lead to increased feeding costs for cattle, threatening higher prices for meat, poultry and dairy products.

And it is not just the US administration that has been leading the charge for biofuels. Brazil has been a pioneer. Nearly half of the world's ethanol is produced from sugar cane in Brazil. Rapid expansion has led to huge deforestation to meet demand, but sugar prices have still risen sharply.

The European Commission has been flexing its legislative powers to promote biofuels. When energy firm Ensus opened a new ethanol factory in Wilton, UK in 2007, one leading grain supplier noted with some excitement that the factory would consume 1.2 million tonnes of wheat every year. The UK had surplus production of 1.6 million tonnes from a total output of 15 million tonnes. The Wilton plant 'would use most of that surplus' leaving little for export.[48] It is small wonder prices have been soaring.

The run-up in food prices has been widely blamed on strong demand in developing economies. This fashionable view was based on the so-called 'two dollar theory'. A rise in poor countries' per capita income from $1 to $2 is supposed to trigger a marked increase in calorific intake, as a growing number of people start to consume more dairy and meat products.[49] Diets become increasingly 'Westernised' as people's incomes rise above subsistence.

It is a neat theory, but it conveniently deflects the blame from where it really lies. Like the belief that surging oil prices are due to strong demand in China, India and elsewhere, it fails to take into account the reality of the intense squeeze on supplies that is ultimately driven by Peak Oil.[50]

Climate Change

The outsourcing of goods production is aggravating the problem of climate change, and not just by hastening the depletion of oil reserves. Rising carbon emissions are taking their toll on food production too. Supplies of wheat were severely damaged in a number of countries by drought and extreme weather in 2007, from Australia, Argentina, Ukraine, to Eastern Europe. According to the International Federation of Red Cross and Red Crescent Societies, 'nearly 500 natural disasters had been recorded in 2007 against 430 in the preceding two years' and it concluded that 'climate change was clearly a factor'.[51]

Rice yields have been hit too, by rising temperatures, and prices have soared. Rice is a staple food for half of the world. A number of countries, including India and Vietnam, have been forced to restrict exports, citing poor harvests. The International Rice Research Institute claims rice yields will 'decrease by 10 percent for every 1 degree increase in growing season minimum temperature'.[52] Scientists in Japan have expressed 'deep concern' over the impact of rising temperatures.

Soaring Commodity Prices and Asset Deflation

For the West, rising oil and food prices will aggravate the collapse of housing markets. The impact on the wallets of US consumers has already been striking. The five-year run-up in energy prices had reduced real disposable income by $235 billion or 2.3 per cent in 2007 alone.[53] It played a part in depressing demand, which central banks offset with housing booms.

Higher oil prices created a demand shortfall because wages failed to rise in tandem. Workers enjoyed little bargaining power even at the top of the strongest housing market since the 1920s. Depressed wages allowed interest rates to remain low. This ensured that central banks could sustain the property bubbles even as oil prices soared. And the rise in oil prices provided a windfall for producers, who promptly recycled their excess funds into the US housing market. For a while, it seemed that nothing could derail the prolonged economic boom enjoyed by the Industrialised West, not even runaway oil prices.

But they did finally push inflation above the target in the UK. It accelerated to 3.1 per cent in March 2007, and the Bank of England Governor, Mervyn King, was obliged to write a letter to the Chancellor of the Exchequer, Gordon Brown. Mr King had to detail the Bank of England's strategy for bringing headline inflation back within target.

There was only one weapon at the central bank's disposal – interest rates – and borrowing costs went up, even though the oil price spike would have only a passing impact on inflation. The core inflation rate was still only 2 per cent. This would soon turn down as the housing market hurt retailer margins and forced record discounting for household goods. There was little risk of a return to the cost-push inflation cycle of the early 1970s.

On that occasion, the sharp run-up in oil prices had precipitated an immediate rise in the core or ex-food/energy inflation rate across all industrialised economies. The core inflation rate moved up in tandem with headline inflation from 1973 onwards (see Figure 5.5). The two are virtually indistinguishable. That stands in marked contrast with today. Headline inflation has been persistently above the core rates (see Figure 5.6).

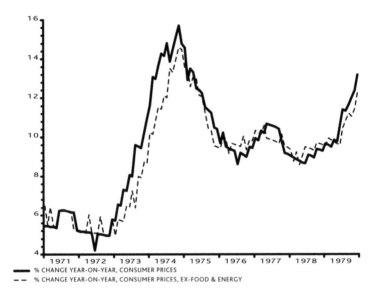

━━ % CHANGE YEAR-ON-YEAR, CONSUMER PRICES
– – % CHANGE YEAR-ON-YEAR, CONSUMER PRICES, EX-FOOD & ENERGY

Figure 5.5   OECD Consumer Prices 1971–79

Source: Organisation for Economic Cooperation and Development.

The same is true of nearly every other major industrialised economy. The transmission mechanism has been broken by globalisation. There have been limited second-round effects from the rise in energy costs, such as airline fares. But soaring energy prices have exerted far less impact on core consumer prices than many economists expected.

Perversely, higher food and oil prices will exacerbate the threat of debt deflation. They may push consumer prices up, but the subsequent squeeze on real incomes will increase the risks of

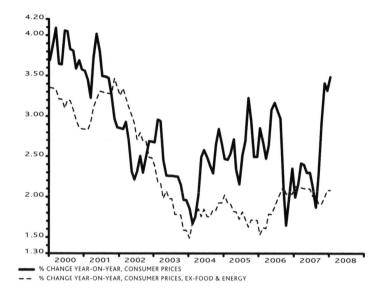

Figure 5.6   OECD Consumer Prices 2000–08

Source: Organisation for Economic Cooperation and Development.

a severe downturn in the housing market. The threat is greater precisely because central banks have seen rising oil prices as a reason to delay rate cuts. Indeed, the run-up in oil prices has been wrongly described as a return of stagflation, an unhappy combination of accelerating prices and slow economic growth that characterised the 1970s and early 1980s.

It is a dangerous analogy. There is a very different dynamic behind today's external price shocks. The persistence of high inflation following the initial oil price shock of 1973 reflected a very different response from wages, which did rise sharply. In economic terms, the rise in oil prices became embedded in expectations. Workers were able to protect their pay against higher prices. There has been a pick-up in inflation expectations in the US and UK over the past two years or so. But the increase has been limited. And crucially, wage pressures have remained extraordinarily weak. The power to offset these increases has been undermined by the threat that companies will relocate to cheaper countries.

For that reason it is absolutely critical for policymakers to differentiate between headline and core measures of inflation. By examining the latter, one is *not* taking a view that higher energy and food costs will be transitory. On the contrary, there are very good reasons to believe that these are secular increases that will continue to exert persistent upward pressure on headline inflation. However, if core inflation diverges from the headline rate, that shows there are few second-round effects. As the housing markets slump, these higher costs will be absorbed, either in real lower wages, or lower company profits. Core inflation therefore becomes even more critical, an indicator of the distress caused by Peak Oil and climate change.

Beyond Rate Cuts

Deep interest rate cuts are not a cure for the forces that precipitate debt deflation. They can mitigate the potential fallout and lessen the chances of a prolonged slump. But they will not prevent a recurrence if governments and central banks fail to understand the forces that created the housing bubbles in the first place.

The Federal Reserve and Bank of England can be criticised for slashing borrowing costs in response to the dotcom collapse, on the specific grounds that they were not addressing the imbalance between capital and labour that created the cycle of boom and bust.

But central banks have no mandate to tackle any of the forces that precipitate such extreme bouts of asset inflation. And in the case of the Bank of England, it is not even allowed to consider the long term consequences of its policy. Financial stability was not mentioned once in the policy objectives set out by the Treasury under Chancellor Gordon Brown in 1997.

Even though it had a less restrictive mandate, the Federal Reserve came under intense pressure at times to let the good times roll, and it also ignored the dangers posed by asset bubbles. In mitigation, Alan Greenspan tried to inject a note of caution in December 1996. But his warning of 'irrational exuberance' caused a stir. Thereafter, he reasoned that the Federal Reserve was 'playing with political dynamite' if it tried to raise interest rates to cool the stock market.[54] It would be easier to deal with the aftermath of bubbles, rather than focus on prevention, Mr Greenspan reasoned.

It is ironic that the consequences of this policy now require the same short term response, which will fail to resolve the underlying tensions driving the boom bust cycle. But the central banks have no choice. Unless they cut interest rates sharply over the next year or two, they will run the risk of repeating the mistakes made by the Bank of Japan in the early 1990s. A delayed response will increase the risks of debt trap, as property prices will fall more sharply, pushing more US and UK homeowners into negative equity.

Missing the Boat

When housing markets begin to deflate, the timing of rate cuts is critical. Leave it too late, and the slide in property values can render rate cuts increasingly ineffective on three grounds. Financial institutions will run into trouble, precipitating a further rise in borrowing costs over and above the increase in key lending rates already prescribed by central banks. These higher borrowing costs will effectively imply monetary policy has been tightened, when it should have been loosened.

Secondly, the availability of credit will deteriorate, feeding into even lower housing demand. Even as interest rates belatedly come down, the contraction in mortgage availability will offset the benefit of lower interest rates. This is tantamount to a further tightening of monetary policy or 'credit conditions'.

Thirdly, there is every possibility that potential homebuyers will be dissuaded from entering the housing market by the sharp fall in prices. Even as interest rates fall and 'affordability' improves, there will be little incentive for buyers to take the plunge. That then fuels a vicious circle. Falling prices act as a deterrent, overwhelming the benefit of rate cuts, precipitating bigger price reversals, 'frightening' buyers even more.

Eventually, it is claimed, the property market will fall far enough that it will be sufficiently cheap and alluring. Buyers will be tempted and the housing market will stabilise of its own accord. It is this mistaken view that leads some commentators to call for central banks to refrain from making more cuts in interest rates. This line of argument has been particularly prevalent in the US, where there has been acute concern in some quarters that rate cuts will 'debase the dollar' and bail out those who deserve to fail.

But there is no reason to suppose the property market will reach a natural floor. If central banks fail to cut in a timely manner, real borrowing costs will go up, not down. Eventually, they will run out of room for manoeuvre and the US will slip into a Keynesian liquidity trap. There is a natural limit to how far market interest rates can fall. As we shall see in Chapter 8, the economist John Maynard Keynes identified 'liquidity preference' as a major obstacle to securing the necessary drop in market rates in his *General Theory of Employment, Interest and Money*. His path-breaking book was published in 1933 in response to the acute difficulties central banks faced at the time trying to prevent a depression. Japan ran into a liquidity trap during the 1990s.

The zero bound for lending rates is a further constraint. Even if central banks struggle to secure lower market rates, they still have the power to set their own lending rate at zero. In theory, it could go below this. But for practical purposes, zero is the limit. There are huge political obstacles to interest rates being cut into negative territory. That would imply central banks were paying banks to take money, which they could then lend. In reality, once a central bank has cut its lending rate to zero, it has nowhere to go. Japan effectively reached that point in 1999. We shall explore the dynamics of Japan's botched monetary policy in more detail in Chapter 7. Only time will tell whether the Federal Reserve, the Bank of England and the European Central Bank can prevent Keynesian liquidity traps taking root. The omens are not encouraging.

6

A GLOBAL CREDIT BUBBLE

The housing slumps of the West may seem daunting, but they are far from an isolated phenomenon. They are merely the flipside of another problem facing the world economy – credit bubbles across a wide swathe of developing countries. Once again, we have to go back to the drive among Western companies to cut labour costs as the starting point. Relocation of production capacity has fuelled a capital flight to these countries, which has effectively been monetised. Fearful of losing out in the global race to attract jobs, emerging market countries have also been accused of mercantilist motives, deliberately holding down their exchange rates to try and remain competitive.

These countries are not just competing with the Industrialised West. They are locked in a competitive battle with each other. If companies have no compunction in shifting jobs out of their own domestic market, 'commercial logic' suggests they will have few qualms moving from one developing country to another, if a cheaper option becomes available.

Vietnam offers lower wages than many of its neighbours and has become the latest hot destination for companies seeking cheap labour. GDP per capita – arguably the most consistent way to compare labour costs across countries – was $2,450 in China during 2007. In Vietnam, it was just $813.[1] Investment into China was strong in the run-up to its accession to the World Trade Organisation, but it has now fallen to its lowest pace since 1991, a modest 1.8 per cent of GDP in 2007. That is well below the inflows seen in the mid 1990s, when they peaked at 5.5 per cent of GDP. By contrast, direct investment into Vietnam has more than doubled in the past two years to a whopping 8.6 per cent of GDP.[2] Companies are choosing cheaper Vietnam over China. Cambodia and Laos are even more cost effective. Investment into Cambodia has been accelerating and is now three times that for China.[3] If the tyrannical regime in Myanmar were ever toppled, one can safely assume this would become the next favourite for companies relocating. Labour costs here are a fraction of those seen across the rest of Asia.[4]

Greater trade integration has, however, gone hand in hand with financial liberalisation. Developing countries have been unable to resist the economic and political pressure for 'financial reform'. Increased trade flows have also eroded the effectiveness of restrictions on capital mobility. Having signed up to free trade in the expectation that it would bring jobs, emerging market economies have been forced to deregulate capital markets. This has precipitated a dramatic increase in capital flows. Globalisation has been marked by large pools of easy finance swirling through emerging market economies.

Attempts to hold exchange rates down, as real and financial capital flooded into these countries, has created asset bubbles that will burst as spectacularly as those in the West. And politically, the fallout may prove more destabilising. Many are rapidly trying to play catch-up with the West, industrialising at a frenetic pace. Their faith in free trade may be shaken when their credit bubbles rupture.

Lopsided

Much of the focus in this book has been directed towards the credit bubbles of the US and UK. But these countries are not alone in suffering from a rapid build-up in debt. If they were, it might be argued that the impact of globalisation on wages was symmetrical. The record debt burdens in the US and UK might reflect a lack of wage growth. But (some) developing countries have at least seen a rise in living standards, prompted by the shift in manufacturing jobs out of the Industrialised West.

Inevitably, so the argument goes, higher wages in these countries should feed through to increased demand for goods and services that will benefit the Industrialised West. This should foster an orderly rebalancing of the global economy, one that cushions the fallout from extreme asset price cycles in the US, UK and Euroland. The pursuit of free trade by large corporations in its current guise, could still be deemed beneficial for the world economy. From this perspective, the trade imbalances and excessive borrowing are temporary problems. The UK, US and others in the West should learn to accept lower wages and higher debt burdens for now, while the rest of the world plays catch-up.

We have already highlighted a number of flaws with this line of argument, in Chapter 4. But there is a bigger problem undermining the efficacy of today's globalisation. The 'strong' growth in developing countries has not been predicated on a rise in wages as these countries industrialise. Of the 189 countries that report to the International Monetary Fund (IMF), more than a hundred have seen private domestic borrowing rise faster than the UK and the US since the beginning of 2000. Many of these have seen their debt levels increase several times the rise recorded in the UK and US (for a full list, see appendix at the end of this chapter).

In relation to disposable income, the UK and US are still well out in front. They have far bigger debt 'burdens'. Their cycles of asset inflation stretch back more than two decades. Since the top of the dotcom bubble, the US and UK have nonetheless been outstripped by a very long list of countries experiencing a far bigger rise in private sector borrowing.

In short, the strong economic growth seen across the globe in recent years, so often touted as defining proof that globalisation works, has not been fuelled by free trade, but by rapid credit growth with bubbles appearing across every continent. If free trade had been the driving force behind the recent world economic boom, there would surely have been little need or place for such excessive credit creation.

Much of the blame for these credit bubbles lies with the same fault-line that created the very real threat of debt traps in the West today. The determination of companies to cut labour costs has underpinned excessive capital inflows, which have proved difficult for central banks in many of these countries to manage. They have either been unwilling or unable to stem the impact of these huge capital flows on domestic credit growth.

Revisiting 1997

It is perhaps worth revisiting the dynamics of the South East Asian crisis in 1997 to understand why the global credit bubble has engulfed so many more countries today. To recap, Thailand, Malaysia, South Korea and Indonesia ran significant current account deficits during the early 1990s. Investors were not perturbed. Direct investment inflows were strong, particularly from Japan, as companies shifted production in search of lower labour costs.

As these economies started to boom, financial capital followed. Money poured into the equity and debt markets. These portfolio flows were followed by a sharp rise in borrowing from foreign banks. Taking these three components together provides a summary of a country's *net financial flows*.

According to the International Financial Statistics compiled by the IMF, net financial flows into Thailand soared to $22.0 billion in 1995 before edging down to $19.5 billion in 1996. In South Korea, they reached a peak of $24.0 billion in 1996, the year before the bubble burst. Indonesia received a record $10.8 billion in 1996.[5] (See Table 6.1.)

Table 6.1   **South East Asia, Balance of Payments 1996 (% of GDP)**

	Current account	Financial flows	Direct investment*	Errors omissions	Overall balance
Thailand	−8.1	10.7	0.8	−1.4	1.2
South Korea	−4.2	4.3	−0.4	0.2	0.3
Indonesia	−3.0	4.3	2.2	0.5	1.8

* In the International Financial Statistics, direct investment is included as part of financial flows.

Source: International Financial Statistics.

The important point about these inflows is that they dwarfed the current account deficits of these countries. The *overall balance*, which combines the current account and net financial flows, was massively in surplus. A positive overall balance implies there is rising net demand for a particular country's currency. Central banks were left struggling to contain huge upward pressure on their exchange rates.

But they were reluctant to allow their currencies to appreciate. Companies were moving production to South East Asia because it was cheap. Governments of the region hardly wanted to kill the goose that laid the golden eggs. Fearful these inflows would cause a loss of competitiveness, central banks intervened extensively on the foreign exchange markets.

Intervention carries significant risks too, however. When a central bank buys US dollars, for example, to keep the value of its currency down, it creates and supplies local currency – in this case baht, won, ringgit or rupiah. The money enters into circulation. The intervention provided the fuel for an acceleration in domestic borrowing. Between 1990 and 1996, the value of notes and coins in circulation surged by annualised rates of 14.0 per cent, 14.1 per cent and 16.3 per cent in Thailand, South Korea and Indonesia respectively.[6]

Malaysia did a slightly better job of limiting the increase, with a rise of 9.0 per cent. But it was still powerless to prevent *quasi money* rising by an annualised 28.1 per cent over the same period.[7] Quasi money is essentially a measure of deposits. Large inflows into these countries helped push quasi money supply up, fuelling the credit bubble. Malaysia's increase in quasi money supply was even bigger than in Thailand, South Korea or Indonesia.

In that respect, it is unsurprising the Malaysian authorities reacted to the crisis of 1997 by imposing draconian capital controls. Stunned investors declared them unworkable. But Malaysia's Prime Minister Mahathir Mohamad rode out the storm of protests. The economy bounced back swiftly, emboldening developing countries to forge a path independent from the clutches of Washington.

No Sterilisation

The central banks could have negated the impact of dollar buying operations on domestic credit growth by sterilising the intervention. Central banks can mop up the excess money created from trying to hold down their exchange rate by issuing government debt in exchange for dollars, or any other reserve currency such as euros, yen or sterling. Central banks can also increase the level of reserves banks are required to hold, to dampen the process of credit creation.

In practice, the sheer scale of the rise in domestic credit showed this never happened in South East Asia prior to 1997. Ultimately, they were swept along by a sense of invincibility. Talk of an economic miracle was widespread, and central bankers are just as guilty of irrational exuberance as investors.

The end result was a bubble in the stock markets across the region, a surge in property prices and inevitably rampant overbuilding. The direct investment inflows and the arrival of new jobs fuelled a pick-up in economic growth. But the surge in domestic credit turned that into an unsustainable boom. Between 1990 and 1996 private domestic borrowing soared by an annualised rate of 24.5 per cent in Thailand, 16.6 per cent in South Korea, 27.8 per cent in Malaysia and 19.5 per cent in Indonesia.[8]

Eventually, the bubble burst, and these countries were forced to devalue their currencies. It was a bitter lesson for the governments and central banks in the region.

Déjà Vu

But a decade on, it is not a lesson many countries seem to have absorbed. Far from persuading governments to pursue more disciplined policies, there has been a rise in the number of countries running huge current account deficits, many far bigger than those that crippled South East Asia in 1997. Globalisation has fuelled an increase in trade imbalances.

Policymakers have fretted for some time that these imbalances will heighten the volatility of currency markets. That is true, but it is only one part of the problem. It is the potential havoc wrought by credit bubbles that should concern the authorities. Many of these countries running large current account deficits have been attracting record financial inflows, leaving their overall balance still in surplus. The trade imbalances have thus coincided with a rapid rise in private sector debt.

In a repeat of South East Asia during the 1990s, that has been countered through extensive intervention by central banks, to stop their exchange rates from appreciating too fast – or not at all if the country is running a currency peg. Foreign exchange reserves have soared.

Between 2003 and 2007, the level of reserves held across all central banks has nearly doubled, climbing to just over $4 trillion. And a large part of that increase has come from developing countries, where reserves have climbed from $1.3 trillion to $3.1 trillion (see Figure 6.1).[9] They now hold reserves more than

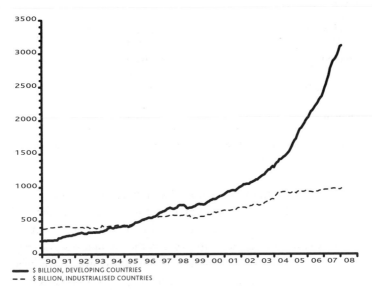

Figure 6.1   Foreign Exchange Reserves

Source: International Financial Statistics.

three times as large as the 'developed' world. This statistic is even more astonishing when it is considered that developing countries account for just under 41 per cent of world imports. 'Developed' countries account for just over 59 per cent.[10]

China had accumulated $1.5 trillion of reserves by the end of 2007. Japan had the second biggest reserves, a hefty $948.4 billion. Other countries with reserves in excess of $100 billion include Russia, Taiwan, India, South Korea, Brazil, Singapore, Hong Kong and Malaysia (see Table 6.2). A number of countries just below this threshold, such as Mexico and Thailand, have been intervening too, to secure a competitive advantage against the West.

Table 6.2   Foreign Exchange Reserves, December 2007

Country	Foreign exchange reserves ($ billion)
China	1,528.3
Japan	948.4
Russia	464.0
Taiwan	270.3
India	266.7
South Korea	261.8
Brazil	179.4
Singapore	162.5
Hong Kong	152.6
Malaysia	100.6
Mexico	86.3
Thailand	85.1

Sources: International Financial Statistics and Directorate-General of Budget, Accounting and Statistics, Executive Yuan, R.O.C. (Taiwan).

And because the intervention has not been fully sterilised, domestic credit growth has exploded. Just as we saw in the mid 1990s, central banks have been unable or unwilling to offset the impact of huge capital inflows into these countries. As 1997 proved, it is a toxic combination. Foreign investors have been rushing into emerging market countries despite very obvious risks that some of their current account positions are unsustainable. In turn, they have been fuelling credit growth and sucking in imports, making their trade deficits even bigger. Thailand, Malaysia, South Korea and Indonesia collapsed because investors pulled the plug. The same fate awaits many countries today.

Eastern Europe's 'Transformation'

By most yardsticks, Eastern Europe has enjoyed quite a transformation since the Berlin Wall came tumbling down in 1989. Accession to an enlarged European Union has sealed a shift away from state-controlled capitalism to free market democracies, and real GDP growth has accelerated across the region. The improvement has been far from smooth. Unemployment remained stubbornly high during the early years, and large scale migration to the West belied a chronic lack of jobs for many. But after many years of rapid growth, unemployment has fallen.

Scratch a little below the surface, and it is clear that Eastern Europe has become consumed by a grotesque credit bubble. Every one of the 16 countries in the Baltic, Balkans and Eastern Europe incurred a current account deficit in 2007. It was a sea of red ink, with Latvia topping the list, running a deficit that hit 23.9 per cent of GDP.[11]

These are scarcely aberrations either. Many of these countries have been persistently in deficit for a decade or more. For seven of them, 2007 saw a record deficit. Nine countries recorded deficits bigger than the shortfall witnessed in Thailand, in the penultimate year before the baht collapsed. Aside from Latvia, the list includes Lithuania, Estonia, Albania, Bosnia, Moldova, Serbia, Rumania and Bulgaria, the latter on a whopping 20.0 per cent of GDP.[12] For many, the deficits are likely to get worse in 2008, as a retrenchment of the Western consumer hits exports of cheap manufacturing goods.

Strong capital inflows ensured that 13 out of these 16 countries ran a surplus on their financial account in 2006. The only one to run a deficit was Slovenia, and that was very small. Two have so far failed to report. And in all but one of these 13 cases, the financial inflows were big enough to offset the current account deficit. In short, they had a surplus on the overall balance. Unsurprisingly, central banks across the region have been intervening to prevent their currencies rising not just in 2006, but for years prior to that. Inevitably, the increase in foreign exchange reserves has not been sterilised, and domestic credit has been soaring.

Top of the list is Rumania, where a 1,870 per cent rise in foreign exchange reserves has driven a nearly identical increase in private debt of 1,908 per cent (see Figure 6.2). Latvia is not far behind with a leap of 1,638 per cent (see Figure 6.3).[13] Albania, Moldova, Bulgaria, Estonia and Lithuania have seen huge increases too. Interestingly, those that have managed to dampen the rise in debt have tended to incur smaller trade deficits, such as Poland, the Czech Republic and Slovakia.

There is an irony here, of course. As we saw in Chapter 4, many of these countries have played a part in accelerating the flood of cheap imports into the UK, making it both possible and, it would seem, necessary for the authorities to create housing bubbles. And yet, they have been overwhelmed by even bigger increases in credit growth than the UK. Once again, it seems

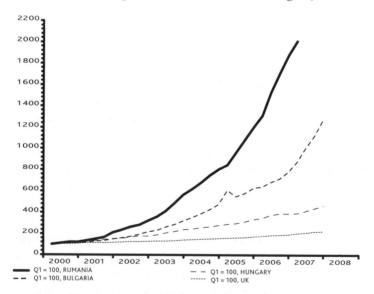

Figure 6.2   Eastern Europe and UK, Private Domestic Debt

Source: International Financial Statistics.

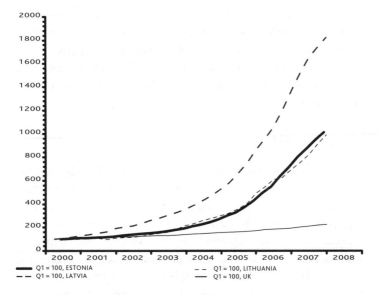

Figure 6.3   Baltic Three and UK, Private Domestic Debt

Source: International Financial Statistics.

that the dramatic rise in 'free trade' has merely destabilised the world economy.

And it is the same for Turkey, another country that has seen its trade surplus with the UK rise, but still managed to incur a huge current account deficit in 2007. That too was financed by massive capital inflows, even bigger than those that swamped South East Asia in the mid 1990s (see Table 6.3).

Table 6.3   Turkey and South Africa, Balance of Payments 2006 (% of GDP)

	Current account	Financial balance	Direct investment	Errors omissions	Overall balance
Turkey	−8.1	11.4	4.7	−0.7	2.6
South Africa	−6.4	5.7	−2.6	2.1	1.4

Source: International Financial Statistics.

South Africa is another country where an economic boom has been funded by waves of foreign capital that have allowed its current account deficit to soar. With commodity prices rising so sharply, it should have been running a surplus. But amidst a global credit bubble, it was too easy to rack up record deficits (see Table 6.3).

Surpluses and Bubbles

In their own right, these deficits are potentially destabilising for the world economy. But the problem does not end here. There are many countries running current account surpluses that have seen even bigger credit bubbles in recent years. In some cases, financial inflows have compounded the current account surplus, pushing the overall balance up even more rapidly. In others, the net financial outflows are small, but fail to offset the current account surplus, leaving the overall balance still heavily in positive territory. The end result has been some extraordinary increases in domestic credit for many countries.

Russia is a case in point. Rising oil prices have yielded a rich dividend for Russia's energy giants, and its current account surplus has soared in recent years. Ordinarily, Russia should be recycling its surplus abroad. But it is not. It was a net importer of capital in 2006. Since the beginning of 2000, Russia has been running a persistent surplus on its overall balance. Russia's central bank has been intervening, and domestic credit has risen by 1,728 per cent.[14]

Azerbaijan is not that dissimilar. It has managed to recycle some of its current account surplus which has soared in response to higher oil prices, but not enough. And domestic borrowing has risen by 1,418 per cent.[15] But it was the only country that was not overrun by capital flooding into the Commonwealth of Independent States (CIS). The financial surpluses for some were astonishing. Georgia's current account deficit may have hit 16.0 per cent of GDP in 2006. But that did not stop investors pouring money into the country, netting Georgia a financial surplus that reached 17.3 per cent of GDP. Domestic credit has jumped by 1,035 per cent since 2000.

But perhaps the biggest risk is Kazakhstan, where the net financial surplus was 20.0 per cent of GDP, nearly double the flows seen into Thailand before its bubble burst. Domestic credit has risen 4,111 per cent so far this decade (see Figure 6.4).[16] Armenia, Belarus, Kyrgyz Republic and Tajikistan have also been quick to embrace capitalism with a recklessness that can only spell trouble as the West battles debt deflation.

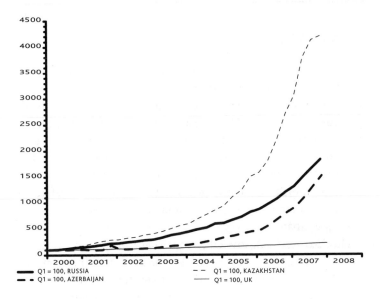

Figure 6.4   CIS, Private Domestic Debt

Source: International Financial Statistics.

In summary, the liberalisation of capital flows, so often hailed as one of the key drivers for today's globalised economy, is in danger of tipping many more countries into debt traps reminiscent of Japan's. Countries running current account deficits have been able to attract record financial inflows that trigger spiralling debt levels. And so have countries running current account surpluses. The net result has been a rise in global credit of eye-popping proportions.

And we should not forget that Japan was running huge trade surpluses too before its credit bubble ruptured in the early 1990s. As we shall see in Chapters 7 and 8, it was this persistent trade surplus and the inability of the Japanese authorities to devalue the yen that made the fallout even more traumatic. It does not matter that much whether a country is running a trade deficit or a surplus: a bubble is a bubble, and there are far too many of them around.

The IMF's View

Unsurprisingly, the IMF's view of the risks posed by capital flooding into emerging markets is rather more benign. It has argued these capital flows are a response to 'favourable worldwide economic conditions'. They are also a reflection of 'strengthened macroeconomic policy frameworks and growth-enhancing structural reforms'.[17] There was very little mention of a key motivation for the huge capital inflows – the determination of Western companies to cut wage bills. And there was no reference to the risks that many countries could become subsumed by debt traps like Japan.

The IMF did acknowledge that these inflows created the 'potential to generate overheating'. But, it noted, these inflows were 'taking place in the context of stronger current account positions for most (but not all) emerging market countries'.[18]

There are indeed a number of countries running very strong current account surpluses, as we have seen. By definition, however, they are offset by countries incurring very large deficits. And it is wrong for the IMF to focus only on the countries with deficits as potential risks. The problem is not just that deficit countries may suddenly suffer a capital flight, as seen repeatedly in the 1990s. The domestic asset bubbles that ineluctably follow are the overwhelming issue. And they are just as prevalent in countries with current account surpluses. In some cases they are bigger.

The IMF was reassured by two further points. Capital inflows were coinciding with a 'substantial acceleration in the accumulation of foreign reserves'. In addition, the 'predominance of net foreign direct investment' relative to portfolio and bank loans, reduced the risks.[19] Since the direct investment inflows are now bigger than they were for South East Asia during the 1990s, there is less reason to be concerned, the IMF argues.

The accumulation of foreign exchange reserves does not provide reassurance, as the IMF and many others contend. It is the core of the problem. Higher foreign exchange reserves are providing the fuel for domestic credit bubbles. Since the focus of the IMF is on countries with current account deficits and not domestic credit bubbles, it wrongly views the creation of foreign exchange reserves as a positive, a safeguard.

And the IMF makes an invalid distinction between the different capital flows. Direct investment inflows (which can create jobs – for the recipients) are seen as more durable, while portfolio and 'other' flows are viewed as less stable, and liable to reversal.

That merely betrays a misunderstanding of or indifference to the underlying dynamics. Capital flooding into countries on the scale seen in recent years has the potential to create credit bubbles irrespective of whether they are driven by the direct investment of firms relocating, or the more speculative portfolio inflows. Indeed, we should be rather more concerned that the capital inflows have been dominated by direct investment flows: it underlines the key point about globalisation today – the unsustainable drive to cut labour costs. But that does not worry the IMF.

Why Intervene?

Inevitably, critics will claim that the issue is not globalisation *per se*, but the response function of central banks across the world, seemingly unable to control their money supply and credit growth. Central banks should have refrained from intervening in their currency markets. Even if they were intent on holding down their exchange rates, they should have made more effort to sterilise the inflows.

But as we have shown before, the South East Asian crisis marked a watershed. The growth enjoyed by these countries during the early 1990s was 'Hailed as the economic success development story of late 20th century'.[20] Unsurprisingly, the turmoil of 1997 left a deep scar. The size of the shock relative to the capital account and the loss of foreign exchange reserves was reckoned by one notable economist to have been 'unprecedented, in recent decades at least'.[21] Table 6.4 shows the huge losses sustained by three of the countries during the crisis. Over two years, $33.8 billion fled Thailand, nearly a quarter of the country's GDP.

Table 6.4   **Capital Flight, South East Asia**

| | *Financial account* | | | | |
	1996 ($ billion)	*1997 ($ billion)*	*1998 ($ billion)*	*Change, 1996–98 ($ billion)*	*% of GDP*
Thailand	19.5	−12.3	−14.4	−33.8	−23.5
South Korea	24.0	−9.2	−8.4	−32.4	−6.7
Indonesia	10.8	−0.6	−9.6	−20.5	−13.5

Source: International Financial Statistics.

And after the bubble burst, IMF staffers were sent to Bangkok, Seoul, Kuala Lumpur and Jakarta to explain 'nearly everything had been wrong', declaring that the economic miracles were a mirage. The IMF imposed tough conditions for loans that still failed to prevent exchange rates collapsing. It demanded a draconian and anti-Keynesian tightening of fiscal policy and drove the economies into recession. For the governments of South East Asia, the IMF's intrusion was seen as a 'violation of sovereignty'.

The actions of the IMF, widely criticised by economists at the time, persuaded central banks in developing countries never to be left so dependent upon the 'West' again, for financial assistance. The calculus for the optimum level of 'precautionary' reserves would no longer include any potential drawdown of IMF quotas.[22] The subsequent rise in reserves became an insurance against IMF borrowing, an attempt to break free from the shackles and intrusion of an undemocratic and unelected 'lender of last resort'.

South East Asia was not alone in suffering a catastrophic capital flight. Mexico, Russia, Brazil, Argentina and Turkey all experienced huge outflows when investors suddenly lost their nerve. Table 6.5 shows the massive reversals in the net financial

Table 6.5 Capital Flight, Various Countries

	Year	Financial account $ billion	Year	$ billion	Change ($ billion)	% of GDP
Mexico (1994)	1993	33.8	1995	−10.5	−44.3	−11.0
Russia (1998)	1997	3.6	2000	−33.9	−37.5	−9.2
Brazil (1999)	1996	33.4	2002	−3.9	−37.3	−4.4
Turkey (2000)	2000	8.6	2001	−14.6	−23.1	−11.6
Argentina (2000)	1998	18.9	2002	−20.7	−39.6	−13.2

The date in brackets shows the crisis year.
Source: International Financial Statistics.

balance during the many crises witnessed since Mexico ran into trouble in 1994. None of the losses were quite as big as Thailand's. But many were bigger than either South Korea's or Indonesia's.

These debacles spawned a wealth of literature on the level of reserves needed to insure emerging market economies against any future external shocks. The IMF was just one of many contributors to a lively debate over how to protect countries against a recurrence of the 1990s. Rather than address the root causes – overinvestment and *financial globalisation* – the emphasis was on building up foreign exchange reserves. It was rather like governments today combating climate change by investing in flood protection instead of tackling carbon emissions.

For many years, financial institutions focused on one simple rule. To provide 'adequate' protection, it was argued, reserves needed to be equal to around three or four months of imports. That might persuade fickle investors not to sell if they knew that central banks were able to maintain the flow of imports during periods of turmoil.

But the rule failed for many of the countries caught out by currency flight since 1994. As Table 6.6 shows, seven of these countries had import cover ratios that satisfied this benchmark. Mexico, Indonesia and Malaysia were within the 3–4 months advocated. Thailand, Turkey, Argentina and Brazil were well above this threshold. And five of the nine countries derailed by capital flight had import cover fulfilling this requirement even after their exchange rates collapsed.

Table 6.6   Import Cover Ratios

	Year before crisis		Year of crisis	
Mexico	1993	3.9	1994	0.8
Thailand	1996	5.6	1997	4.5
South Korea	1996	2.3	1997	1.4
Malaysia	1996	3.6	1997	2.7
Indonesia	1996	3.9	1997	3.3
Russia	1997	2.3	1998	2.0
Brazil	1998	7.1	1999	6.8
Argentina	1999	9.6	2000	9.1
Turkey	1999	6.1	2000	4.6

Source: Economist Intelligence Unit.

Not surprisingly, the search was on for a new benchmark. And one that gained acceptance was the so-called Greenspan–Guidotti rule, named after the former Federal Reserve chairman and an ex-Argentine finance official. Greenspan and Guidotti argued that developing countries needed to amass enough reserves to cover all short term external debt obligations falling within a year.

When a crisis looms, however, it is not just the holders of short term debt that are liable to sell. 'Long term' investors rarely remain inert once the selling begins. Increasingly, economists and policymakers began to stress the need to accumulate reserves in line with total external liabilities. After all, the main source of uncertainty lay not so much with the current account deficit, but the threat of sudden capital outflows, whatever their maturity. Russia was not even running a current account deficit before it was hit by a sudden exodus of capital. The deficits in Brazil, Argentina and Turkey were not onerous compared to those seen in South East Asia during 1997 (see Table 6.7). Central banks, it was argued, needed to look at the entire financial risks facing each country.

And the risks had risen dramatically. As noted earlier, emerging market economies have come under concerted pressure to liberalise financial markets and dismantle capital controls in recent years. Financial globalisation is the price developing countries have been obliged to pay for increased access to the Western consumer.

Table 6.7   Balance of Payments, Year Before Crisis

	Current account ($ billion)	Financial balance ($ billion)	Direct investment (%) of GDP	Errors omissions (%) of GDP	Overall balance (%) of GDP
Mexico, 1993	−5.8	8.4	N/A	−0.8	1.8
Russia, 1997	0.0	0.9	0.4	−2.5	−1.6
Brazil, 1998	−4.0	2.4	3.5	−0.3	−1.9
Argentina, 1999	−4.2	5.1	7.8	−0.2	0.7
Turkey, 1999	−0.7	2.7	0.1	0.9	2.9

Source: International Financial Statistics.

Many have seen a sharp rise in their external debt. Ironically, some countries have seen their borrowing rise even though in net terms – taking into account assets – their external position has improved.[23]

Such is the paradox of financial globalisation. Diversification with the help of more liquid capital flows was meant to spread the risks. In reality, it spawned bigger debt levels and bigger risks, even for countries running massive current account surpluses, such as China.[24]

In this context, the rapid run-up in reserves should not be seen as merely an attempt to take jobs from the West, but also as a response to the increased risks from financial globalisation. The point was encapsulated by one Chinese economist writing in the official newspaper *People's Daily*:

> If Thailand had had sufficient foreign exchange reserves, the 1997 crisis would not have worsened or extended to other areas. If South Korea had a large stockpile of foreign exchange reserves, the government would not have to resort to drawing funds from the people to get through difficult periods. Hong Kong survived the 1997 crisis because it had large foreign exchange reserves.[25]

A large stockpile of reserves might not provide a complete insurance against a run on the currency, but it might act as a deterrent to footloose investors. It would give central banks more ammunition to ambush speculators attempting to build large positions in currency markets designed to profit from the collapse of an exchange rate. Equally, high reserves would also provide investors with a degree of reassurance.

Ultimately, because it failed to address the underlying causes, it merely increased the risks. Insurance that allows house builders to build on flood plains only serves to heighten the potential collective loss.

And for some countries, the increase in foreign exchange reserves has not even provided increased 'insurance', because the rise in debt has been so astonishing. The ratio of foreign exchange reserves to external liabilities has fallen sharply, even though central banks in these cases have been intervening aggressively. In these instances, the capital inflows have simply been out of control. Notable examples include the Baltic Three and Hungary.

A Conundrum

At this point, it is important to address an apparent misconception. Because the US has received enormous capital inflows from Asia, oil exporters and other emerging market economies, it is assumed that these countries are net exporters of capital. In reality, many of them, particularly the emerging market economies, are net importers of capital. The two apparently conflicting statements are reconciled by one important point that goes to the heart of the global credit bubble. The capital inflows into the US are funded significantly by the intervention of central banks, as they recycle their huge foreign exchange reserves principally by buying US assets. Thus it is possible for the US to have net capital inflows, and for many emerging market countries too. Put another way, the financial account for the world is not equal to zero, as it is for the current account.

And the sequence of events should be noted. The capital flows into emerging market economies typically begin with Western companies looking for cheap labour, which causes a widening of the trade imbalances. With hot money following on the back of that, the central banks then intervene and that leads to a recycling of reserves back to the West.

It is instructive to see that more than half of the countries with the largest reserves shown in Table 6.2 (above) have been enjoying net capital inflows over recent years, including China, Russia, India, Brazil, South Korea, Thailand and Mexico.[26]

It was wrong, therefore, of the Federal Reserve to shift the blame for housing bubbles in the West on to governments of so-called developing economies. Their 'excess savings' were driven *a priori* by capital flows in search of cheaper labour, a policy which governments of the West sanctioned and enthusiastically promoted.

Too Much Intervention?

Unsterilised intervention may have been the fuel driving the domestic credit bubbles that have sprung up across the developing world. But a vicious circle has taken hold, where central banks have been intervening, stimulating credit growth, driving asset prices up, attracting more speculative inflows, thus necessitating more intervention, and so on. It is unsustainable.

And where central banks have been able or willing to sterilise their intervention, the costs are rising. They are unlikely to keep accumulating reserves at such a frenetic pace. We may soon be arriving at a crunch point, where the costs of intervening and holding down currencies are so great, that many central banks will be forced to give up. The data is only tentative at this point, but after the credit crunch erupted in August 2007, the rate of intervention slowed sharply.[27]

That has to be the logical outcome of the forces unleashed by globalisation. The collapse of the housing market is driving interest rates in the US down sharply. Euroland and the UK will follow. Housing deflation has long since pushed Japanese interest rates down to rock bottom. They look set to hit zero again this year. All four major reserve currencies will soon have interest rates that will be very unattractive for emerging market countries looking to recycle the proceeds of intervention.

Domestic credit bubbles have also pushed inflation up in emerging market economies, widening the differential in borrowing costs, exacerbating the fiscal costs of sterilising intervention. Across the developing world, inflation has been accelerating. Like the West, much of this has been confined to food and energy. But many of these countries are more vulnerable to climate change and Peak Oil, as food and energy constitutes a far bigger proportion of their inflation indices. It is becoming impossible for these countries to hold down both inflation and their exchange rates, and sterilise the subsequent intervention without punitive costs.

This dynamic is aggravated by speculative inflows, seeking to take advantage of rising domestic interest rates, necessitating more intervention, thus perpetuating the cycle. A globalisation that relies upon such excessive domestic credit creation at its core is patently unstable.

That is certainly true for China, where on some estimates the authorities were losing $4 billion a month sterilising its foreign exchange intervention towards the end of 2007.[28] China's soaring current account surplus finally forced it to break its peg against the dollar in July 2005. The Chinese authorities still tried to limit the renminbi's appreciation.

For a while, higher interest rates in the US than at home implied that the dollars held by the Chinese central bank earned more than it was paying out in local currency bills. But as the logic of outsourcing eventually forced interest rates down in the US and up in China, sterilisation became expensive. The renminbi is now being allowed to rise more rapidly. And the costs of sterilising intervention will keep on rising as the US housing market continues to tumble and US interest rates are forced even lower.

The risks posed to the balance sheets of central banks engaged in extensive intervention cannot be ignored either. They will be forced to go cap in hand to governments for bailouts, if the losses on their reserves rise too far.[29] Once the People's Bank of China concedes defeat and stops intervening, the renminbi will soar.

Belatedly, some governments have been introducing selective capital controls, to limit the destabilising influence of investors piling into a country's financial markets. Argentina (since 2005),

Thailand (since 2006) and Colombia (since May 2007) have imposed unremunerated reserve requirements on selected types of capital inflows – effectively a tax. Others, such as Brazil, Kazakhstan and South Korea have introduced measures to limit short term inflows through the banks. And India has placed restrictions on commercial borrowing overseas.

The Decoupling Myth

These measures have been limited and come far too late in the day to prevent a more debilitating adjustment. Excessive credit growth has made these countries more vulnerable to events in the West, undermining one popular assumption that emerging markets will be able to decouple from the West. Decoupling became a fashionable concept during 2007. Developing economies, it was argued, could detach themselves from the Industrialised West because they now trade with each other so much more. That is certainly true. China is not buying from the US, it is importing from other developing countries. It is a point already highlighted in Chapter 4, in the context of why trade deficits have risen so sharply in the US and UK.

Decoupling overlooks two critical points. Eventually, the accumulation of foreign exchange reserves will have to slow, and that will trigger an abrupt drop in credit growth. Apart from the increasing costs of sterilisation, the bubble will also be punctured by a drop in demand from the Western consumer, already underway. That will worsen the trade positions of these countries. A number of countries highly dependent upon large capital inflows saw a marked deterioration in their trade position in 2007.

Those running deficits will see them get bigger. Other countries will see their surpluses decline. China's trade surplus, for example, is beginning to turn down because of a slump in US consumer spending. The overall balance of payments surplus of countries dependent upon the Western consumer will fall. Some will slip into the red. There will be less pressure to intervene, less fuel for the credit bubbles. Some central banks may even be forced to stop their currencies depreciating. Reserves will then shrink, causing domestic credit growth to brake even more sharply.

The capital inflows will also drop. Companies may still be keen to relocate. Indeed, the pressure to shift jobs might even intensify, if a slump in demand from the Western consumer causes profits to slide. But other financial flows will seize up. A deepening of the credit crunch in the West will make investors risk averse and lead to a sharp drop in capital inflows, as Western banks and investors are forced to retrench. Stock markets in the region will fall, leading to a drop in portfolio inflows, and the property bubbles will start to unravel too. The two will feed off each other, as the bubbles deflate quickly.

All this underlines the problems with the way globalisation has developed. Transferring jobs abroad is boosting wages in developing countries, but there is still a shortfall in consumer demand across the world economy. Outsourcing necessarily implies there will be a reduction in aggregate wages. It is not only the West where the authorities have filled the gap with record debt. It is happening across the world. The extent to which domestic credit has fuelled the strong growth of these economies should trouble the IMF rather more than it has.

Appendix: Private sector domestic credit, by world region

List of countries with credit growth faster than the UK and US since January 2000

EUROPE		% increase since January 2000
Albania	Q3 07	1,181.9
Armenia	Q4 07	381.1
Azerbaijan	Q4 07	1,417.8
Belarus	Q3 07	6,138.4
Bosnia	Q4 07	181.6
Bulgaria	Q3 07	1,019.9
Croatia	Q4 07	274.5
Denmark	Q4 07	194.5*
Estonia	Q4 07	913.1
Georgia	Q4 07	1,035.3
Greece	Q4 07	192.9*
Hungary	Q3 07	339.4
Iceland	Q2 07	753.8
Ireland	Q4 07	277.0
Kazakhstan	Q4 07	4,111.2
Kyrgyz Republic	Q4 06	369.5
Latvia	Q3 07	1,638.5
Lithuania	Q3 07	809.6
Luxembourg	Q4 07	217.4
Macedonia	Q3 07	204.7
Moldova	Q4 07	1,153.7
Poland	Q3 07	149.7
Rumania	Q1 07	1,908.4
Russia	Q4 07	1,727.8
Serbia	Q4 07	651.4**
Spain	Q4 07	256.5
Tajikistan	Q3 07	1,088.9
Turkey	Q3 07	1,064.3
Ukraine	Q4 07	2,996.8
United Kingdom	*Q4 07*	*125.9*

NORTH AMERICA		
Mexico	Q4 07	127.3
United States	*Q3 07*	*80.1*

CENTRAL AMERICA		
Belize	Q4 07	140.1
Costa Rica	Q4 07	523.8
Guatemala	Q4 07	226.8
Honduras	Q4 07	265.5
Nicaragua	Q4 07	191.6

SOUTH AMERICA		% increase since January 2000
Brazil	Q4 07	231.6
Chile	Q4 07	158.1
Colombia	Q4 07	210.9
Ecuador	Q4 07	177.2
Suriname	Q4 07	1,331.9
Venezuela	Q3 07	1,313.2

CARIBBEAN		
Dominican Rep.	Q3 07	239.8
Haiti	Q3 07	152.0
Jamaica	Q3 07	169.0
Trinidad & Tobago	Q3 07	161.6

MIDDLE EAST		
Bahrain	Q3 07	204.8
Iran	Q3 07	441.7
Jordan	Q4 07	166.8
Kuwait	Q4 07	290.7
Qatar	Q4 07	661.0
Saudi Arabia	Q4 07	273.3
Syria	Q3 07	283.6
United Arab Emirates	Q3 07	322.6
Yemen	Q4 07	451.3

AFRICA		
Algeria	Q4 07	561.0
Angola	Q4 07	103,922.9
Benin	Q3 07	157.0
Botswana	Q3 07	298.4
Burkina Faso	Q3 07	166.6
Burundi	Q3 07	173.5
Chad	Q2 07	166.6
Congo, Dem. Repub.	Q2 07	1,118.4**
Equatorial Guinea	Q2 07	505.4
Ethiopia	Q3 07	152.6
Gambia	Q3 07	243.3
Ghana	Q4 07	736.2
Guinea	Q3 07	299.4

AFRICA		% increase since January 2000	ASIA		% increase since January 2000
Liberia	Q4 07	246.1	Bangladesh	Q4 07	236.9
Madagascar	Q4 07	273.9	Bhutan	Q2 07	573.1
Malawi	Q2 07	511.6	Brunei	Q2 07	140.8
Mauritius	Q4 07	189.2	Cambodia	Q4 07	718.6
Morocco	Q4 07	136.9	China	Q3 07	174.8
Mozambique	Q3 07	187.2	India	Q3 07	303.3
Namibia	Q4 07	224.9	Indonesia	Q4 07	335.1
Niger	Q3 07	234.2	Maldives	Q4 07	834.1
Nigeria	Q3 06	424.3	Mongolia	Q2 07	1,971.9
Rwanda	Q1 06	177.8	Pakistan	Q4 07	239.9
Sao Tome	Q1 07	2,460.1	Sri Lanka	Q1 06	145.3
Seychelles	Q3 07	196.8	South Korea	Q3 07	127.1
Sierra Leone	Q4 07	866.7	Vietnam	Q4 06	322.4
South Africa	Q4 07	185.8			
Sudan	Q3 07	2,426.6	**AUSTRALASIA**		
Swaziland	Q4 07	311.9	Australia	Q2 07	129.4
Tanzania	Q4 07	913.8	Solomon Islands	Q3 07	329.1
Uganda	Q3 07	212.0	Tonga	Q3 07	160.2
Zambia	Q4 07	832.6	Western Samoa	Q4 07	185.1

*   Start Q1 2001.
** Start Q1 2002.

7

JAPAN'S BEAR MARKET

The story of Japan's bear market is an economic calamity unparalleled in modern times. At the turn of the 1990s, Japan was the envy of the world. The people of Japan were enjoying untold prosperity as the stock market soared and property prices rose exponentially. Unemployment was negligible. The Japanese economy was a powerhouse to be revered and respected. Japanese banks were the biggest in the world. Companies everywhere were trying to emulate the Japanese way of doing business. It seemed that Japan could do no wrong.

The swift reversal in Japan's fortunes from the booming 1980s to a decade or more of tumbling asset prices was a classic illustration of the damage inflicted by excessive speculation. It provided a warning of the dangers in allowing property prices to soar out of control, and then failing to respond quickly when the bubble inevitably bursts. Japan's experience has also been a painful lesson in the costs of not confronting the threat of debt deflation early enough. It was evident from as early as 1991 that Japan was at risk of slipping into a liquidity trap that would ultimately bring down many of its once mighty banks. All the subsequent tinkering with monetary and fiscal policy failed to arrest years of stagnation.

Japan was largely dismissed as an idiosyncrasy by foreign commentators. Many claimed the country's problems were unique and that 'it could never happen here'. Some even revelled in the sudden downturn in the country's fortunes. It showed that the once unbeatable Japanese were not so invincible after all. The remarkable rise of Japan from its defeat at the end of the Second World War had left many in awe. The spectacular growth of Japanese industry and the world domination achieved by so many of its leading companies had been viewed with considerable envy.

As Japan spluttered and dipped into repeated recession, its government became inundated with advice from abroad. Much of this counsel was misguided. It reflected a popular belief that Japan's problems would not have been so endemic if it had moulded its economy on the Anglo-Saxon model. Successive US administrations proved notably trenchant, arguing that a policy more receptive to market forces would have brought an early end to the decline. In reality, it was the last thing Japan needed. The inexorable slide into a liquidity trap had been initiated by uncontrolled asset inflation, record borrowing and corporate excess. This could happen to any country that failed to check the forces of unbridled speculation.

Ichi ban

Japan seemed a good place to be in 1989. Four and a half decades on from its humbling defeat at the end of the Second World War, it had been completely transformed. Its economy had become the envy of the world. Many Japanese people were wealthy beyond their wildest dreams. Japan was a materialist's paradise.

The triumphant mood was encapsulated neatly by the phrase 'ichi ban'. Translated, it simply means 'number one'. The phrase was made popular in Japan in 1979 with the publication of Ezra Vogel's book *Japan as Number One*,[1] which tried to identify reasons for the country's success.

The trappings of Japan's success story were evident for all. At the height of the property rush, Japanese investors were stampeding into the US property market. Mitsubishi Estate bought New York's Rockefeller Center for $84.6 billion in 1989. Mitsui Fudosan had acquired the Exxon Building in New York for $61.0 billion three years earlier. Shuwa Corporation had purchased the Arco Plaza in Los Angeles for $62.0 billion in 1986.[2]

The world art market was dominated by cash-rich Japanese bidders too, snapping-up masterpieces at record prices. Between

40 and 50 per cent of impressionist and modern paintings on sale at Sotheby's and Christie's auction houses were being acquired by Japanese dealers.[3] Japanese companies were among the largest in the world. Mitsui & Co., Sumitomo Corp., Mitsubishi Corp., Marubeni Corp. and C Itoh all had larger sales than America's biggest company, General Motors.[4]

US magazine *Forbes*'s list of 'world billionaires' was headed by Japanese railway and golf course magnate Yoshiaki Tsutsumi. His business empire was conservatively thought to be worth $37 billion.[5] Rising standards of living were also matched by the world's longest life expectancy.[6] Japan's affluent citizens were travelling the world in record numbers.[7] A prosperous Japan was seeking more clout on the world stage.[8]

The people of Japan had been swept along by the euphoria of becoming the world's most dynamic economy. Success was intoxicating. The transformation of Japan since 1945 had been secured by hard work. Once Japan started to overtake its peers, its people began to believe in their invincibility. The confidence was understandable on one level. There was little getting away from the fact that the 'Japanese way of doing business' had helped build one of the world's most dynamic economies.

But egotism was to prove Japan's undoing. The success enjoyed by the Japanese economy had long gone hand in hand with higher property and share prices. For the most part, the rise in asset values had been steady, measured and far from spectacular.

From the middle of the 1980s, however, there was a marked sea change. Both equity and real estate prices started climbing much more quickly than could be justified even by the extraordinary strength of the Japanese economy. The confident mood engendered by rapid increases in standards of living and very low unemployment can provide fertile conditions for speculation to become rife. And so it was in Japan.

By the early months of 1988, much more of Japan had become consumed by a speculative frenzy. An equivalent plot of land now cost 30 times more in Japan's capital city than in London, 50 times more than in San Francisco and 99 times more than in Los Angeles.[9] The average annual income of a Tokyoite could buy just 4.4 square metres of residential land. By contrast, the average income of a Londoner would have bought 48.4 square metres, while the average Los Angelean could have bought 309.9 square metres. When 220 flats were put up for sale in the city of Kobe, the developer was so overwhelmed with applicants that it had to draw lots. Prospective buyers had a one in 60 chance of being successful.[10]

The boom years were not without costs. The pressure to work hard was unrelenting. Sudden death from excessive work – *karoshi* – was becoming increasingly common.[11] Japan's work culture was also coming under heavy criticism from abroad. US workers demonstrated, claiming Japanese importers were stealing their jobs. Widespread apprehension that newly rich Japanese were 'buying up' America was fuelling 'a virtual tidal wave' of anti-Japanese sentiment.[12]

The property boom was also proving highly divisive back home, creating tensions between the haves and have-nots.[13] House prices rose so far out of reach for some ordinary working Japanese they simply gave up trying to get on the property ladder. Many were forced to commute two hours or more to work in central Tokyo.[14] An increasing number of people were getting into debt using multiple credit cards. Nearly half of those seeking help from the Japan Credit Counselling Association in Tokyo during 1989 had 'between eleven and twenty credit cards'.[15] Skyrocketing land prices led to a shortage of affordable burial plots. This was prompting a proliferation of underground multi-storey mausoleums or 'condominium graves'.[16]

Quick and easy gains from an inflated stock market were a temptation to all. Criminals were targeting specific share prices and manipulating the market.[17] Politicians were not immune to the allure of rising share prices. Recruit Cosmos, a recruitment company, had tried to bribe as many as 60 leading Japanese politicians by offering shares in the company before its flotation.[18] The scandal that shook Japan's political world to its core resulted in the resignations of Prime Minister Noboru Takeshita, Finance Minister Kiichi Miyazawa and the leaders of two opposition parties.[19] It was small wonder that many saw

Japan as a ruthless and materialist competitor that was merely interested in making money.[20]

The speculative tumult that had gripped the nation could not last. When the stock market closed for business on the final day of 1989, few investors imagined that share prices would never see such levels again. Few believed that the bull-run of the 1980s would descend into a prolonged and painful bear market stretching for nearly two decades. Few could have conceived that house prices, which had risen year in, year out, since 1945 would slide uninterrupted for 16 years.[21] And few could have anticipated the chaos that would be wreaked on Japan's banks, threatening the very foundations of the financial system. The demise of Japan's once powerful economy holds many lessons for those in the West.

Capitulation and Liquidation

The sheer scale of the fall in share prices witnessed during the 1990 crash was partly a response to the excessive borrowing that drove the stock market boom in the first place. As the Bank of Japan forced interest rates up, the pain of servicing the high levels of debt incurred during the bubble years rose steadily. Higher interest rates were initially not a problem. So long as share prices continued to soar, investors had little to fear. Capital gains far outweighed the rise in interest payments. But the higher borrowing costs eventually took their toll and share prices inevitably faltered.

Many people in Japan had borrowed heavily to finance their share purchases. Few had wanted to miss out on the chance to make a quick and easy profit. The banks were certainly not shy in playing their part in fuelling the merry-go-round. Investors took advantage of lax lending criteria to jump on board the great bull-run of the late 1980s. Once the market started to fall, large numbers of investors were forced to unwind their holdings. What started as an orderly correction soon snowballed. Enforced liquidations intensified and the market tumbled even more quickly.

The speed of the decline in share prices was aggravated by a series of policy mistakes by the Bank of Japan. It was under few illusions that share prices had been pushed up to such extreme levels by heavy borrowing. It had made repeated references during the boom to the culpability of banks in fuelling the speculation. The very nature of the rise in share prices in the first place implied any downturn would be fraught with dangers. There was always a risk that the slump in the stock market would cause serious financial distress, sending large numbers of companies to the wall. That was overlooked by the Bank of Japan. The threat of an uncontrolled slide in share prices inflicting significant damage on the economy, leading to the collapse of numerous banks, was never taken seriously.

On one level, it was not difficult to see why the Bank of Japan became so entrenched. The rise in asset prices during the second half of the 1980s had been quite astonishing. By the end of 1989, it was fighting a rearguard battle to contain the forces of speculation. As interest rates rose, Japan's central bank governor Satoshi Sumita became increasingly unpopular, not least among politicians. Many leading members of the ruling Liberal Democratic Party had enjoyed a considerable rise in their personal fortunes from the surge in share and property prices. They were certainly not happy with Mr Sumita's insistence that this was unsustainable. The battle of wills between an increasingly isolated Bank of Japan and the ruling political elite was intense. Mr Sumita was under pressure to let the good times roll.

The Inflation Puzzle

It would be wrong to pin the blame for the collapse of the stock market solely on tensions between the Bank of Japan and the government. The Bank of Japan had also become obsessed with the spectre of inflation. Central banks across the world had spent much of the 1980s fighting to bring inflation under control. Paul Volcker's arrival at the helm of the US Federal Reserve in 1979 had marked a sea change in the determination of central banks worldwide to quell the build-up in inflation pressures.

It was hard to see why the Bank of Japan was so worried. By the end of the 1980s, inflation dynamics had begun to change in many countries, not least in Japan. The rapid growth witnessed in the economy during the second half of the decade was not the threat to price stability widely claimed at the time. Consumer demand was rising strongly, but so was capital spending. A growing share of Japan's GDP was being used to expand production capacity. The ratio of investment spending to GDP had soared from 12.6 per cent at the beginning of the 1980s to 18.5 per cent by the end of the decade. By contrast, the proportion of the country's output being absorbed by consumer demand was falling.[22] The economy was booming, but it was a supply-driven expansion, not a demand-led one. Japan was in the throes of an overinvestment cycle, one financed by record levels of debt.

The distinction is important. The economy was actually coping comparatively well with the 'strains' of rapid growth. Unemployment had fallen to just 2.1 per cent at the end of 1989, and wages were rising more quickly.[23] But, the surge in capital spending implied that the threat from wage inflation was overstated. Heavy investment expenditure was pushing productivity up quickly enough to pay for the higher wages. Unit labour costs were falling.[24]

The Bank of Japan conceded that productivity was improving rapidly in the manufacturing sector. However, it believed the inflation risks lay in the service sector, where it would not be possible to secure the same gains in efficiency. Productivity in services could not match the impressive advances witnessed in manufacturing. But it was still wrong to argue there was such an inflation risk. Productivity in manufacturing was rising quickly enough to compensate for the less dynamic service sector.[25] The Bank of Japan's analysis reflected a consensus that had emerged during the late 1970s and 1980s, of an automatic trade-off between economic growth and inflation.

Bursting the Property Bubble

One of the Bank of Japan's key arguments for maintaining such an aggressive monetary policy focused on the need to bring property prices down from stratospheric valuations. Soaring share prices had contributed in no small measure to the extraordinary wealth gains witnessed in the late 1980s. But the real estate market had been a bigger culprit in the eyes of the Bank of Japan. Shares were widely owned. But property holdings were still worth ten times the average Japanese stock market portfolio.[26]

The sharp rise in borrowing during the boom implied that any attempt to precipitate a gradual decline in property prices could backfire. Here again the Bank of Japan misread the early warning signs. There was already convincing evidence that the most overheated area of the housing market was turning down before interest rates started to rise in 1988. House prices had shot up by 67 per cent in Tokyo during 1987 in response to a series of interest rate cuts that pushed the discount rate down to a low of 2.5 per cent.[27] Valuations became so stretched and unaffordable that many people wanting to buy their first home started looking far beyond the capital city. Banks had also begun to exert some self-restraint with 'less aggressive financing'.[28] The property market soon cooled and during the following year prices rose by just 0.4 per cent.[29] Prices had also eased off in a number of Tokyo satellite cities, including Kawasaki, Yokohama and Kanagawa. Average prices in Kanagawa had dropped by 8.7 per cent during 1988 after surging 85.7 per cent the year before.[30]

By the spring of 1989, house prices in Tokyo had started to slip. A report in the National Land Agency's official gazette revealed that house prices were falling in 'almost all areas of Tokyo and Kanagawa prefectures'.[31] Another survey conducted by real estate company Misawa Homes had found that 'medium to large' house prices in Tokyo were going down at an annual rate of 8 per cent.[32] Yet another report released by the Tokyo Metropolitan Government on 2 October 1989 confirmed that residential property prices were declining year-on-year for the first time since 1975.[33] Commercial property prices had also started trending down. After galloping ahead by 61.1 per cent during 1987, prices had risen by just 3 per cent in the following year, and then started to drift down.[34]

The property bubble had its seeds in the capital city. The downturn in the Tokyo market was a warning that the Bank of Japan had started raising interest rates far too late into the boom. House prices in the rest of Japan were still climbing sharply during 1989. But they were largely playing catch-up with Tokyo. After prices leapt in the capital city, there was the inevitable knock-on or 'centrifugal' impact on the rest of the country. The extraordinary rise in house prices in Tokyo during 1987 had 'triggered a chain reaction in urban centres in the neighbouring prefectures as well as in other major cities'.[35] Indeed, urban centres located near to Tokyo, such as Urawa and Omiya in Saitama Prefecture, saw prices rise by an average of just 0.4 per cent during 1988. By contrast, municipalities between 40 and 60 kilometres from the centre of Tokyo, such as Kumagaya and Fukaya, saw an average rise of 17.1 per cent.[36]

By the time the discount rate had been pushed up for the fifth time in the summer of 1990, it was clear that land prices were cooling across the whole country (see Figure 7.1).[37] It was an early

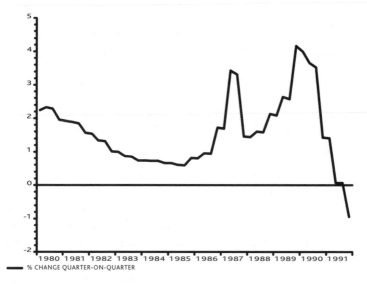

Figure 7.1   Japan Land Prices, Nationwide

Source: Japan Real Estate Institute with Thomson Calculations.

indication that successive rate increases had already quashed the 'land price myth'. But the Bank of Japan wanted more convincing evidence of a slowdown in property prices before it would relent.

It did not have to wait long. On 8 November, the Construction Ministry reported that prices in the condominium market had fallen by as much as 30 per cent during the third quarter of 1990 in Tokyo, Osaka and Nagoya.[38] Another survey released on 13 December 1990 showed that land prices had fallen by between 5 and 10 per cent in the three biggest urban areas – Tokyo, Kinki and Nagoya.[39] By the end of 1990, official figures showed that real estate prices were starting to fall in Japan's six largest cities for the first time since the 1973–74 oil crisis (see Figure 7.2 and Table 7.1).[40] Asset speculation had been tamed. The widely held belief that property prices would always rise was suddenly in doubt.

Table 7.1   **Japan Property Prices – the Turning Point**

	Q1 1990 (%)	Q2 1990 (%)	Q3 1990 (%)	Q4 1990 (%)
Commercial	27.5	9.3	9.0	–2.3
Residential	35.4	12.2	11.8	–6.8
Industrial	26.7	10.6	10.3	–2.5
Overall	29.7	10.7	10.4	–3.9

Largest six cities in Japan. Annualised changes.
Source: Japan Real Estate Institute.

Credit Squeeze Ignored

Perhaps the most compelling warning that Japan was heading into trouble came from the slump in money supply. Ironically, the biggest reversal was seen in the measure targeted by the Bank of Japan, M2+CDs. During the final three months of the boom, M2+CDs had been expanding at an annualised rate of 15.1 per cent. But within the space of a year, this had dropped to a mere 2.0 per cent (see Figure 7.3).[41] The absolute level of M2+CDs even contracted over the final two months of the year, by an annualised rate of 0.6 per cent. The turnaround in money supply growth was unprecedented, and showed asset deflation was hurting the economy.

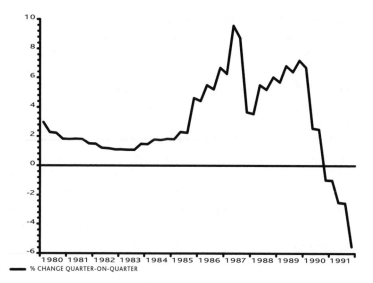

Figure 7.2   Japan Land Prices, Six Largest Cities

Source: Japan Real Estate Institute with Thomson Calculations.

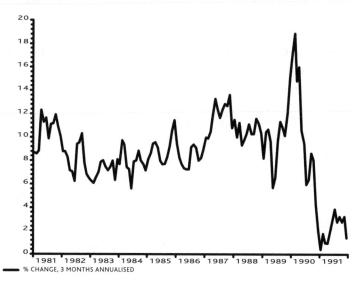

Figure 7.3   Japan Money Supply, M2+CDs

Source: Bank of Japan.

But the collapse in money supply growth was never taken seriously. The superficial resilience of the economy during the early stages of the bear market led many to conclude that the money supply numbers were unreliable. The role of money supply had after all been discredited during the second half of the 1980s. The monetarists' heyday had come and gone. The credit growth witnessed in many countries during the 1980s had failed to translate into the rapid inflation predicted by many monetarists.

The general distrust of money supply numbers was understandable on one level. The reputation of monetarists had been tarnished by arguments over the most appropriate money supply aggregate to use. For those who had never been won over by the monetarist doctrine, this constant shuffling between various measures of money supply was proof of the discipline's shaky intellectual foundations.

When the bubble burst in Japan during 1990 however, there could be little doubt over what was happening to money supply. All measures slumped. And there was clear evidence that credit growth was turning down too. As the growth in bank lending slammed to a halt, it was evident the Bank of Japan had hit the brakes too hard.[42]

The new Bank of Japan governor, Yasushi Mieno, refused to accept that Japan was on the verge of a credit squeeze. Numerous excuses were made why the money supply numbers should be ignored. Perhaps the most disingenuous argument of all was the claim that the relationship between money supply and the economy had broken down because of the collapse in asset prices. The slump in money supply growth simply reflected the sharp fall in property and share prices, which naturally reduced the demand for credit. That was precisely the point. By allowing money supply growth to plummet, the central bank was aggravating the impact of the property crash on the economy.

The central bank was paying far more attention to developments on the foreign exchange market than events closer to home. The Japanese government had come under considerable pressure during the mid 1980s to resolve the chronic trade imbalances that emerged vis-à-vis the US. The US had claimed Japan was not doing enough to stimulate demand at home, and the Bank of Japan was cajoled into cutting interest rates on five occasions during 1986 and 1987. The rate cuts had been instrumental in fuelling the easy credit conditions that triggered the sharp rise in asset prices. So long as the yen remained firm, the Bank of Japan appeared reasonably relaxed about the low interest rates. The strong yen acted as a constraint on inflation.

However, the yen started to come under heavy selling pressure during the course of 1989. The trade imbalances that had pushed the yen up so sharply during the mid 1980s were now starting to unwind. The US trade deficit was improving. The Bank of Japan became fixated with the risks that a falling yen would aggravate the inflation outlook.[43] As share prices started to slide early in 1990, the yen continued to fall. Having fretted about the exchange rate for so long, the Bank of Japan found it hard to ignore the currency markets during the early months of the bear market (see Figure 7.4). It was unable to shift its attention towards tumbling asset prices. That was a critical error.

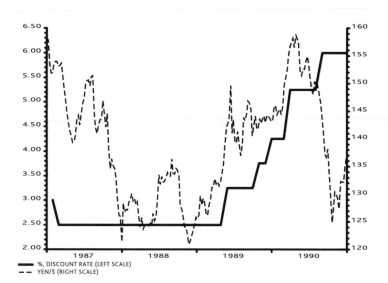

Figure 7.4   Discount Rate and Yen/$

Sources: Bank of Japan and Datastream.

Sliding Towards a Liquidity Trap

The Bank of Japan ignored the warning signs because the economy seemed unaffected. But there were simply very long lags in play. The slump in money supply growth would impact in time, with a vengeance. By failing to cut interest rates quickly, the economy began its inevitable slide towards recession.

After the bubble burst in the spring of 1990, the Bank of Japan delayed cutting interest rates until the summer of the following year. When rates did start coming down, the decline was agonisingly slow. Real borrowing costs went up, not down. The intensity of the overinvestment boom witnessed in the late 1980s always implied there was a risk that inflation would fall quickly once the bubble eventually burst. Even a modest downturn in demand would squeeze the ability of companies to raise prices at all. By the spring of 1991, factory gate prices were already turning down (see Figure 7.5).[44]

By the summer of 1993, inflation had all but disappeared.[45] But still the central bank dithered. Astonishingly, interest rates

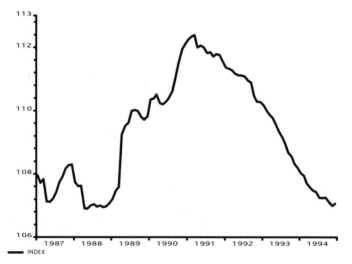

Figure 7.5   Japan Domestic Wholesale Prices

Source: Bank of Japan.

did not come down at all during 1994, even though the spectre of deflation was looming and the yen was climbing remorselessly. By the end of the year, Japan was officially in deflation.[46] The central bank relented in 1995. Interest rates were cut to 0.5 per cent, but the Bank of Japan had lost the chance to secure a meaningful fall in real borrowing costs.

There was still room for the discount rate to come down by another 0.5 per cent before they hit bottom. And eventually they did – four years later. That was never going to make much difference. With property prices in freefall, Japan had already slipped into a liquidity trap.

The Bank of Japan's mistakes were compounded by government policy. The banks came under intense pressure from the government to raise lending margins. As bankruptcies climbed, the Ministry of Finance cajoled the banks to raise operating margins to help pay for the costs of debt write-offs. Operating profits at the banks jumped sharply during the early years of the downturn.[47] Interest rates were falling belatedly, but lending rates charged by banks were even slower to come down. The widening differential was good for banks' profits, it was claimed.

The policy of trying to raise lending margins was futile. Operating profits might go up. But the failure to pass on the benefit of lower rates to borrowers meant that more of them would default. Any short-term boost to operating profits from wider lending margins would soon be lost as more and more borrowers defaulted, pushing debt write-offs up.

The government should have instead made every attempt to avoid sending companies under. The principle of moral hazard suggests companies should ordinarily be allowed to default if they have overreached themselves. But this principle became an unaffordable luxury once the economy had slipped into a liquidity trap. There was little to be gained by 'teaching debtors a lesson' once the bubble had burst.

The time to worry about excessive borrowing was during the boom, not in the depths of a bear market. Attempts to dispose of bad debts created more selling pressure in the real estate market as banks were forced to sell repossessed properties. And the Bank of Japan lost the ability to offset the deflationary impact of these property disposals once interest rates had hit a floor.[48] Effectively, they had no way of alleviating the distress caused by rising bankruptcies. The debt disposals aggravated the slide in property prices, which in turn increased the risk of more companies going under. Crucially, the level of debt in real terms went up, not down. It proved to be the ultimate vicious circle.

It's the Banks' Fault, but …

Throughout Japan's long fight against debt deflation, banks became the targets of considerable criticism. They were seen as one of the biggest engineers of the boom and subsequent collapse. Much of the opprobrium heaped on Japan's bankers by the public reflected the intense anger at the huge loss of wealth suffered during the bear market. People felt they had been duped and needed someone to blame. The banks were an obvious target given their complicity in allowing the bubble to inflate.

As the economy slipped deeper into trouble, the banks were also accused of prolonging the crisis. They were heavily criticised for failing to dispose of their bad debts. By leaving so many non-performing loans on their books, the banks were accused of strangling the provision of credit to new companies. Weighed down by these bad debts, it seemed that banks were in no position to extend fresh loans to growth industries and support an economic recovery. Too many defunct companies were being kept afloat, stifling the creation of new businesses, it was claimed.

The banks did have huge amounts of bad debts on their books, and they were slow in getting rid of them. They were sometimes reluctant to let companies fold too. Many companies were kept on life support even when it seemed their cause was a lost one. The close ties that had been forged with companies dissuaded banks from pulling the plug. The *keiretsu* system that bound many companies to the banks had been one of the cornerstones of stakeholder capitalism. It had been a key factor behind the extraordinary success of the Japanese economy during the post-war era. Many bankers found it hard to break the ties that were seen as instrumental to the Japanese way of doing business.

Nevertheless, it was disingenuous to suggest that the banks alone were guilty of prolonging the debt crisis. Disposing of their bad debts even more quickly would have made the problem worse. Once deflation had set in and interest rates had hit rock bottom, any attempt to dispose of these bad debts would have created yet more deflation and even higher bankruptcies. Without the power to control real borrowing costs, accelerated debt disposals would lead to a sharper fall in prices.

Call off the Debt Collectors

However, critics argued that the level of bad debts would have fallen if the banks had not carried on lending to so many struggling companies. As property prices started to tumble, many companies in trouble were successful in securing additional loans from their banks. Had the banks been more ruthless from the outset, the economy would not have slipped into a liquidity trap, it was claimed. The attempt to dispose of bad debts would have led to a lower level of non-performing loans.

This argument is wrong on a number of counts. Firstly, bank lending growth did turn down sharply following the 1990 stock market crash. The banks may have been 'too accommodating' with respect to some of their larger *keiretsu* borrowers. But by the same token, credit lines were cut to numerous smaller companies. By the end of 1993, bank lending growth was down to just 0.5 per cent year-on-year. Lending growth went negative in 1994, before turning down decisively again in the spring of 1997. By the summer of 2005, the total level of bank loans outstanding was 27.0 per cent below its March 1996 peak.[49]

Furthermore, once deflation had started to take root back in 1993, the scope to get real interest rates down to ultra-low levels was diminishing. There was still room for interest rates to come down, at both the short and long end of the yield curve. But time was running out. Not lending to companies in trouble would have accelerated the downturn in the economy. At this juncture the banks should have been stopped from making companies bankrupt. The government should have intervened.

But from January 1993 onwards, Japan embarked on a fire sale that would ultimately precipitate a series of debilitating financial crises. The banks were cajoled into selling their non-performing loans to debt-collecting agencies, which then attempted to recover as much of the loans as possible, often by selling the collateral through court auctions.

The collapse in property prices was precipitous. The first of the debt-collecting agencies, the Cooperative Credit Purchasing Company, struggled to sell repossessed properties, in part because of the myriad of competing claims over repossessed properties, and in part because of criminal activities. But the real problem was that prices collapsed from a glut of supply. The recovery rate from these collateral disposals just imploded.[50]

The folly of the debt disposals finally caught up with the banking system in 1995, when a number of credit cooperatives collapsed, sparking panic among depositors. Instead of changing tack, the government persevered with the wholesale selling of repossessed properties. Another debt-collecting agency, the Housing Loan Administration Corporation, was set up following the crisis at the mortgage lenders, and the selling continued.

By the spring of 1997, the Japanese economy had suffered a further shock when Nissan Mutual Life Insurance went under. There was now a palpable fear that collapsing financial institutions would destroy people's savings. The savings ratio started to rise sharply. When Yamaichi Securities and Hokkaido Takushoku Bank went under in the autumn of 1997, the savings ratio soared again. Bankruptcies were eroding confidence and aggravating the downturn in the economy. The policy of asset disposals was backfiring. By the end of 1997, land prices were going down faster than at any point since the bear market began. But the government failed to see the flaw in its strategy.

The anxiety spread. Distrust of the banks caused many people to withdraw their deposits and hold their savings in cash. People began to hoard. Some moved their money from the smaller banks to some of the bigger and supposedly stronger banks. Others shifted their money out of deposits with fixed maturities (time deposits) into accounts with instant access. Once rumours started to fly that a bank was in trouble, depositors were able to withdraw their money quickly. Demand for gold soared. Everywhere, there was a tangible fear that more banks and insurance companies could still go under, that savings would be lost.

The Bank of Japan was forced to inject huge amounts of liquidity to satisfy the public's demand for notes and coins. That caused some measures of money supply growth to balloon and the velocity of circulation to tumble (see Figure 7.6).[51] Ironically, when the growth in the narrow measures of money supply soared during the late 1990s, many economists concluded that the Bank of Japan had secured a turnaround in the economy. But it had not. Surging demand for notes and coins was a measure of the uncertainty felt by many.

We've Been Here Before

But Japan's experience was nothing new. Historians only have to go back to the 1930s to find numerous parallels with Japan's bear market. The theory of debt deflation – falling prices brought on

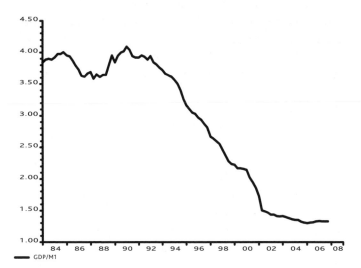

Figure 7.6   Japan Velocity of Circulation

Sources: Cabinet Office (Japan) and Bank of Japan.

by excessive borrowing – was first postulated by the US economist
Irving Fisher in response to the depression that had gripped the
US. He had lost a personal fortune during the Wall Street crash
of October 1929, after proclaiming just months earlier that 'stock
prices have reached what looked like a permanently high plateau'.[52]
He set out to explain in his book *Booms and Depressions* why the
economic malaise of the early 1930s was proving so intractable.
His analysis held important lessons for the Bank of Japan, many
of which were ignored.

The starting point for Fisher's analysis of debt deflation was,
rather obviously, the accumulation of excessive debt. Fisher was
at pains to emphasise that there was no absolute level of debt
that should automatically be considered too dangerous. Much
would depend upon the level of debt in relation to underlying
fundamentals, such as income. The nature of the debt also had
to be considered. Debtors with short term liabilities, for example,
would be far more vulnerable to a sudden shift in sentiment,
particularly if they had borrowed from financial markets.

Fisher went on to stress that it did not matter what triggered
the turning point in the debt cycle. Sentiment could shift for no
other reason than speculators had simply judged that asset prices
were too high. Whatever the cause, high levels of debt could
precipitate distress selling. Once debtors were forced to sell, there
was a risk of what he termed stampede liquidation. As the selling
began, more debtors would be forced to liquidate in response to
the slide in prices.

Fisher's analysis was mirrored by Japan's experience during
the crash of 1990. Numerous speculators ran into trouble just
months after share prices started to slide. The collapse of Tokyo-
based dealer Akebono Kikaku in early May of that year was an
obvious warning. It was the third biggest corporate default in
Japan's post-war history. By the summer, trading company Itoman
had run into severe trouble. And by the end of the year, a number
of high-profile bankruptcies had shattered any illusion that the
economy would remain immune to the slump in share prices.[53]

The banks were already feeling the effects of the crash too.
Taiheiyo Bank was teetering on the brink of default. The

'Sumitomo shock' was also reverberating across the financial system. Banks were quickly cutting their loan exposures after Sumitomo Bank's revered chairman had been forced to resign in the wake of a damaging loan scandal.

The next stage of Fisher's theory was influenced by the economist's strong monetarist leanings. As debtors were forced to liquidate, this would lead to a reduction in money supply or credit. The very act of repaying a loan would cause the level of deposits held by banks to contract, depressing the total stock of money supply. Ordinarily, the bank could use the proceeds of a repaid loan to lend again to another borrower. That would prevent money supply growth from turning down. Once prices had started to fall, however, it might prove difficult to tempt speculators to borrow.

This stage of Fisher's theory was again reflected in Japan's experience, as money supply growth collapsed within months of share prices starting to tumble. The failure to recognise the significance of the money supply numbers was arguably the single biggest policy blunder committed by the Japanese authorities during the first year of the crash.

Fisher also suggested that a sudden decline in money supply would be a warning that liquidation could push price levels down even more sharply. A downturn in the credit aggregates implied that debtors were being forced to repay their loans and that no new loans were being created. That would effectively mean there was a shortfall of buyers to stop prices from spiralling down.

It might not be necessary for new borrowers to enter the market to stabilise prices. Speculators with deep reserves or savings might be attracted into the market by the lower prices. In this sense, it could be said that money supply might not be an accurate indicator of the potential impact of distress selling on prices. If a speculator buys assets from a forced seller using his or her savings, then a contraction in money supply need not be a true measure of the potential selling pressure.

However, the high level of debt that accumulated during the boom years implied it was unlikely there would be enough speculators in such a position. It seemed reasonable, therefore, to assert that a sudden lurch down in money supply growth would reflect significant distress selling. And in this respect, money supply or credit growth was a crucial indicator of how far forced liquidation might trigger a chain reaction of events that eventually led to debt deflation.

Once money supply growth started to turn down, Fisher warned there was a risk that inflation would start to tumble, raising the spectre of deflation. This was another stage of the debt deflation theory that reflected Fisher's monetarist inclinations. Strictly speaking, the causality between these two stages outlined by Fisher is not a necessary condition for a country to slip into a debt trap. The price level can also sink because of overinvestment. Indeed as we have already seen, over the years, overinvestment has quite often been accompanied by extreme borrowing.

For Fisher, money supply played a critical role in propagating debt deflation. But in fact, the theory of debt deflation is better viewed in terms of real business cycle dynamics. The accumulation of debt and the subsequent distress selling may cause money supply growth to soar and then collapse. But money supply was merely a reflection of the sharp swings in borrowing that drove the boom and bust phases of the economic cycle. Money supply was still a critical indicator, as it provided timely evidence of what was happening in the real world. But it was not the money supply growth *per se* that determined the swings in the business cycle. It was the unbridled exuberance, the overinvestment and subsequent collapse of confidence that wreaked so much havoc.

Hoarding and the Velocity of Circulation

Whatever the precise transmission mechanism, Fisher then warned that companies and individuals could go bankrupt, profits would be squeezed hard and unemployment would start to rise. In Japan's case, unemployment was slow to rise. The social pact between employers and employees, not to mention the excess level of labour demand at the peak of the economic cycle, implied it would be some time before a significant rise in unemployment materialised. But the signs of a collapse in profits were clear-cut.

Profits had soared during the final stages of the bull market. But within three months of share prices peaking, they had begun to turn down sharply. By the end of 1992, corporate profits had fallen by nearly half.[54]

As confidence wilted, people would start to hoard too, Fisher warned. Pessimism would cause people to defer spending. Individuals would hold on to their money a little longer, spend it more slowly, and the velocity of circulation would fall. Once again, Fisher invoked a strict monetarist interpretation when outlining the role played by a falling velocity of circulation.[55]

But in fact, it was probably better to see hoarding as a real phenomenon too. It was simply a reflection of fear. The evidence of hoarding in Japan was certainly compelling. The surge in demand for gold, the rush to install home-safes, particularly in the aftermath of the 1997 financial crises, were classic symptoms. Manufacturers of safe-deposit boxes were facing unprecedented demand. Many banks were renovating their branches to install more boxes.

One of the more compelling illustrations of the fear was the increase in demand for notes with high denomination. Between 1992 and 2002, the demand for ¥10,000 note bills rose by 82.0 per cent. By contrast, demand for ¥5,000 bills increased by 16.4 per cent. Demand for ¥1,000 notes edged up by just 6.2 per cent, while the number of ¥500 notes in circulation fell by 7.8 per cent.[56]

Neither hoarding nor a falling velocity of circulation need necessarily precipitate more deflation. A slowing velocity of circulation will only cause the price level to decline if the money supply is assumed to remain unchanged. But that is unlikely. The demand for cash in all probability would push up the growth rate for narrow money supply. A falling velocity of circulation would increase the demand for money and trigger a rise in the supply. It would only lead to more deflation if the authorities refused to acquiesce to the higher demand for money. And as such, there is no evidence this occurred in Japan. The fear implicit in hoarding may well have exerted a significant depressing effect on economic activity, but not necessarily in the strict monetarist sense postulated by Fisher's theory of debt deflation.

The Curse of Real Debts

All of this brings us to arguably the most protracted stage of the debt deflation theory. The falling price level would raise the real value of debts and the real rate of interest. Taken together, this would cause more forced selling. Efforts to repay debt by the liquidators would push the level of real debts up, not down, implying the economy was in a debt trap. The economy would be snared by a high level of indebtedness, as evident in the US during the early 1930s. Indeed, Fisher remarked at the time how 'all the liquidation that had been accomplished down to 1932 left the unpaid balances more burdensome (in real dollars of 153 cents apiece) than the whole debt burden had been in 1929, before liquidation had began'.[57]

It was a refrain that would be repeated by many Japanese bankers nearly 70 years later. 'No matter how much we write off, bad debt does not seem to come down', was a common refrain.[58] But the Bank of Japan was oblivious to these difficulties. It failed to recognise that the scale of the decline in the stock market during 1990 implied over-leveraged individuals and companies could soon run into trouble. In turn, it underestimated the financial problems that were likely to play a major role in depressing the economy.

8

POLICY FAILURES IN A LIQUIDITY TRAP

Had interest rates come down quickly during the immediate aftermath of the crash, the Bank of Japan would have been able to get real borrowing costs down. Deflation could have been averted.[1] Instead, property prices continued to slide and the economy slithered from one recession to another (see Figure 8.1). The stock market carried on falling, hitting successive new lows and crumbling to a fraction of its 1989 peak.

The government came under enormous pressure to consider alternative policies to reflate the economy. Some economists urged the government to cut taxes and boost spending. Others argued that the only way out of the mire was to pursue supply-side reform. The Bank of Japan was cajoled into doing more. It should either print money or monetise the government's budget deficit. Inflation targets were advocated while others believed currency devaluation proffered a better solution. There was no shortage of policy prescriptions on offer. Few of them worked.

Why Did 'Keynesian' Policies Fail?

The government's first response to the economic downturn was to try to reflate through demand management policies. Virtually every fiscal policy option was tried in a bid to end the decline. The first emergency supplementary budget was introduced in the spring of 1992. A total of ten emergency budgets had been crafted worth a massive ¥126.4 trillion, before Prime Minister Junichiro Koizumi came to power in April 2001.[2] This total included an element of double counting. The ruling Liberal Democratic Party regularly massaged the size of the spending initiatives in a bid

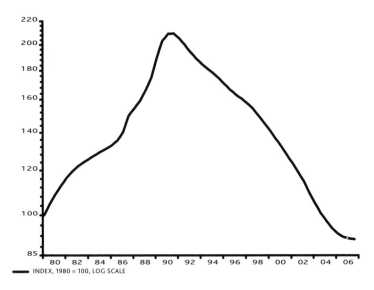

Figure 8.1 Japan Nationwide Land Prices

Source: Japan Real Estate Institute with Thomson Calculations.

to impress financial markets that it was serious about reflation.[3] Nevertheless, the scale of the fiscal stimulus during the early years in particular was still impressive. Large sums were pumped into building new roads, bridges and dams to keep construction companies in business.

It was to no avail. No matter how hard the politicians tried, the economy would only respond for a short while before sliding back into recession. Failure to reverse the decline did not deter the politicians. They reasoned that without the stimulus, the economy would be in even more trouble. The experience of spring 1997 in particular convinced many that the government had no choice but to keep incurring record budget deficits, otherwise Japan would slip further into difficulty. The tax increases introduced in April 1997 were followed by an alarming dip in the economy. The decision to tighten fiscal policy was blamed by many for pushing the country into recession.

In reality, Japan was in trouble well before the tax hikes took effect. A number of economic indicators suggest that the economy had already peaked in October 1996 and was turning down by the time they were implemented.[4] The failure of Nissan Mutual Life Insurance Co. in the spring of 1997 caused people to panic, pushing the savings rate up sharply. Within a year, it had risen by more than 3 per cent (see Figure 8.2).[5] The tax hikes were not the primary cause of the recession that gripped Japan later in the year.[6]

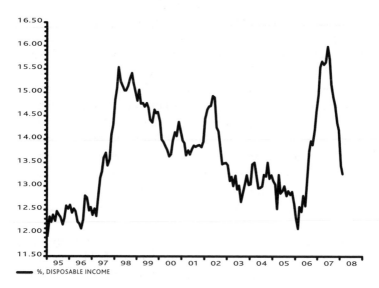

Figure 8.2   Japan Savings, Worker Households

Source: Statistics Bureau of Ministry of Internal Affairs and Communications.

But as the economy deteriorated over the summer, many economists concluded it was because of the higher taxes. Prime Minister Hashimoto came under enormous pressure to reverse the tax hikes and provide even greater stimulus. Not until the reforming Mr Koizumi came to power in the spring of 2001 did the government pledge to keep a lid on its borrowing. Even then, demands from factions within the Liberal Democratic Party to boost spending forced the government to announce yet another supplementary budget by the end of 2002.[7]

Given that the curse of deflation was insufficient demand, it is perhaps puzzling that the government's fiscal policies failed.

Japan had fallen into a liquidity trap and was unable to get real borrowing costs down. Attempts to stimulate demand seemed to make sense. That seemed to be the lesson of Keynesian economics. Keynes had argued that a government should try to spend its way out of recession when a country was in a liquidity trap. Indeed, successive Japanese prime ministers invoked the legacy of Keynes to justify the increase in public spending.

However, Keynes had stressed that the *first* priority for an economy in recession was to reduce interest rates as far as possible. In his view, there was always a risk that the 'marginal efficiency of capital' or the rate of return on investment could collapse quickly following a boom, triggering a slide in share prices. He explicitly warned of the risks should the authorities fail to push interest rates down quickly during a property market slump.[8]

In this important respect, Japan failed the Keynesian test. The Bank of Japan dithered and allowed real interest rates to remain too high during the early years of the bear market. Furthermore, there was a clear implication from Keynes' writings that fiscal policy should only be used *when* interest rates had hit a floor. The first priority was monetary policy.[9]

Here again, Japan did not adhere to Keynesian philosophy. The government tried to spend its way out of trouble long before interest rates were cut to zero. The first big increase in government spending came more than three years *before* the discount rate was trimmed to 0.5 per cent. As a result, its actions delayed the fall in borrowing costs required to stabilise property prices. Nearly every time the government announced higher spending or tax cuts, bond investors began to bet that economic recovery was imminent. Bond yields would rise intermittently, as investors anticipated that higher interest rates would follow.

This had an immediate and direct impact on borrowing costs. Bank lending rates are indirectly tied to government bond yields.[10] The premature use of fiscal policy by Japanese governments caused bond yields to rise temporarily, triggering more bankruptcies and short-circuiting economic recovery (see Figure 8.3).[11] This was the classic 'crowding out' effect long highlighted by critics of demand management economics. In short, the announcement of successive fiscal initiatives had considerable side-effects that were ignored.

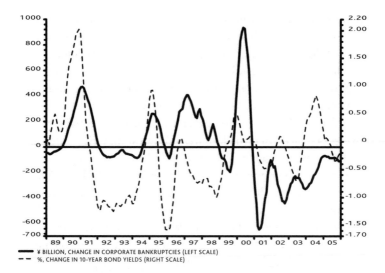

Figure 8.3   Japan Corporate Bankruptcies and Bond Yields

Sources: Tokyo Shoko Research and Datastream.

This 'crowding out' has long been the subject of fierce debate between Keynesians and advocates of supply-side reform, who argue that the government should minimise its role in the economy. Here was compelling evidence that the private sector was being squeezed out.

The experience of Japan still did not constitute a refutation of Keynesian economics. Keynes' prescription was a specific response when monetary policy had failed. The Japanese authorities tried reflating the economy before this point had been reached. Demand management policies should only have been invoked once interest rates had hit a floor. Japan's experience has in effect not been a failed exercise in Keynesian economics. It has been a misunderstanding of what Keynes was saying when he outlined the risks of a liquidity trap.

Causes of a Liquidity Trap

Keynes also warned that interest rates could not always be relied upon to fall quickly enough in an economic downturn. Investors might simply find it hard to believe that inflation and, therefore, interest rates will fall so low. There might be a natural aversion towards low borrowing costs, particularly among bondholders.[12] The low running yield on bonds might be seen as insufficient cushion against the *perceived* risk that interest rates could rise.

As Keynes pointed out, a 4 per cent running yield on bonds would provide adequate compensation up to the point where investors 'feared that the long-term interest may rise faster than by 4 per cent of itself per annum, i.e. by an amount greater than 0.16 per cent per annum'. He went on to add, 'if however, the rate of interest is already as low as 2 per cent, the running yield only offset a rise in it of as little as 0.04 per cent per annum. This, indeed, is perhaps the chief obstacle to a fall in the rate of interest to a very low level.'[13] In short, the relationship was far from linear. As bond yields fell, the safety margin against a possible rise in interest rates would diminish rapidly.

Keynes referred to this aversion as rising liquidity preference, but it could just as easily be summed up by the notion of money illusion. When an economy is sliding towards a possible liquidity trap, interest rates need to fall quickly. But investors have become so used to high borrowing costs during a boom that they find it difficult to adjust. One of the many curious features of a low inflation environment is that savers can feel worse off just because nominal interest rates have dropped. They might fail to recognise that in real terms they may not have lost out. The problem is even more acute in a time of deflation. Deposit rates of 0.01 per cent still provided a real return for savers in Japan.

This money illusion might slow down the necessary reduction in interest rates. But eventually, Keynes argued, it could even stop them from falling altogether.[14] When this point was reached, the economy was in a liquidity trap. The central bank could inject all the liquidity it wanted into the money markets. But if investors did not believe that interest rates could fall any lower, the increase in liquidity would have no effect. These risks were all the more critical precisely because the heavy investment spending witnessed during a boom could cause the marginal efficiency of capital to fall sharply. If there was a natural limit to how far interest rates could fall, then there was clearly a possibility that monetary policy would be rendered inoperable.

Keynes' belief that bondholders could play a significant role in preventing interest rates from falling resonates with Japan's experience. Even though the Bank of Japan was tardy in cutting short term interest rates, bondholders were even slower to respond to the changing economic environment. Significantly, Keynes thought that there might be a floor to long term interest rates 'which may perhaps be as high as 2–2½ per cent'.[15]

In Japan's case, it is clear the floor was not as high as Keynes feared. Bond yields did eventually fall below these levels towards the end of 1997. Nevertheless, there was still a risk that 'the long-term interest rate may be more recalcitrant when once it has fallen to a level which, on the basis of past experience and present expectations of future monetary policy, is considered "unsafe" by representative opinion'.[16]

In other words, the speed of the decline in long term interest rates was important, as well as the existence of any particular floor. And in Japan's case, the failure of long term interest rates to fall quickly contributed in no small measure to the prolonged bear market. Had bond yields fallen in line with short term rates, deflation could have been averted. Japan would never have slipped into a liquidity trap, even with the slow pace of decline in short term interest rates witnessed during the early 1990s.[17]

The failure of long term interest rates to fall partly reflected the crowding out effects from the premature use of demand management policies. Bond yields did fall during 1991 once it became apparent the stock market crash had triggered a downturn in the economy. By the end of the year, ten-year yields were less than 1 per cent above the discount rate.

From the spring of 1992, however, there was a marked divergence between short and long term rates. The fall in bond yields repeatedly lagged behind the drop in the discount rate. By the summer of 1994, the gap between ten-year bond yields and the discount rate had widened to nearly 3 per cent.[18] It was only after a succession of financial collapses rocked the nation in 1997 that the yield curve (the gap between bond yields and short term lending rates) started to flatten. By the time it was clear that Long Term Credit Bank was running into trouble in the summer of 1998, the differential had fallen back below 1.0 per cent (see Figure 8.4). It was not until eight years or more into the bear market that bond investors began to accept the economic environment had changed.

Figure 8.4   Japan Yield Curve

Sources: Bank of Japan and Datastream.

The very sensitivity of bond market investors to an expansionary fiscal policy was also a function of the slow adjustment to a low inflation environment. In effect, these two factors – the premature use of fiscal policy and money illusion – were 'bound up' in each other. Bond investors feared that higher government spending would eventually trigger a rise in inflation.

But the failure of bond yields to fall as quickly as short term interest rates during the early years of the bear market was critical.[19] The full effect of the Bank of Japan's cut in interest rates was diluted by money illusion or liquidity preference among bond investors.

The Supply-Side Fallacy

The failure of demand management policies was seized upon by supply-side economists who saw it as proof that Japan needed more reform to break out from its debt trap. The government has certainly got little to show for getting heavily into debt. Seventeen years of grappling with asset deflation has caused the government's debt burden to more than double. Public sector debt is now 180 per cent of GDP, more than four times that of the US and UK (see Figure 8.5).[20] Attempts to alleviate the symptoms of a debt problem in the private sector have merely spawned another debt headache in the public sector.

There was no getting away from it: Japan's experiment with *its* interpretation of Keynesian economics failed to pull the country out of a liquidity trap. This does not mean the supply-side economists were right either. The crucial point made by Keynes during the early 1930s was still valid: when an economy is in a liquidity trap, the remedy lies with demand reflation. Furthermore, any attempt to make companies rationalise and cut costs would backfire.

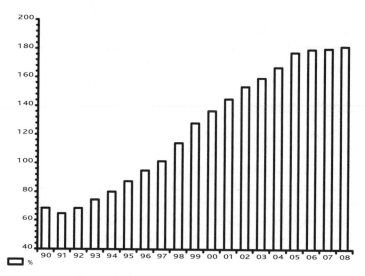

Figure 8.5   Japan Government Debt

Source: Organisation for Economic Cooperation and Development.

Keynes had been moved to write *The General Theory of Employment, Interest and Money* precisely because of heated arguments on this issue with the classical economists of the time. When the UK economy fell into a depression during the 1920s, the classical economists argued that the problem lay with the imperfect workings of the supply mechanism. Unemployment was rising because wages were not flexible enough, they claimed. If there was an excess supply of workers, they were obviously being paid too much. The remedy for mass unemployment was to cut wages to make it more attractive for prospective employers to hire. It was the pressure to cut wages in a bid to restore full employment that culminated in the British General Strike of April 1926.

The origins of the classical school can be traced back to the early nineteenth century. The French economist J.B. Say first propounded the proposition that 'supply creates its own demand'. What became known as 'Say's Law' was then invoked by David Ricardo in *On the Principles of Political Economy and Taxation*, published in 1817. He argued that wages would adjust quickly to ensure that unemployment would be no more than a transitory phenomenon. From time to time unemployment would occur, but the correct policy prescription would be to facilitate the adjustment by allowing wages to fall. By the early 1920s, full employment was considered to be the natural order.

On one level, it was hard not to disagree with the classical economists. If there was excess supply of a commodity, it usually meant that the price was too high. To bring demand and supply back into line, prices would ordinarily have to fall. However, as Keynes rightly pointed out, workers cannot be compared to any other commodity. Reducing the take-home pay of employees will have significant second-round effects on the economy that cannot be ignored.[21] In short, what made sense for an individual company might not work in aggregate. A cut in nominal wages would lead to a commensurate decline in nominal aggregate demand. In real terms, there would be no gain.

Once the different marginal propensities to consume between workers and shareholders were taken into account, it is quite likely that lower nominal wages might even lead to a fall in real take-home pay. Furthermore, by pushing prices down, Keynes warned there was a risk that individuals with high debt burdens could be pushed to the point of insolvency.[22] In other words, cutting nominal wages in a liquidity trap would increase the risks of a deflationary spiral. Attempts to reduce nominal wages could lead to lower economic activity and even higher real unit labour costs.[23]

There may be times when workers price themselves out of a job. In some respects, the pendulum may have swung too far following the heyday of the classical economists in the 1920s and early 1930s. Wages became increasingly inflexible in many Western countries during the 1960s and 1970s. The share of national income accruing to workers rose steadily. By contrast, the proportion of national income accruing to companies fell.[24] As a result, investment spending as a percentage of GDP declined, reducing the potential growth path for the economy.[25] But consumer demand was still rising quickly, fuelled by the strong gains in take-home pay. The end result was higher inflation and eventually a rise in unemployment, as governments were forced to slam on the brakes.

However, Keynes' argument was specific to a time of deflation. He correctly reasoned that putting the burden of adjustment onto workers would only exacerbate the liquidity trap. The authorities had no way of offsetting the deflationary effects of cutting wages. Any attempt to reduce wages to try to clear the labour market would push the economy deeper into recession.[26] Unemployment would rise, not fall. The disastrous experience of classical or supply-side economics during the early 1930s should have been a warning that a similar prescription would not work for Japan in the 1990s.

Unfortunately, many of the lessons from this period went unheeded. Instead, reformists were emboldened by the success of their policies in revitalising some Western economies during the 1990s. They reasoned that if it had worked for these countries, it was the right way forward for Japan.

Supply-siders overlooked a crucial point. The US, for example, was able to adjust real interest rates to offset any deflationary fallout from corporate restructuring. A judicious use of supply-side policies may raise the potential growth path of an economy. But to realise this potential, interest rates have to be adjusted accordingly.

When US companies started taking radical action to boost productivity during the early 1990s, the Federal Reserve was able to offset the impact on confidence. US companies were embarking on concerted drives to boost their profit margins, and many shed large numbers of workers. Downsizing became a popular euphemism to describe management efforts to make companies more efficient. At the time, many worried over the potential impact such heavy job losses would have on sentiment and the wider economy.

The Federal Reserve correctly asserted that if productivity was improving quickly, there was no need for interest rates to rise. In addition to the aggressive rate cuts witnessed during the recession of 1990–91, the Fed reduced interest rates a further three times during the tentative upswing of 1992 to ensure real interest rates remained low (see Figure 8.6).[27] The recovery took hold and many of the workers made redundant in old industries found jobs in new and expanding areas of the economy. Supply-side policies 'worked' because the Federal Reserve was able to accommodate the inevitable stresses and strains that reform creates.

A Social Contract

The contrast with Japan should be evident. Once inflation had turned negative in the mid 1990s, the Bank of Japan lost the chance to secure low real borrowing costs.[28] Thereafter, any attempt to impose a similar prescription on Japan was never going to work. Supply-side economists trumpeted the case for reform, but Japan was in no position to accommodate the deflationary impact of corporate restructuring.

Given the implicit social contract that had built up between employers and workers under the job-for-life system, this was even more pertinent. Japan had prided itself on full employment. Even now it still does not possess the social security net to accommodate

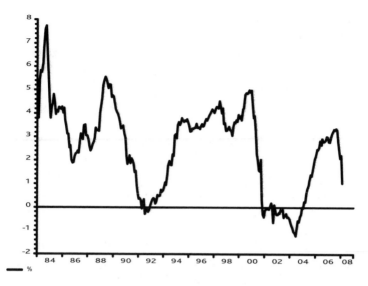

%

Figure 8.6   US Fed Funds Target Adjusted by Core Consumption Deflator

Sources: Federal Reserve and Bureau of Economic Analysis.

large-scale unemployment. The impact of job losses on confidence would be more debilitating than in other Western countries.

Japanese people had also been brought up to believe their company would take care of them through to retirement. The company was the social security net, not the government. Redundancies would prove even more demoralising for this reason. But many hardliners saw the guarantee of a job for life as one of the key weaknesses of the Japanese economic model. It was, and still is, one of the major differences between the Japanese way of doing business and the Anglo-Saxon approach. In Japan, workers' interests have traditionally been placed ahead of shareholders'. Japanese management reasoned that company loyalty to the workforce would be rewarded in the long run. It was actually in the interests of companies to promise job security, as they would benefit more in return from a committed workforce. It was not just cultural values that drove Japanese companies to avoid redundancies at all costs. It was good business sense too.

Mr Hayami's Mistake

One of the most ardent reformists was the Bank of Japan governor, Masaru Hayami. On his appointment in the spring of 1998, Mr Hayami declared that the economy would never recover unless the country was prepared to accept the pain that went with corporate restructuring.

Mr Hayami believed there was a danger companies would defer the necessary changes that would secure an improvement in corporate profitability. Without that, the stock market would never recover. The central bank governor led a concerted campaign to convince sceptics of the case for a rise in interest rates. Higher borrowing costs would force companies to take more drastic action to cut labour costs. Short term interest rates were eventually pushed up in August 2000. The policy soon backfired. In little more than a year, the Nikkei 225 had broken below 10,000. The decline in property prices accelerated as the economy again slipped into recession.[29]

The premise for the rate hike was flawed, but was typical of the misunderstanding that lay at the heart of the supply-side argument. Mr Hayami believed that a recovery in corporate earnings was crucial to a turnaround in the economy.[30] And when profitability started to improve during the course of 1999, he assumed that this would filter through to higher wages, boosting consumption and creating a virtuous cycle of rising economic prosperity.

But Japan's version of trickle-down economics failed. Wages fell sharply during 1999 and remained depressed in 2000 (see Figure 8.7). Profits were rising because wages were being cut. There was no positive knock-on effect, precisely because Japan was embedded in a liquidity trap.

Money Supply in a Debt Trap

One of the most vocal arguments for resolving the debt crisis was put forward by monetarists. They argued that it would be easy to reflate the economy. All Japan had to do was increase the money supply and then prices would stop falling. If the Bank of

Figure 8.7   Japan Compensation of Employees

Source: Cabinet Office (Japan).

Japan pumped enough liquidity into the money markets, banks would start lending again. Money supply growth would rebound, bringing an end to deflation.

Writing in the *Wall Street Journal* in late 1997, Milton Friedman declared, 'There is no limit to the extent to which the Bank of Japan can increase the money supply if it so wishes.' And he argued,

> The Bank of Japan can buy government bonds on the open market, paying for them with either currency or deposits at the Bank of Japan. Most of the proceeds will end up in commercial banks, adding to their reserves and enabling them to expand their liabilities by loans and open market operations. But whether they do so or not, the money supply will increase.[31]

The argument was wrong, as subsequent events proved. It is questionable how much a central bank can directly affect money supply growth, even under normal circumstances. In today's deregulated world, credit growth is largely influenced through varying the cost of borrowing. Once Japan had fallen into a liquidity trap, the Bank of Japan lost the power to stimulate money supply growth. It could try and change the stock of money supply outstanding. But without the ability to influence real interest rates, it would be impossible to exert any impact on the demand for money and secure an increase in credit growth. Attempts to inject liquidity into the money markets would fail.

The earliest signs of this difficulty emerged in the spring of 1999. After interest rates were cut to 0 per cent, the Bank of Japan injected liquidity aggressively into the money markets. It promised to provide 'ample funds', but it soon became clear that the banks did not need the money.[32] Time after time, the Bank of Japan would inject liquidity into the financial system, only to see the bulk of the funds end up in the hands of short-term money market brokers, or *Tanshi*. They would simply re-deposit the funds at the central bank. The Bank of Japan had injected more money than was needed, and the excess was parked in accounts held at the central bank.[33]

The problem resurfaced two years later. After interest rates were cut to 0 per cent for a second time, the Bank of Japan tried to stimulate money supply with an explicit policy of quantitative easing. Short term interest rates would no longer be targeted now that they were down to zero. Instead, the Bank of Japan (BoJ) would focus on the level of reserves held by the banks. Specifically, it would target the level of current account balances the banks held at the BoJ. This target was initially set at ¥5 trillion, but by the end of October 2002 it had been raised to ¥15–20 trillion. In March 2003 it was hiked again to ¥17–22 trillion, before being pushed up to a peak of ¥30–35 trillion in January 2004.[34]

The rationale behind the policy was straightforward. Banks earned no interest on their current account balances. By forcing them to hold large amounts of reserves, banks would have every incentive to lend the money. They would be compelled to accelerate their lending, triggering a recovery in money supply.

On 2 May 2001, the Bank of Japan attempted to inject liquidity into the money markets, but the banks were unwilling to sell the required volume of securities to the central bank. The Bank of Japan tried to pump ¥1.6 trillion into the money markets in two ¥800 billion purchasing operations. It only received offers for ¥702.9 billion in discount bills and ¥716.6 billion in short term government bills. It was another striking illustration of the impotence of monetary policy in a liquidity trap.

Over the next two weeks, the Bank of Japan's liquidity operations repeatedly drew insufficient demand. It responded by increasing the range of securities that were eligible for repurchase. That made little difference. It allowed the central bank to hit its new reserves target, but it failed to trigger a recovery in credit growth.

None of this should have come as a surprise. The banks had seen one company after another run into trouble. There was not much incentive to lend while companies were defaulting in such heavy numbers. There was not much loan demand either. Money supply growth was being squeezed by deflation. Monetarists had the direction of causation back to front. Money supply would only accelerate once prices had stabilised in the first place. The authorities had to forcefully intervene and frustrate deflation before conventional policy remedies would have any effect.

Let the Printing Presses Roll

The monetarists were not easily dissuaded. The Bank of Japan came under intense pressure to 'print money' or monetise the government's budget deficit. A central bank can print money if it agrees to underwrite government spending. Under normal circumstances, government borrowing is covered by the issuance of bonds to the general public. But if the Bank of Japan simply provided the money to fund a budget deficit, it would effectively be creating money out of 'thin air'. It could buy the bonds directly from the government. If the private sector could not be persuaded to accept the liquidity through the course of normal money market operations, then the authorities should generate money supply itself.

Again, the policy advice was flawed. The economy was in a liquidity trap, and any attempt to fund the government's borrowing directly from the printing press would not change the money supply. There might be more deposits created by the Bank of Japan in circulation. But there would be fewer bonds in circulation too. The two would offset each other. It was just a simple switch between two different liabilities. Instead of the public lending money to the government, it would be the Bank of Japan.

The decision to print money could leave more money in the hands of financial institutions. The banks were big buyers of government bonds during the depths of the crisis (see Figure 8.8).[35] They would have fewer bonds to buy if government borrowing was being funded via the printing press. Theoretically, the deposits that were being used to buy government bonds could have backed fresh loans. In essence, printing money could remove the pressure of the private sector to fund the government's enormous budget deficit.

The banks were not reluctant to lend, however, because of a shortage of funds. The banks were awash with deposits. In November 2000, Japan's banking system passed an unwelcome

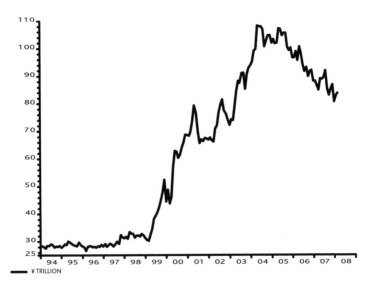

Figure 8.8   Japan Banks Assets, JGBs

Source: Bank of Japan.

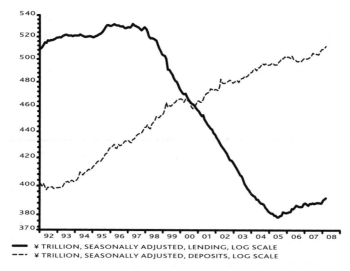

Figure 8.9   Japan Bank Lending and Deposits

Source: Bank of Japan.

milestone, when the level of deposits rose above the level of loans for the first time in the post-war era (see Figure 8.9).[36]

It was a fear of deflation that caused banks to hold back. They had been heavy buyers of bonds precisely because they did not want to lend. There was little loan demand either. The monetarists' argument ignored the pivotal role of bond purchases in pushing interest rates down. Monetisation does not work simply by injecting extra funds into financial markets. It works by influencing interest rate expectations. And since these were already close to rock bottom, there was not much room for conventional policy to reflate the economy.

The monetarists were undeterred. Some argued that monetisation would work through the demand effects of increased government spending. Even if the monetary effect could not be relied upon, then there was still the positive impact of running an even bigger budget deficit. Central bank purchases of bonds would hold long-term interest rates down while government spending rose. In short, it could help obviate the crowding out effects that had caused demand management policies to fail for much of the 1990s.

In many respects, this was right. And had this policy been followed from the outset, Japan would have stood a better chance of avoiding a liquidity trap. However, this prescription was simply an extension of Keynesian demand management policies. The argument for monetisation was reduced to nothing more than a plea for more fiscal stimulus, albeit reinforced by quantitative easing to prevent crowding out.

The Bank of Japan was determined not to cave in to demands to underwrite government spending. Previous experiences of printing money had been disastrous. The government's budget deficit had been monetised immediately after the end of the Second World War, prompting a collapse of the yen and an outbreak of hyper-inflation. The Bank of Japan was keen to avoid a repeat. A new constitution enacted in 1947 had made it illegal for Japan's central bank to print money.[37]

The Bank of Japan also feared monetisation could send bondholders running for cover. Any announcement that the government would finance its borrowing by printing money, they argued, would drive up yields.[38] The government has already acquired a huge debt burden trying to spend its way out of trouble. Investors might conclude that a concession from the Bank of Japan to print money would open the floodgates to more profligate spending and a bigger debt burden. Bondholders might demand an insurance premium against these risks, and that would mean higher borrowing costs, precipitating more deflation. Since the whole problem of debt deflation had been caused by an inability to reduce borrowing costs, the decision to print money could easily backfire.

Monetarists rightly argued that if the Bank of Japan was printing money, then there was little reason why investors should worry about the size of the public sector debt burden. If the government simply sold the bonds to the central bank, another public sector financial institution, then there would be no risk of default.

In the end, the Bank of Japan acceded to the pressure and did start to buy bonds more aggressively. It did not buy them directly from the government, but on the secondary market.[39] The central bank was not directly monetising the government's huge borrowing, although some economists argued it was the same as printing money.[40] It was a way of circumventing the constitutional ban on monetisation.

The Bank of Japan's holdings of Japanese government bonds soared and by the end of 2005, the central bank's balance sheet had swollen to 30.9 per cent of GDP (see Figure 8.10).[41] The policy had some limited success. By keeping bond yields low, it did facilitate some improvement in bank lending, which stopped contracting in the summer of 2005. The stock market did recover some lost ground, and the rate of decline in property prices slowed. In some cities, land prices rose swiftly, again, notably Tokyo.

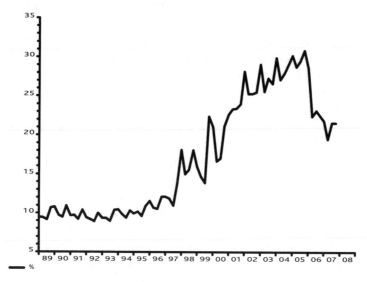

Figure 8.10   Japan, BoJ Assets/GDP

Sources: Bank of Japan and Cabinet Office (Japan).

But money supply remained dormant and economic growth was largely driven by a strong world economy, which boosted exports. By the spring of 2008, Japan was in serious trouble again. Consumer confidence had tumbled, wages were falling and the stock market was sliding. The yen was soaring too, threatening more deflation. Quantitative easing was the right policy, but the

Bank of Japan had dithered for too long, waiting eleven long years before sanctioning a move that might have prevented Japan from slipping into a liquidity trap.

Drive the Yen Down

These problems did not stop a number of prominent economists suggesting that the liquidity trap could be eliminated by encouraging the yen to fall. The argument was predicated on the belief that Japan is a 'structural net savings surplus economy'.[42] Because the population is ageing rapidly, it has a tendency to save more than can be invested profitably at home. Demographics naturally led Japan to run a structural savings surplus.

As the economy was already suffering from overinvestment, it would have been unwise to try to match the high rate of savings by raising the level of capital spending. That would have exacerbated the twin problems of deflation and low rates of return. Japan could, therefore, only secure the requisite level of savings by running large trade surpluses. As a result, the excess savings had to be exported. The poor profitability of much of Japan's investment at home also implied it would be better for savers to put their money overseas.

According to this school of thought, the trade surplus ought to have been allowed to get even bigger. The Bank of Japan should have intervened to force the yen down when the bubble burst during the early 1990s. And it was argued that some form of monetisation would have helped to secure a lower yen. But with trade tensions rising, devaluation was not an option. Japan was warned by the US and Europeans not to export its way out of trouble. The yen thus rose during the first five years of the downturn, adding to the deflation pressures within the economy.

There can be little doubt that the strong yen complicated the central bank's task of preventing the slide into deflation. By the end of the 1990s, the Bank of Japan came under intense pressure to support the government's attempts to drive the yen down. It was initially urged to refrain from sterilising any intervention on the foreign exchange markets. The devaluation camp believed that unsterilised intervention would prove more effective in driving the yen down.

The clamour for unsterilised intervention was essentially a call for some form of monetisation. It had always been customary practice for the Bank of Japan to neutralise any intervention it carried out on behalf of the Ministry of Finance. When the government sold yen for dollars, the implicit increase in the provision of yen would be offset by money market operations to absorb the extra domestic currency in circulation.

The calls went unheeded, much to the government's dismay. The central bank correctly argued that switching to unsterilised intervention could not secure a weaker yen. The case was made powerfully by policy board member, Kazuo Ueda.[43] The government believed that creating an excess supply of yen would automatically cause it to depreciate.

This view fell into the same trap as the reflation case put forward by orthodox monetarists. There was already an excess supply of yen since the economy was in a liquidity trap. A decade of asset deflation had also made banks and other financial institutions risk averse, and reluctant to take the risk of investing overseas.

For this reason, unsterilised intervention could never succeed where sterilised intervention had failed. In short, monetisation could not drive the yen down. Attempts to create an excess supply of yen could only work if there was room for interest rates to fall, encouraging investors to move their money abroad. Since interest rates had hit rock bottom, there was no transmission mechanism between monetary policy and a weaker yen.

Indeed, it was notable that economists calling for yen devaluation would routinely omit any explanation of the precise dynamics that would trigger a weaker currency. Invariably, there would be an unwritten assumption that printing money or unsterilised intervention would magically cause 'capital flight'.

There was one further flaw. A currency devaluation essentially constitutes a one-off terms of trade shift. A distinction needs to be made between a rise in anticipated inflation pressures and a one-off price movement caused by an external 'shock'. The real cost of borrowing is nominal interest rates minus anticipated or expected inflation, not actual inflation. A fall in the yen would not necessarily lead to a rise in anticipated inflation.[44] Some countries have successfully used currency devaluations as a cure for debt difficulties. For this to work, people have to believe that the currency devaluation is likely to be continuous and sustained. And that will only happen if a country is running a current account deficit.

Even in these cases, there is a self-limiting break on how far currency devaluations can be used to support a policy of reflation. A weaker currency will eventually reduce the current account deficit and, in turn, that will put a cap on how far the exchange rate can depreciate. Monetarists argued that people could be convinced that devaluation would lead to higher inflation if an 'expansionary' monetary policy was simultaneously put in place. But expectations are largely adaptive, and since there is no direct mechanism between printing money and capital flight, it becomes impossible to create the self-fulfilling cycle of a depreciating currency.

Finally, there is no obvious reason why an ageing population should lead to such a persistent trade surplus. An external surplus simply means that a country has generated excess savings over and above any rate of investment in both the private and public sectors combined. It does not mean that it has created enough savings *per se*. Japan does not need to run a trade surplus just to save. Seventeen years after the initial stock market crash, Japan has seen huge amounts of financial wealth evaporate despite running trade surpluses throughout the bear market.

The biggest destroyer of people's savings has been deflation itself. Running bigger trade surpluses would eventually lead to further upward pressure on the yen, and increase the risk of more jobs being lost to low-cost countries such as China. Targeting a higher net surplus of savings will ultimately put more downward pressure on prices, and lead to a *lower* level of aggregate savings. Far from encouraging Japan to run large external surpluses, the correct policy prescription should be focused on how to reduce the marginal propensity to save and in turn shrink the trade surplus. That would lead to a higher level of aggregate savings and higher levels of wealth for an ageing population to draw down in retirement.

The excess savings fallacy is reminiscent of the mistake made by the classical economists in the late 1920s and early 1930s. The 'structural surplus' school of thought effectively implies that savings and investment are exogenous variables. Taking the so-called structural problems of an ageing population into account, it is assumed they will automatically create a high level of excess savings. But as Keynes pointed out, 'savings and investment are the determinates of the system, not the determinants. They are the twin results of the system's determinants, namely, the propensity to consume, the schedule of the marginal efficiency of capital and the rate of interest.'[45]

Inflation Targeting

Other economists stressed the need for Japan to consider inflation targets as a remedy for the debt crisis. This school of thought rightly recognised that Japan was suffering from insufficient demand, which could not be resolved by cutting interest rates any further. It also accepted that the government had reached the end of the road too, as its finances were stretched to breaking point after years of heavy spending. Deflation was the problem, and it was being exacerbated by the expectation that prices would keep on falling. Why buy today when the prospect of a fall in prices meant that it would be cheaper to wait? It paid to defer spending.

The only way to eradicate deflation would be to convince the Japanese public that prices would start to rise. By setting an inflation target, it was argued, the public will start to believe that inflation rather than deflation would prevail tomorrow. People would not be tempted to wait and would start buying now. Once a country was in a liquidity trap, monetary policy could only operate through its effect on expectations. By raising inflation expectations, the Bank of Japan would effectively be reducing real interest rates in a manner that could not be achieved through other policy avenues. This theory won backing from a number of respected economists.[46] On paper, inflation targeting made sense. But in practice it was never likely to succeed, as subsequent events proved.

The pressure on the Bank of Japan to adopt inflation targets started to mount in 1999, when the Ministry of Finance publicly suggested that the central bank should adopt an inflation target of '1 to 3 per cent, to be achieved in six years'.[47] By the spring of 2001, the Bank of Japan had relented in part and set a target. It would aim for price stability.[48] The goal was not as aggressive as some would have liked. Nevertheless, it marked a decisive step in the direction demanded by advocates of inflation targeting. But seven years have elapsed since the target was unveiled, and Japan continues to suffer from deflation. By the end of 2007, the consumption deflator was still in negative territory, falling on an annual basis, despite the sharp run-up in oil prices (see Figure 8.11).[49]

There are a number of reasons why the inflation target has not succeeded. It had to be supported by specific policy measures that the public would understand, otherwise it would lack credibility. Inflation targeting was usually linked with a call for some form

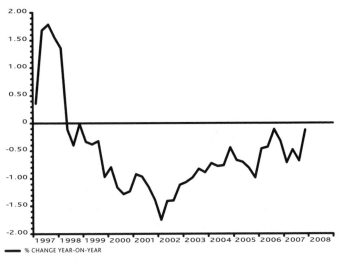

Figure 8.11   Japan Consumption Deflator

Source: Cabinet Office (Japan).

of monetisation.[50] One of the most vocal advocates of inflation targeting suggested in the spring of 1999 that the government should produce 'attention grabbing increases in the monetary base' to 'convince the private sector that inflation rather than deflation will prevail tomorrow'.[51]

The Bank of Japan had already been easing aggressively even before it adopted an inflation target. By the spring of 2001, the central bank's balance sheet had already swollen to a massive 22.7 per cent of GDP.[52] Quantitative easing did mark a further intensification of the central bank's attempts to stimulate a recovery in money supply. But the failure of previous attempts to inject liquidity into the money markets meant there was little reason to believe the latest policy would work.

The obvious riposte was that the efficacy of monetary policy was being undermined by the 'fatalism' of the Japanese authorities. Mr Hayami was less than convinced that quantitative easing would succeed. Other Bank of Japan policy board members, notably Kazuo Ueda, had written extensively about the limitations of monetary policy.[53] Advocates of inflation targets argued that the policy would only work if the central bank itself believed in it.[54] The public could hardly be hoodwinked into expecting prices to rise if the authorities were not convinced themselves. The public scepticism displayed by the central bankers undermined the policy from the outset.

This criticism missed the point. The Bank of Japan and the government had declared time and time again that Japan was poised for economic recovery. Policymakers' credibility was at a low ebb. The country's slide into such a protracted slump had destroyed many people's faith in the ability of the authorities to reflate the economy. Once it became apparent that headline-grabbing increases in the monetary base also made little difference, the credibility of the authorities would have been damaged even further.[55]

A Philosophical Footnote

It is perhaps worth stressing how many of the points raised in this chapter go to the heart of the age-old battle between Keynesian economists and monetarists. Keynesian economics has been widely criticised following the inability of successive Japanese governments to resuscitate the economy through the use of fiscal policy. This has been deemed a failure of demand management policies and led many to search for alternatives. But the supply-side or monetarist solutions made matters worse. Keynes' analysis was far more relevant to the problems facing Japan.

Firstly, it was Keynes who warned of the irrationality that was characteristic of an extended overinvestment cycle.[56] Classical economists were inclined to play down the risks. Their philosophy that markets tended towards equilibrium, and usually at full employment, disregarded the possibility that an overinvestment cycle could cause an extended slump. Indeed, one of Keynes' criticisms of the classical school of economics was the almost laissez-faire attitude towards the risks of a capital spending boom.[57] For this reason alone, it is hard to see how the monetarists' case – which is largely an extension of the classical analysis of the 1930s – can offer the right policy prescription for an economy facing the threat of a debt trap.

Secondly, it was Keynes who rightly warned that monetary policy might become ineffective during the downturn following an overinvestment cycle. It was not just the risk that interest rates would fail to fall quickly enough. He also emphasised the possibility that demand for 'loanable funds' would collapse because of the slide in the 'marginal efficiency of capital', making it also hard to use monetary policy to stabilise the economy. Even when interest rates were finally brought down to their limits, there was a chance that loan demand would remain so weak that a recovery would be impossible without government intervention.

Thirdly, Keynes correctly asserted that attempts to cut costs and squeeze workers would backfire. He passionately warned of the need to maintain nominal wages to support aggregate demand.[58] By putting so much pressure on companies to dispose of bad debts and boost profitability, the Japanese government inadvertently sent wages spiralling down, fuelling deflation and boosting real borrowing costs.

In short, it is hard to call Japan's experience a failure of demand management policies when many of the policies the government was pursuing were in direct contravention of Keynesian philosophy. The fact that fiscal policy aggravated the slide into a liquidity trap was not an indictment of Keynesian economics. Indeed, once monetary policy had become inoperable, Keynes argued that government efforts needed to be focused on boosting confidence, so that people would save less. By aggravating the glut of property sales, the government's policy had the opposite effect.

Lastly, it is worth pondering the many overlaps between Fisher's analysis of a debt trap outlined in Chapter 7, and the Keynesian view expounded in this chapter. Given Fisher's strong monetarist inclinations, it seems somewhat incongruous to have used his analysis of a debt trap alongside a Keynesian interpretation of events in Japan. But there are significant parallels between the two seemingly diametrically opposed philosophies. The phrases 'debt deflation' and 'liquidity trap' have been used interchangeably. There are many similarities between Fisher's debt trap and the Keynesian liquidity trap. They are both caused by a failure of real borrowing costs to fall quickly. They both reflect the problem of money illusion when prices tumble. And both economists were at pains to explain how an economy could fall into a trap after a period of rapid debt accumulation.

9
WHERE ARE WE HEADING?

As this book goes to print, time is running out for the Federal Reserve and the US administration. US officials have been frantically pulling the levers, trying to avert a meltdown of the financial system.

The collapse of Bear Stearns in March 2008, the fifth largest US investment bank, sent shockwaves across Wall Street. The Federal Reserve's response, a forced sale to JP Morgan, yet another rate cut down to 2.25 per cent and more liquidity injections, provided some respite. But the housing market has continued to head down. House prices are on track to fall 25 per cent across all major cities in 2008.[1] In the UK, house prices are starting to slide too. Property prices now look poised to fall further and faster than the dark days of negative equity in the early 1990s, following the Lawson Boom.[2]

Deflating an asset bubble of such extremes was never going to be easy. Central banking has become a high-wire act. Cut rates too soon, then there is a risk the euphoria will return, and markets will soar. Leave it too late, they will slide uncontrollably, it would seem, into the very debt trap that has snared Japan for so long. The Federal Reserve left it too late. And the Bank of England has been dithering too.

Rate cuts are not working because property prices are sliding too fast. Tumbling house prices are causing losses to accumulate among banks. In just over a year, they had been forced to write off an estimated $181 billion.[3] Banks in turn are failing to cut mortgage rates, as they seek to rebuild their balance sheets. The lenders have gone into their bunkers. The transmission mechanism between rate cuts and the housing market has been blunted by the sheer scale of the losses inflicted by the collapse in the housing market.

The Federal Reserve is making many of the mistakes committed by the Bank of Japan. Both central banks delayed cutting until property deflation had become endemic. When they did start bringing rates down, they were too timid in the critical early months. And once it was clear that lower lending rates *per se* were not going to do the trick, they resorted to liquidity injections to shore up the banks.

Liquidity injections alone will not work. The US is heading for a Keynesian liquidity trap. As we saw in Japan during the 1990s, liquidity traps imply central banks can inject infinite funds into the banking system, but once the credit mechanism is broken, that will not be enough. For sure, a seizure of the money markets, with banks frightened to lend to each other, has aggravated the financial crisis facing the West in 2008. In that respect, liquidity injections can help at the margin.

But it is not the core of the problem. That is falling house prices. And the housing market can only be stabilised by driving down borrowing costs. If the authorities fail on this score, millions more properties will foreclose. The homeless crisis will intensify and tent cities will proliferate. More banks will fail. Economic depression may then follow recession. Governments will then be forced to intervene, to 'frustrate' deflation, by taking foreclosed properties off the market through public sector bodies, renting them out to the homeless. The government will have to become a major landlord.

Quantitative Easing Now

There is only one monetary policy option that is likely to work at this late stage. That is quantitative easing. And if they do use that soon, there is a risk that will not work either. The Bank of Japan dithered, delaying the introduction of quantitative easing until 2001, eleven years after Japan's bubble burst. Quantitative easing, or central bank buying of government bonds to drive yields down, would push mortgage rates lower – if done soon enough.

Comparisons with the Savings and Loan Crisis

It is instructive to look back at the Savings and Loan crisis of the early 1990s to see how monetary policy eventually put a floor under the housing market. The Federal Reserve started easing in the summer of 1989. Mortgage rates fell sharply. The 30-year fixed rate dropped by 4 per cent between 1990 and 1993.[4] The one-year variable rate dropped by 5 per cent. House prices fell for a short while, before stabilising in 1994.

By contrast, the 30-year fixed rate had dropped just over 1 per cent from its high by late March 2008. Disconcertingly, the one-year variable rate had carried on *rising*, hitting a new high of just over 7 per cent. The Federal Reserve was belatedly slashing interest rates, but some mortgage rates were going up, not down.

Further rate cuts seem more than probable. But if they do not work, the Federal Reserve will be obliged to try and drive bond yields lower. Fixed rate mortgages are priced off bond yields, and if they can be forced lower, then borrowing costs for homeowners may ease. That might eventually help to stabilise the housing market.

But to get mortgage rates down by the same margin as seen in the early 1990s would require the Federal Reserve to push bond yields down a long way. That may need to fall to levels seen in Japan, when yields dropped to 1.0 per cent and lower. With headline inflation at 4.0 per cent, bond investors are not going to accept negative yields on that scale lightly. There is a clear market failure that requires aggressive intervention by the authorities.

Quantitative easing, however, has only a limited shelf life. If house prices are allowed to fall too fast, lower mortgage rates might not even do the trick. Potential homebuyers may choose to stay on the sidelines. Furthermore, with interest rates so much lower than they were in the early 1990s, there is a practical limit to how far they can fall.

And as the losses among banks continue to mount, it might be even more difficult to get mortgage rates down, even with quantitative easing. If we reach that point, the game is up for monetary policy. The Federal Reserve will be redundant. It will be the US Treasury that will be forced to act, rescuing more banks by injecting public sector capital and, ultimately, taking many into public ownership and instigating large-scale nationalisation.

The current US administration may find that difficult to swallow ideologically. But it will have little choice. Unless it intervenes, the collapse of more and more banks will drive the US economy deeper into recession. So far, 243 mortgage lenders have gone out of business.[5] Their destruction has been a critical source of stress, precipitating a contraction of credit, which has accelerated the collapse of the housing market.

And while house prices are sliding, the economy has only just gone into recession. The rise in unemployment has been modest to date. If it starts to climb quickly, delinquencies will rise further and foreclosures will jump again. A vicious circle beckons.

Regulatory Backlash Not the Complete Answer

The backlash has already begun. Talk of heightened regulation to rein in banks is understandably rife. In the UK, the Financial Services Authority has admitted to 'blunders' in its supervision of Northern Rock. And there is no question that the regulators failed in their job. The party got out of hand, and on both sides of the Atlantic there were too few dissenting voices during the heady boom.

More regulation is inevitable. But if we pin the blame for the housing bubbles on the regulators, central banks or even 'greedy' bankers, we will fail to redress the real causes. They were almost certainly all culpable. But they were mere actors. Regulation was lax because it suited the politicians of the day, who wanted the economic growth that came from allowing borrowing to spin out of control. Interest rates were kept too low because financial stability was never considered important. Governments needed housing bubbles, as they were wedded to a free trade model that was inviting wage destruction for the masses amidst an unsustainable drive to cut labour costs. They were happy for jobs to be shipped to cheaper countries, and failed to see that the rising debt levels at home were the inevitable counterpart. For more than a decade, governments presided over an economic strategy that now lies in tatters.

The political discourse over what went wrong has barely begun because few are willing to acknowledge the real cause of the housing crisis. A thriving blame industry has emerged, with much hand-wringing by the politicians. Presidential hopeful Hillary Clinton blames the Republican-led Administration. Alan Greenspan and Ben Bernanke, both with strong Republican leanings, are also cited. But it was the Democrats that signed up to many of the trade deals that stripped the US of so many manufacturing jobs, and paved the way for boom and bust. Hillary now rails against policies championed and implemented by husband and former president Bill.

And in the UK, the Conservatives attack New Labour for economic *incompetence*. The emphasis should be noted. There was nothing wrong with the free trade model *per se*, or the underlying economic policy, they imply. It was just a lack of competence at the Financial Services Authority and within the Treasury, that saw it all unravel.

In truth, the Conservatives supported the free trade policies that underpinned New Labour's economic mirage. Some of their critiques over the split in the Bank of England's responsibilities, which undermined its ability to monitor the financial system, are accurate.

But Northern Rock was not just a regulatory failure. It was allowed to grow so rapidly with few checks and balances because of the prevailing political climate. And while it may have been the most highly leveraged bank in Europe, it was hardly alone. Six months after it collapsed requiring government support, more and more UK banks are running into trouble. There is systemic failure, one born of a failed economic policy that gave too much power to corporates to roam the globe, and too little protection to workers.

A regulatory backlash provides a convenient smokescreen for more fundamental reform to economic policy. A more equitable balance of power between capital and labour will have to emerge, otherwise protectionist pressures will intensify. Securing that, will be no small task. This book does not pretend to have all the answers to that vexing issue. Its primary aim is to diagnose the problem and suggest some immediate remedies that might at least mitigate the fallout.

There are, however, a number of important points to be noted. The concentration of corporate power through mergers, acquisitions and leveraged takeovers has to be reversed. The ability of large multinationals to control and drive labour costs down, by moving jobs around from one country to another, lies at the heart of the debt problems facing the West. Until we recognise that point, the West will not be able to shake its destructive dependence on housing bubbles. We will continue to lurch from boom to bust, with debt traps and debt deflation threatening prolonged economic stagnation.

There are two ways to even out the playing field: reduce corporate power, or increase the strength of labour. Many argue for the latter, and among emerging market economies in particular, the case for greater labour regulation is overwhelming. The commercial logic for outsourcing would be far less appealing for transnational companies if Chinese workers had the same rights as their Western counterparts. Free trade deals were signed by Western politicians on both sides of the political spectrum without anywhere near enough attention to worker rights in developing countries.

But persuading the Chinese authorities to introduce full union rights for its 300 million or so workers may prove nigh on impossible. A quicker alternative may be to reduce the ability of companies to expand profit margins by cutting labour costs. Big companies can hold on to their profits for longer. Smaller companies create more competition, allowing the 'benefits of free trade' to be disseminated more quickly to workers and real wages to rise. That would make consumers less reliant upon debt.

Whatever the remedies, the immediate task is to prevent debt deflation taking root. Central banks and governments have presided over the biggest credit bubble in modern history. We have to hope they are up to the task.

NOTES

Preface

1. See 'Closure put back at Burberry site', *BBC News*, 8 November 2006.
2. See 'Squaring up to Burberry', *Observer*, 25 March 2007.
3. See 'Burberry workers to fight closure', *BBC News*, 7 September 2006.
4. See 'Factory closure saves Burberry only 1% of profit', *Guardian*, 18 April 2007.
5. See 'Burberry warns on profit', *Wall Street Journal*, 16 January 2008.
6. In the US, the Wilshire 5000, peaked at 14,751.6 on 24 March 2000, and by the end of February 2008, it had closed at 13,456. In the UK, the FTSE 100 peaked at 6,930.2 on 30 December 1999. It closed at 5,884.3 at the end of February 2008. In Japan, the Nikkei 225 peaked at 20,833.2 on 12 April 2000. By the end of February 2008, it had fallen to 13,603.0. And in Germany, the DAX 30 peaked at 8,065.0 on 7 March 2000. By the end of February 2008, it had fallen to 6,748.1.

1 Introduction

1. Auction houses have routinely been selling foreclosed properties with discounts of 50 per cent and more since the summer of 2007. And by February 2008, homebuilders were being forced to give huge discounts to remove properties from their books. In February 2008, D.R. Horton announced price cuts of 'up to 50 per cent' in an attempt to clear a backlog of 399 unsold homes in Southern California.
2. See 'Don't forget the Northern Rock of 1878', *The Times* (of London), 22 September 2007. The City of Glasgow Bank collapsed on 2 October 1878. Its liabilities of £12 million exceeded the bank's assets of £7 million.
3. See 16 March 2005 Budget speech, when the Chancellor, Gordon Brown, began by asserting that 'Britain today is experiencing the longest period of sustained economic growth since records began in the year 1701.'

4. See 'Japanese wages fall as cost of raw material hits companies', *Financial Times*, 1 February 2008.
5. Source: Organisation for Economic Cooperation and Development (OECD). The index of unit labour costs across the whole economy in Japan fell from 104.3 in 1998 to 89.2 in 2006, a drop of 14.5 per cent. Unit labour costs declined in every year, and are now at their lowest level since 1983. The index for manufacturing unit labour costs slipped from 109.8 to 89.1 over the corresponding period, a decline of 18.8 per cent.
6. Source: Bureau of Economic Analysis (BEA). The ratio of current profits from production to GDP in the US climbed to 12.0 per cent in Q3 2006, its highest level since Q1 1966.
7. Source: Bureau of Labor Statistics (BLS). The ex-food/energy/shelter inflation rate was 2.0 per cent in the US by January 2008. Source: Office for National Statistics (ONS). The ex-food/energy/alcohol and tobacco inflation rate was 1.3 per cent in the UK by January 2008. Source: Eurostat. The ex-food/energy/alcohol and tobacco inflation rate was 1.7 per cent in Euroland for January 2008.
8. Japan finally bailed out one of its troubled banks with public money in 2003, after it had also started printing money. But had it resisted the mantra to 'let the market work' and nationalised banks many years before, the crisis might never have reached that point. Japan might not still be afflicted with declining property prices across large areas of the country. See Chapter 6 for more.
9. Source: Royal Institution of Chartered Surveyors. The number of surveyors reporting a rise in prices peaked in March 2004, with a net balance of 45.7 per cent of surveyors reporting that prices were rising. The net balance fell sharply from June onwards to hit –35.9 per cent in January 2005, and then carried on falling to a low-point of –45.9 per cent in May 2005. In other words, a net balance of 45.9 per cent of surveyors reported that prices were falling.
10. Source: BLS. Unemployment rose from a low of 5.481 million in April 2000 to 9.266 million in June 2003, an increase of 3.785 million.
11. This was a common view, that pressure from the US on Japan to reflate sewed the seeds for Japan's property and stock market bubble in the late 1980s. In reality, the first seeds of the crisis of over-accumulation were being sewn. Japanese companies were relentlessly pursuing market share overseas, retaining profits in the pursuit of rising investment levels, and reluctant to concede anything other than modest wage increases. As a result, Japan's growth was lopsided, with insufficient consumer demand and overinvestment. That led to the build-up in trade surpluses, and the subsequent cut in interest

rates to 2.5 per cent, and a double-digit expansion of the money supply. Furthermore, that inflation peaked at comparatively low levels and fell so quickly in the subsequent downturn, underlined the lack of wage pressures during the economic boom, and the crisis of over-accumulation by corporates.

12. Source: International Financial Statistics, IMF. World real GDP growth has averaged 5.2 per cent y/y in the three years to 2006. That was the best performance since the 1971–73 period, when GDP rose by an average 5.6 per cent y/y.

13. In a speech to the American Economic Association in San Diego on 4 January 2004, Ben Bernanke, then a governor on the Federal Reserve Board, suggested that 'The high level of markups is an important and perhaps insufficiently recognised feature of the current economic situation. To the extent that firms can maintain these markups, profits will continue to be high, supporting investment and equity values. To the extent that product-market competition erodes these markups, as is likely to occur over time, downward pressure will be exerted on the inflation rate, even if, as is likely, the recent declines in unit labour costs do not persist.'

14. See 'Wheat forecast slashed for the second time', *Financial Times*, 31 October 2007.

15. Source: Bundesbank. Hourly negotiated wage rates, adjusted for the consumer price index, fell on an annual basis in 41 out of 44 months between April 2004 and December 2007.

16. Source: Eurostat. Euroland retail sales fell by an average annual rate of 0.7 per cent in the three months to January 2008, the worst performance since the data series began in 1996.

17. Source: Eurostat. Spain retail sales fell by an average annual rate of 1.3 per cent in the three months to January 2008. The six-month rate showed a contraction of 6.7 per cent on an annualised basis.

18. See 'Wal-Mart, a nation unto itself', *New York Times*, 17 April 2004.

19. See 'China has trouble as a global engine', *Wall Street Journal*, 26 October 2007.

20. See 'China emerges as profit source for big firms', *Wall Street Journal*, 9 October 2007.

21. See 'Why Plutocracy endangers emerging market economies', Martin Wolf, *Financial Times*, 7 November 2007.

2 Global Contagion

1. Chronologically, Japan's financial crisis was the first overinvestment debacle.

2. Charles P. Kindleberger, *The World in Depression*, University of California Press, 1986, pp. 44–5. The volume of instalment credit outstanding rose from $1.375 billion to $3 billion between 1925 and 1929.

3. The most notable decline was in rubber and plastic products, where prices fell by 47.8 per cent between 1926 and 1929. Other commodities experiencing deflation included lumber and wood, metals and metal products and non-metallic mineral products. Source: *Historical Statistics of the United States: Colonial Times to 1970*, Department of Commerce, 1975, p. 199.

4. Kindleberger, *The World in Depression*, pp. 44–5.

5. Source: *Historical Statistics of the United States: Colonial Times to 1970*, p. 199.

6. John Maynard Keynes, *The Economic Consequences of the Peace*, Labour Research Department, 1920, pp. 133–7. Reparations created a capital shortage in Germany and contributed to hyperinflation. Strictly speaking, therefore, they were just a transfer from one country to another, and did not accelerate the pace of overinvestment globally *per se*. But the motivation for the reparations reflected the dominant political ideology of the time.

7. Keynes, *The Economic Consequences of the Peace*, pp. 133–7.

8. For a fuller discussion of the impact of reparations in plunging Germany into economic decline, see Kindleberger, *The World in Depression*, pp. 131–2.

9. Source: Bureau of Labor Statistics (BLS). The ex-food/energy CPI rose to a high of 5.6 per cent in January and February 1991. Excluding shelter, it climbed to a high of 5.6 per cent in February 1991.

10. John Kenneth Galbraith, *The Culture of Contentment*, Houghton Mifflin, 1992.

11. Source: BLS. The US unemployment rate rose to a high of 10.8 per cent in November 1982. A decade later, the peak in unemployment was 7.8 per cent, three percentage points lower.

12. Source: Bank of Thailand. Exports in baht terms rose 19.5 per cent y/y in Q4 1993, 21.5 per cent y/y in Q4 1994 and 19.2 per cent y/y in Q4 1995. However, by Q4 1996, exports were down 2.9 per cent y/y. It is a similar pattern for exports in US$ terms. Exports rose 20.3 per cent y/y in Q4 1994, 18.3 per cent y/y in Q4 1995, and then fell 4.2 per cent y/y in Q4 1996. The deceleration was led by exports of electrical appliances, where the annual rate slowed from 36.4 per cent y/y in Q4 1994, to 19.7 per cent y/y in 1995 and then dropped to –9.2 per cent y/y in Q4 1996 (baht terms). Electrical appliances accounted for 7.7 per cent of exports.

Source: National Statistic Office, South Korea. There was a similar slowdown in South Korea, with exports growth in US$ terms dropping from 36.4 per cent y/y in Q3 1994 to a low of –7.8 per cent in Q3 1996, and then continuing into 1997, with a decline of 5.8 per cent y/y in Q1 of that year. The deceleration in Won terms was less pronounced.

Source: Statistical Office, Malaysia. Exports growth in US$ terms slowed from 34.4 per cent y/y in the final quarter of 1994 to just 0.8 per cent y/y in the second quarter of 1997. Exports growth also decelerated sharply in Taiwan.

13. Yamaichi Securities announced its closure on 24 November 1997, after admitting off-book losses of ¥264.8 billion.

14. Sources: Department of Commerce and Bureau of Economic Analysis (BEA). The real non-residential investment to GDP ratio reached a peak of 13.0 per cent in 1929. As profits collapsed following the stock market crash, capital spending fell sharply. It took more than 70 years for capital spending to reach these heights again, rising to a high of 12.7 per cent of GDP in Q3 2000.

15. There has been considerable debate about the significance of rising investment to GDP ratios in real terms, since in nominal terms the increase was far less pronounced. Sharp falls in the price of capital goods helped to push the investment deflator down in the late 1990s. Indeed, it was falling prices that helped drive the real investment to GDP ratio up. However, this does not change the conclusions drawn about the importance of overinvestment. Falling capital goods prices can allow a smaller share of nominal national income to be taken by capital goods, and thus allow wages to rise as a proportion of real GDP, and prevent collapses of pricing power when the bubble bursts.

16. Other notable examples included WorldCom.

17. Source: BEA. Profits from current production (i.e. profits with inventory valuation adjustments (IVA) and adjustment for depreciation charges (CCADJ)) were $835.2 billion in Q1 1997. They rose to $895.5 billion in Q3 1997, before slipping steadily to $832.6 billion in Q1 2000.

18. Source: BEA. The durables consumption deflator fell 0.2 per cent y/y in September 1995, and the decline accelerated, reaching a peak for the 1990s of –3.1 per cent y/y in March 1998.

19. Source: BEA. The index for durables consumption deflator peaked in April 1995, and the decline from that point through to March 2000 was a cumulative 9.5 per cent.

20. The technology-ladened Nasdaq peaked at 5,048.6 on 10 March 2000. But arguably the one event that seemed to trigger the reappraisal

of investment returns on high-tech stocks was the release of a bearish assessment on Amazon from an analyst at US investment bank, Lehman Brothers. By the time the note was released (23 June 2000), the Nasdaq had already dropped by 22.0 per cent from its peak. But the research note fuelled concerns that the highly vaunted business model that had underpinned the explosive growth in such a wide number of fledgling e-commerce companies was now unravelling. Ironically, Amazon went on to prosper. But numerous e-tailers failed. See 'Amazon shares plunge 19 per cent on Lehman analyst's report', *Wall Street Journal*, 26 June 2006.

21. Source: BLS. Payrolls in the computer and electronic products sector fell from 1.865 million at the end of 2000, to 1.319 million at the end of 2003, a drop of 29.3 per cent.

22. Sources: BEA and BLS. The deflator for consumer durables was falling at a y/y rate of 1.4 per cent when the Nasdaq peaked in March 2000. By October of 2003, the annual rate had dropped to a low of 4.3 per cent. The ex-food/energy inflation rate fell from 2.4 per cent in March 2000 to a low of 1.1 per cent in November 2003.

23. 'Deflation: Making Sure "It" Doesn't Happen Here', Remarks by Governor Ben Bernanke before the National Economists Club, Washington DC, 21 November 2002.

24. Source: BEA. The current account deficit reached a peak of 0.5 per cent of GDP in 1972. That compares with a shortfall of 6.2 per cent of GDP in 2006.

3   Addicted to Debt

1. Source: Office for National Statistics (ONS). Total financial liabilities, households and nonprofit institutions.

2. Sources: ONS and Office for Economic Cooperation and Development (OECD). The personal sector debt to disposable income ratio was 126.5 per cent in Canada, 89.6 per cent in France, 104.8 per cent in Germany and 57.7 per cent in Italy.

3. Source: ONS. Total financial liabilities, households and nonprofit institutions and non-financial corporations, and GDP at market prices.

4. The 'Lawson Boom' was named after Chancellor of the Exchequer Nigel Lawson, who presided over a sharp increase in borrowing and inflation during the late 1980s.

5. Sources: OECD and Council of Mortgage Lenders (CML). Between 1990 and 1995, 345,130 homes were taken into possession.

6. Source: ONS. There is a question with compatibility between the two numbers, but it does not alter the validity of comparison. Up until

1997, the debt numbers were based on 'personal sector'. This data series was discontinued in 1997. From 1987 onwards, the numbers were based on 'households and nonprofits'. The increase in debt under the Conservatives is based on the former. The increase in debt under New Labour is based on the latter.

7. Source: Federal Reserve, Flow of Funds (FoF). Financial liabilities for households and nonprofit institutions.

8. Sources: Bureau of Economic Analysis (BEA) for disposable income, and Federal Reserve for financial liabilities for households and nonprofit institutions.

9. Source: ONS. Between Q2 1987 and Q2 1997, the personal sector debt burden went up from 80.6 per cent to 93.4 per cent.

10. Sources: ONS, BEA and Federal Reserve. From Q1 1997 to Q3 2007, disposable income rose by an annualised rate of 5.4 per cent in the US and 4.8 per cent in the UK. Personal sector debt rose by an annualised 9.4 per cent in the US and 9.9 per cent in the UK.

11. Source: Federal Reserve, FoF. Total private debt in the US went up from 172.1 per cent to 219.5 per cent between Q2 1997 and Q3 2007.

12. Source: Office of Federal Housing Enterprise Oversight. House prices went up 104.5 per cent between Q2 1997 and Q2 2007.

13. Source: Halifax Building Society, Halifax House Price Index.

14. Source: Nationwide Building Society, Nationwide Monthly Average House Price Index.

15. Source: OECD.

16. See 'Current Monetary Policy Issues', speech by Rachel Lomax, 22 November 2007.

17. Source: OECD.

18. Source: OECD.

19. Source: OECD.

20. Source: OECD. Between 1990 and 1999, the ratio of corporate equities held by households to disposable income rose from 52.1 per cent to 190.9 per cent.

21. See 'Mutual Funds and the US Equity Market', Federal Reserve Bulletin, December 2000. By 1998, 49 per cent of US households had either a direct or indirect ownership of US shares.

22. Source: OECD.

23. Source: OECD. The ratio of household corporate equities/disposable income fell from 190.9 per cent in 1999 to 88.8 per cent in 2002.

24. See 'Mutual Funds and the US Equity Market', Federal Reserve Bulletin, December 2000. By 1998, households with incomes over $100,000 accounted for 91 per cent of all direct and indirect shareholdings.

25. See 'Review of Housing Supply', Kate Barker, March 2004.
26. Sources: Department of Commerce and BEA. From January 1993 through to its peak in January 2006, housing starts rose by 89.4 per cent. Household formation climbed by 14.5 per cent from Q1 1993 until December 2007.
27. Source: CML.
28. See 'Homeownership at the crossroads', CML Housing Finance, Issue 02 2007.
29. Source: Department of Commerce.
30. Source: Reuters. Speaking in Vancouver on 24 January 2008.
31. Source: Department of Commerce. By Q4 2007, homeownership was down 1.1 per cent y/y, comfortably the biggest drop since records began in 1966.
32. See 'Losing Ground: Foreclosures in the Subprime Market and Their Cost to Homeowners', Center for Responsible Lending, December 2006.
33. 'Foreclosure Crisis Worsens', Housing Predictor, 26 November 2007. www.housingpredictor.com, 6 March 2008.
34. 'Paulson Dismisses Mortgage Rescue Plan', *Financial Times*, 28 February 2008.
35. Source: Federal Reserve. Home mortgages, households and nonprofits (FoF Liabilities).
36. Source: Federal Reserve. Household debt payments as percentage of disposable income, financial obligation, homeowner.
37. Source: CML.
38. Source: CML.
39. Source: CML. The median income multiple was 3.17 months for all house purchases, and 3.38 for first-time buyers. This compares with 2.13 and 2.31 respectively in 1990.
40. Source: CML. At the top of the lending cycle, in August 2007, 17,500 out of 67,900 mortgages taken out by home movers were 'interest only with repayment vehicle not specified'. For first-time buyers, 7,300 out of 34,800 mortgages were taken out on a similar basis.
41. From May 1997, the target was initially set at 2.5 per cent for RPIX (retail price index, all items excluding mortgage interest) inflation. In December 2003, set a new target, 2 per cent, based on the CPI (Consumer Price Index).
42. Without the rise in borrowing, there would also have been a significant shortfall in GDP growth and unemployment would have been much higher. In the UK, real GDP would have been 4.6 per cent lower, and unemployment would have been 474,000 higher after ten years of slower borrowing. In the US, real GDP would have been

3.7 per cent lower, while unemployment would have risen 632,000 over and above that seen.

43. Source: ONS.

44. Source: ONS. RPIX fell below the target of 2.5 per cent in April 1999 and carried on falling, reaching 1.5 per cent in April 2002.

45. See for example 'Practical issues in UK Monetary Policy, 2000–2005', 20 September, 2005, by Stephen Nickell. 'Household Debt, House Prices and Consumption Growth', 14 September 2004, by Stephen Nickell. 'How important is housing market activity for durables spending?', Bank of England Quarterly Bulletin, Summer 2005, and 'House prices and consumer spending', Bank of England Quarterly Bulletin, Summer 2006.

46. There were three fiscal initiatives: the Economic Growth and Tax Reconciliation Act of 2001, the Job Creation and Workers Assistance Act of 2002, and the Jobs and Growth Tax Relief Reconciliation Act of 2003.

4   'Free Trade' and Asset Bubbles

1. See 'The roots of the mortgage crisis', *Wall Street Journal*, 12 December 2007.

2. Source: Bureau of Labor Statistics (BLS). The median usual weekly earnings of full-time wage and salary workers in constant (2006) dollars fell from $678 in 2001 to $671 in 2006.

3. Source: Office for National Statistics (ONS). In 2007, average earnings rose by 3.9 per cent y/y. Adjusted for the retail price index, average earnings fell 0.4 per cent y/y. At the peak of the dotcom cycle (January–March 2000) average earnings rose by 3.2 per cent y/y, adjusted for the retail price index. In the final three months of 2007, they fell 0.4 per cent y/y.

4. Source: ONS.

5. In the UK, a minimum wage of £3.60 for adults was introduced on 1 April 1999, benefiting 1.9 million employees. In the US, the Senate voted to increase the minimum wage in July 1996, from $4.25 to $5.15.

6. See 'The Level and Distribution of Economic Well-Being', Ben Bernanke, 6 February 2007 and 'Embracing the Challenge of Free Trade: Competing and Prospering in a Global Economy', Ben Bernanke, 1 May 2007.

7. See 'Education and Economic Competitiveness', Ben Bernanke, 24 September 2007.

8. Because of the association of deflation with the 1930s, falling prices conjures up images of economic decline. But there were long periods

of falling prices in the late 1800s that were associated with growth
and prosperity. See for example, 'Fear of falling? Relax, global
deflation might be good for you', *International Herald Tribune*,
30 January 1999.

9. See 'The Global Saving Glut and the U.S. Current Account Deficit',
Ben Bernanke, 10 March 2005. 'Global Imbalances: Recent
Developments and Prospects', Ben Bernanke, 11 September 2007.
See also 'Testimony of Chairman Alan Greenspan', Federal Reserve
Board's semiannual Monetary Policy Report to the Congress,
20 July 2005 and 'International Imbalances', by Alan Greenspan,
2 December 2005.

10. Source: Economist Intelligence Unit (EIU). Malaysia ran the largest
surplus, 13.2 per cent of GDP, followed by Thailand, 12.7 per cent
of GDP, and then South Korea, 11.7 per cent of GDP. Indonesia also
ran a surplus, of 3.9 per cent of GDP.

11. Source: EIU. China's current account surplus is likely to have reached
11.6 per cent of GDP in 2007.

12. Source: EIU. Argentina's current account swung from −1.4 per cent
of GDP in 2001 to a surplus of 8.6 per cent in 2002, and remained
in surplus thereafter. Brazil ran in a deficit of 1.5 per cent of GDP
in 2002, but thereafter was in surplus.

13. Source: EIU. Mexico's deficits have been quite modest over the four
years to 2007, averaging 0.6 per cent of GDP. Russia's current account
balance rose from 0.1 per cent of GDP in 1998 to 12.6 per cent of
GDP in 1999, and averaged 9.7 per cent between 2000 and 2006.

14. See Chapter 6.

15. Source: EIU. New Zealand's current account deficit was 8.1 per cent
of GDP in 2007. Iceland's current account deficit was 12.4 per cent
of GDP.

16. Source: EIU. The current account deficits for Spain, Greece, Portugal
and Ireland were 9.5 per cent, 12.5 per cent, 8.5 per cent and 5.9
per cent of GDP respectively in 2007.

17. Source: International Financial Statistics. Private sector credit rose
by 264.5 per cent between January 2000 and December 2007. The
increase was 111.2 per cent in Portugal and 306.4 per cent in Ireland.
In Greece, private sector credit rose 205.2 per cent between January
2001 and December 2007.

18. See 'Eurozone bond yields diverge', *Financial Times*, 15 February
2008, and 'Eurozone bond yields diverge', *Financial Times*,
26 February 2008.

19. Source: EIU. After oil prices fell below $9 per barrel in 1986, Saudi
Arabia's current account deficit reached 13.3 per cent of GDP a
year later.

20. Source: EIU. Saudi Arabia's current account surplus rose to 13.1 per cent of GDP in 2003.
21. Source EIU. Kuwait's surplus in 2003 was 19.7 per cent of GDP. Qatar's was 24.3 per cent of GDP, while that of the United Arab Emirates was 8.6 per cent of GDP.
22. Souce: EIU. Iraq had a deficit of 8.8 per cent of GDP, and Lebanon had a deficit of 24.9 per cent of GDP.
23. Source: EIU.
24. Source: EIU.
25. See 'Global Imbalances: Recent Developments and Prospects', Ben Bernanke, 11 September 2007.
26. See 'The Global Saving Glut and the U.S. Current Account Deficit', Ben Bernanke, 10 March 2005.
27. Source: Bureau of Economic Analysis (BEA). The savings ratio fell to 0.4 per cent in 2006, its lowest level since current records began in 1959.
28. Source: BEA. The personal sector savings ratio fell from 5.6 per cent in January 1995 to 1.6 per cent in December 1999.
29. Source: ONS. The savings ratio fell to 2.4 per cent in Q1 2007, the lowest level since current records began in Q1 1963. Mervyn King was speaking on 22 January 2008, in Bristol at a dinner hosted by the Institute of Directors South West and the Confederation of British Industry at the Ashton Gate Stadium.
30. See 'Testimony of Chairman Alan Greenspan', Federal Reserve Board's semiannual Monetary Policy Report to the Congress, 16 February 2005.
31. See 'The Mortgage Market and Consumer Debt', Alan Greenspan, 19 October 2004.
32. Ibid.
33. See 'Foreclosures in the Subprime Market and Their Cost to Homeowners', Center for Responsible Lending (CRL), December 2006.
34. Source: Office of Federal Housing Enterprise Oversight.
35. See 'Foreclosures in the Subprime Market and Their Cost to Homeowners', CRL, December 2006.
36. Source: BEA. Profits from 'current production', or with IVA (inventory valuation adjustment) and CCADJ (capital consumption adjustment) rose to a high of 12.3 per cent of GDP in Q1 1966, higher than the peak of 12.0 per cent reached in Q3 2006.
37. Net direct investment outflows climbed from $2.6 billion in 1960 to $7.2 billion in 1971. During that period, the current account fell from a surplus of $2.8 billion to a deficit of $1.4 billion.
38. Source: BEA. Profits from 'current production', or with IVA and CCADJ, rose from 7.3 per cent of GDP in Q4 1990 to 10.1 per cent

in Q4 1996. Gross direct investment outflows accelerated from 0.6 per cent of GDP in 1990, to 1.3 per cent in 1996.

39. Source: EIU. Japan's net direct investment outflows were particularly strong in the late 1980s, reaching a peak of 1.6 per cent of GDP in 1990.
40. Sources: EIU and Department of Commerce.
41. Source: ONS. The current account deficit was initially reported to have reached 5.73 per cent of GDP in Q3 2007, before it was revised down. This compares with a high of 5.69 per cent in Q3 1989.
42. Source: ONS.
43. Source: ONS.
44. Source: ONS.
45. Source: ONS.
46. Source: ONS. Total employment rose to a record 29.4 million in November 2007.
47. Source: ONS.
48. Source: ONS.
49. Source: Department of Commerce. The US external debt to GDP ratio was 19.2 per cent of GDP in 2006, based on current cost.
50. Source: ONS. The net investment income balance fell into deficit in Q1 2007. For the first three quarters of 2007, the deficit was £5.9 billion.
51. Source: ONS. 'Other Investment' recorded a deficit of £28.6 billion in the year to Q3 2007, helping to push net investment income into a deficit of £5.1 billion over the corresponding period.
52. Source: BLS. Manufacturing payrolls fell from 17.299 million in January 1997 to 13.774 million in December 2007, a drop of 20.4 per cent.
53. Sources: BEA and ONS. Imports as a percentage of GDP were 16.8 per cent of GDP in the US in Q4 2007, compared with 30.7 per cent in the UK.
54. See 'Who Calls the Shots in the Global Economy', Hedrick Smith, 16 November 2004, www.pbs.org.
55. See 'The Wal-Mart Effect', Economic Policy Institute, 26 June 2007.
56. Source: IMF, *Direction of Trade Statistics*.
57. Source: IMF, *Direction of Trade Statistics*.
58. Source: IMF, *Direction of Trade Statistics*.
59. Source: General Administration of Customs, China. The trade surplus for textile manufactures reached $140.5 billion in 2007. The surplus for machinery and electronic equipment rose to $147.0 billion.

60. Source: General Administration of Customs, China. In the final three months of 2007, Chinese exports to the US were up 10.7 per cent y/y.
61. The S&P IFCG Composite rose 211.5 per cent from 1 January 2003 to 1 December 2006, and carried on rising in 2007, climbing a further 42.5 per cent.
62. See 'China's smog shutdown', *Wall Street Journal*, 28 February 2008.
63. See 'Democratic rivals clash over economy', *Financial Times*, 15 February 2008.
64. See 'Where Ricardo and Mill Rebut and Confirm Arguments of Mainstream Economists Supporting Globalisation', Paul A. Samuelson, *Journal of Economic Perspectives*, vol. 18, no. 3, Summer 2004, pp. 135–46.
65. See 'Greenspan's '63 Essay Foretold Subprime Inaction', *Bloomberg*, 19 December 2007.

5   Dealing With the Fallout

1. Irving Fisher, *Booms and Depressions*, Adelphi Company, 1932. Also see Chapter 7 in this book.
2. The Federal Reserve cut on 18 September 2007 from 5.25 per cent to 4.75 per cent. It then cut on 31 October, from 4.75 per cent to 4.5 per cent. The third reduction came on 11 December, from 4.5 per cent to 4.25 per cent. An emergency rate cut was delivered on 22 January 2008, from 4.25 per cent to 3.5 per cent. A fifth move followed on 30 January, from 3.5 per cent to 3.0 per cent. The Bank of England cut its official lending rate from 5.75 per cent to 5.50 per cent on 6 December 2007. It cut again on 7 February 2008, from 5.50 per cent to 5.25 per cent.
3. Source: National Association of Realtors (NAR). The median house price peaked in September 2005 on the new home sales basis at 13.6 per cent y/y, and in October 2005 for existing home sales, at 16.9 per cent y/y. The Mortgage Bankers Association (MBA) new purchase index for mortgage applications peaked in September 2005.
4. Source: S&P/Case-Shiller.
5. Source: MBA. Foreclosures started for residential mortgages rose to 0.88 per cent of all loans in Q4 2007, the highest since current records began in 1979.
6. Source: NAR. Existing home sales had fallen from a peak of 7.210 million (annualised) in September 2005 to 5.03 million two years later. New home sales had dropped from a peak of 1.389 million (annualised) in July 2005 to 0.693 million in September 2007.

Although the September reports were not yet published by the time the Federal Reserve finally delivered is first rate cut, the available reports showed sales had still plummeted.

7. Discount rate was cut from 6.25 per cent to 5.75 per cent on 16 August 2007.

8. According to a report from the Boston Consulting Group released in May 2007, 55 per cent of homeowners thought their home would sell for more than a year before. That was a drop of just 4 percentage points from a year earlier.

9. Source: Datastream. When the US housing market peaked in June 2005, the price to earnings ratio for the S&P 500 stock market index was 19.9. When the stock market peaked in March 2000, it was 31.4.

10. Source: Bureau of Economic Analysis (BEA). Corporate profits from 'current production', or with IVA (inventory valuation adjustment) and CCADJ (capital consumption adjustment), were still rising at an annual rate of 22.7 per cent y/y in Q3 2006. Overseas profits remained strong through most of the following year, rising 36.5 per cent y/y in Q3 2007.

11. Source: BEA.

12. Source: BEA. The current account deficit was 5.5 per cent of GDP in Q2 2007 and fell to 5.1 per cent of GDP in Q3 2007. But the goods and services deficit rose from $174.0 billion in Q3 2007 to $179.9 billion in Q4. That suggested the current account was unlikely to fall in Q4 2007.

13. Source: BEA. Net International Investment Position of US at Current Cost.

14. Source: BEA. The net investment income balance was in surplus, by $22.2 billion in Q3 2007, even though the government income balance was –$39.1 billion.

15. Source: BEA.

16. Source: Federal Reserve. Home Mortgages, Issuers of Asset Backed Securities. Data is annualised. Issuance fell from an annualised $272.4 billion in Q2 2007 to –$234.6 billion in Q3 2007, and then –$268.1 billion in Q4 2007.

17. See 'The man who saw it coming', *Wall Street Journal*, 29 August 2007.

18. Source: Bureau of Labor Statistics (BLS). Import prices rose 13.6 per cent y/y in February 2008.

19. Source: BLS. US import prices for goods from China rose 3.4 per cent y/y in February 2008.

20. Source: BEA.

21. See 'The Wal-Mart Effect', Economic Policy Institute (EPI), 26 June 2007.
22. Source: BLS. At the end of 2006, import prices for consumer durables were rising 2.1 per cent y/y. By February 2008, they were up 1.9 per cent y/y. But consumer durable prices at the CPI level fell 1.4 per cent y/y and 1.0 per cent y/y over the two respective periods.
23. Source: Office for National Statistics (ONS).
24. Source: ONS.
25. The West Texas Intermediate had touched or passed this level twice before but had retreated before the end of closing. See 'Oil prices close above $100 for the first time', *Wall Street Journal*, 20 February 2008.
26. Kenneth S. Deffeyes, *Hubbert's Peak: The Impending World Oil Shortage*, Princeton University Press, 2001, and *Beyond Oil: The View From Hubbert's Peak*, Hill and Wang, 2005.
27. Souce: BEA.
28. Deffeyes, *Hubbert's Peak* and *Beyond Oil*.
29. Matthew R. Simmons, 'Twilight in the Desert: The Risk of Peak Oil', Presentation to Minnesota House of State Representatives, Minnesota, 4 February 2008.
30. See Lester R. Brown, 'Is World Oil Production Peaking?', Earth Policy Institute (EPI), 15 November 2007.
31. See 'Oil majors hit by slump in Gulf findings', *Financial Times*, 10 March 2008.
32. Matthew R. Simmons, 'Another Nail in the Coffin of the Case Against Peak Oil', November 2007.
33. Source: International Energy Agency (IEA): See 'Oil Market Report', January 2008.
34. Source: IEA.
35. Matthew R. Simmons, *Twilight in the Desert: The Coming Saudi Oil Shock and the World Economy*, John Wiley and Sons, 2005.
36. Matthew R. Simmons, 'Twilight in the Desert: The Risk of Peak Oil', Presentation to Minnesota House of State Representatives, Minnesota, 4 February 2008.
37. Source: IEA. Russia's oil production continued to rise in 2007, climbing to 10.07 million barrels per day from 9.84 million barrels per day in 2006. But that was the smallest annual increase since 1999.
38. Simmons, 'Twilight in the Desert'.
39. See 'True scale of CO_2 emissions from shipping revealed', *Guardian*, 5 January 2008.

40. C. Ford Runge and Benjamin Senauer, 'How Biofuels Could Starve the Poor', *Foreign Affairs*, Council on Foreign Relations, vol. 86, no. 3, May/June 2007.

41. Ibid.

42. See 'Studies suggest biofuels can worsen warming', *Wall Street Journal*, 7 February 2008.

43. See Lester R. Brown, 'Ethanol Demand Could Send Grain Price Soaring', EPI, 5 January 2007.

44. Runge and Senauer, 'How Biofuels Could Starve the Poor'.

45. See Lester R. Brown, 'Why Ethanol Production Will Drive World Food Prices Even Higher in 2008', EPI, 24 January 2008.

46. See Brown, 'Ethanol Demand Could Send Grain Price Soaring'.

47. See Brown, 'Why Ethanol Production Will Drive World Food Prices Even Higher in 2008'.

48. See 'Biofuel plant to boost UK wheat prices', *Farmers Weekly*, 16 November 2006.

49. See 'Double blow puts wheat at record peaks', *Financial Times*, 18 December 2007.

50. See Brown, 'Why Ethanol Production Will Drive World Food Prices Even Higher in 2008'.

51. See 'Natural disasters reach new high', *Financial Times*, 13 December 2007.

52. See 'Rice Harvests More Affected Than First Thought by Global Warming', International Rice Research Institute, 29 June 2004.

53. Source: BEA. The increase in costs of gasoline, oil, gas and electricity was costing US consumers an extra $248.1 billion compared with 2003, equal to 2.8 per cent of total consumption.

54. Alan Greenspan, *The Age of Turbulence*, Penguin Books, 2007, p. 178.

6   A Global Credit Bubble

1. Source: Economist Intelligence Unit (EIU).

2. Source: EIU.

3. Source: EIU. GDP per capita was $649 in 2007 for Laos, and $569 for Cambodia. Net direct investment inflows into Cambodia were 5.9 per cent of GDP in 2007.

4. Source: EIU. GDP per capita for Myanmar was $306 in 2007. Net direct investment inflows were 1.6 per cent in 2007.

5. Source: International Financial Statistics (IFS). The IFS does not publish data for Malaysia during this period.

6. Source: IFS.

7. Source: IFS. Between 1990 and 1996, quasi money supply rose by an annualised rate of 15.8 per cent, 17.5 per cent and 24.9 per cent in Thailand, South Korea and Indonesia respectively.

8. Source: IFS.

9. Source: IFS. World foreign exchange reserves rose from $2.12 trillion in December 2003 to $4.06 trillion in December 2007. Reserves for developing countries climbed from $1.30 trillion to $3.08 trillion.

10. Source: *Direction of Trade Statistics*, IMF. Developed countries accounted for 59.1 per cent of world imports in the year to December 2007. Developing countries accounted for 40.9 per cent of world imports over the corresponding period.

11. Source: EIU.

12. Source: EIU.

13. Source: IFS.

14. Source: IFS.

15. Source: IFS.

16. Source: IFS.

17. See IMF, *World Economic Outlook*, October 2007, chapter 3, 'Managing Large Capital Inflows'.

18. Ibid.

19. Ibid.

20. See 'The Fuss About Foreign Exchange Reserves Accumulation', Charles Wyplosz, May 2007.

21. See 'International Reserves in Emerging Market Countries: Too Much of a Good Thing?', Jeanne Olivier, Brookings Papers on Economic Activity.

22. After 1997, Thailand had its IMF quota increased from SDR573.9 million ($797.6 million) to SDR1,081.9 million ($1,477.4 million). South Korea's quota was increased twice, from SDR799.6 million ($1,111.3 million) to SDR2,927.3 million ($4,332.5 million), while Indonesia's quota was raised from SDR1,497.6 million ($2,081.3 million) to SDR2,079.3 million ($2,839.4 million).

23. See 'The Foreign Exchange Buildup: Business as Usual?', Charles Wyplosz, March 2007.

24. Source: IFS. China's International Investment Positions (IIP) Liabilities rose from $637.1 billion in 2004 to $964.5 billion in 2006.

25. 'Large forex reserves do more good than harm', Xie Taifeng, *People's Daily Online*, 14 November 2006 (http://english.people.com.cn).

26. Source: IFS. In the four years to 2006, the net financial surpluses averaged 2.9 per cent of GDP in China, 0.2 per cent in Russia, 3.2 per cent in India, 0.6 per cent in Brazil, 1.8 per cent in South Korea, 2.1 per cent in Thailand and 1.8 per cent in Mexico.

27. Source: IFS. In the three months to May 2007, foreign exchange reserves held by developing countries rose by $229.0 billion. In the three months to October 2007, the increase dropped to $90.7 billion, before rising to $148.3 billion in the three months to December.
28. 'Beijing begins to pay price for forex "sterilisation"', *Financial Times*, 1 February 2008.
29. 'Are High Foreign Exchange Reserves in Emerging Markets a Blessing or a Burden?', Russell Green and Tom Torgerson, Treasury Department, Office of International Reserves, March 2007.

7 Japan's Bear Market

1. At the time, the book was the largest selling non-fiction translation in Japan.
2. See 'Mitsubishi faces grim choices after Rockefeller failures', *Nikkei Weekly*, 15 May 1995.
3. See 'Japanese businessman pays $78.1 million for Renoir work', *Japan Times*, 19 May 1990. See also 'Japanese snapping up masterpieces', *Japan Times*, 9 January 1990 and 'Going once ... going twice ... sold!', *Japan Times*, 2 December 1989.
4. See 'Five largest companies are Japanese', *Japan Times*, 9 July 1991.
5. See 'Tokyo real estate tycoon tops list of world's richest people', *Japan Times*, 9 July 1991.
6. See 'Life expectancy decreases slightly, but Japanese still live the longest', *Japan Times*, 12 August 1988.
7. See 'Record 8.43 million Japanese took overseas trips in 1988', *Japan Times*, 24 May 1989.
8. See 'Tokyo seeks more clout on world stage', *Japan Times*, 4 October 1989.
9. See 'Japan tops world land price survey', *Japan Times*, 18 April 1989. Survey undertaken by the Japanese Association of Real Estate Appraisal in January 1988, just as land prices were beginning to peak in Tokyo. See also, 'Land prices are triple those of US', *Japan Times*, 5 October 1989.
10. See 'Kansai land costs, demand soaring', *Japan Times*, 20 March 1990.
11. See 'No end in sight to overwork problem', *Japan Times*, 17 June 1989. 'Sudden death an increasing threat to employees', *Japan Times*, 4 July 1989. 'Death rate due to overwork on the increase for employees', *Japan Times*, 28 November 1989. 'Death after overtime ruled covered by law on accidents', *Japan Times*, 18 May 1989.

12. See 'Americans blame Japan for deficit woes', *Japan Times*, 28 April 1989. See also, 'Cross-shareholdings raises ire', *Japan Times*, 11 August 1989. 'Japan doubles US assets, becoming top investor there', *Japan Times*, 1 July 1989. 'Japanese property investors have shifted from Hawaii to California dream houses', *Japan Times*, 16 August 1989. 'Cash-rich Japanese pay Broadway bills', *Japan Times*, 17 November 1989.

13. See 'Danger seen in financial asset boom', *Japan Times*, 15 June 1990.

14. See 'Tokyo land prices force buyers out', *Japan Times*, 1 June 1990 and 'Land boom has driven price wedge between Tokyo and rest of country', *Japan Times*, 6 November 1989.

15. See 'Increase in credit card insolvencies spurs plans for consumer education', *Japan Times*, 20 December 1989. See also 'Growing numbers seek debt counselling', *Japan Times*, 19 May 1989.

16. See 'Bell tolls for traditional graves in Tokyo', *Japan Times*, 8 May 1989. See also 'Skyrocketing land prices have gravediggers delving deeper', *Japan Times*, 2 March 1991 and 'Tokyo will try out compact tombs', *Japan Times*, 18 April 1989.

17. See 'Wealth of Japan's capital markets is drawing underworld into the game', *Japan Times*, 4 April 1989.

18. See 'Investigators get general idea of route Recruit shares took', *Japan Times*, 11 January 1989. Recruit Cosmos was floated in the autumn of 1996. The company 'acquired' 900,000 shares and offered to sell them to 60 influential people in business, political and government circles before floatation. Because the share price was likely to go up after floatation, the share sales were considered as cash gifts.

19. See 'Ex-official denies bribery as Recruit trial kicks off', *Japan Times*, 25 November 1989.

20. See 'Japan is only interested in profits, Kaifu told', *Japan Times*, 4 September 1989.

21. Source: Japan Real Estate Institute. The land price index started to fall in Q4 1991, and has continued falling without interruption, through until Q3 2007, when it was still going down 0.2 per cent q/q. Over this period, land prices have fallen 56.6 per cent.

22. Source: Cabinet Office (Japan). The investment to GDP ratio carried on rising until it reached a peak of 19.6 per cent in the first quarter of 1991. The ratio of consumer spending fell from 56.1 per cent during the first quarter of 1980 to 53.8 per cent during the final quarter of the year. All figures quoted are in real terms.

23. Source: Ministry of Labour. The unemployment rate had dropped to a low of 2.1 per cent at the end of 1989. It subsequently fell to a new low of 2.0 per cent in August the following year. Source: Management and Coordination Agency. Average wages rose by 4.7

per cent y/y during 1989 compared to an average 2.5 per cent y/y during the previous three years.

24. Source: Organisation for Economic Cooperation and Development (OECD). Unit labour costs in the business sector were 3.2 per cent lower in 1989 compared to 1984.

25. Source: OECD. Productivity growth in the business sector averaged 3.7 per cent y/y during the second half of the 1980s.

26. Source: Cabinet Office (Japan). The ratio of property to equity assets in the personal sector was 10.1 at the end of 1990.

27. See 'Tokyo residential land boom overshadowed by Osaka rise', *Japan Times*, 10 March 1989.

28. See 'Land prices in Kanto expected to cool down', *Japan Times*, 13 January 1989.

29. See 'Land prices found easing in Tokyo but still skyrocketing in other cities', *Japan Times*, 17 May 1989.

30. See 'Tokyo residential land boom overshadowed by Osaka rise', *Japan Times*, 10 March 1989. A National Land Agency report showed that the 'Tokyo area posted a relatively low year-on-year gain of 0.4 per cent per cent in residential zones.'

31. See 'Land prices stable in Tokyo but rising fast in Nara, Osaka', *Japan Times*, 1 April 1989.

32. The survey was conducted by MRD, an affiliate of Misawa Homes Co. The survey was conducted on 1 December 1988 on housing lots of 130 square metres or more in 439 locations in Tokyo and the prefectures of Kanagawa, Chiba, Saitama and Ibaraki. The survey showed that the annual rate between December 1987 and December 1988 had plunged from 73.5 per cent to 8.4 per cent. The average price fell by 8 per cent y/y in Tokyo, by 6.2 per cent y/y in Kanagawa. But prices were still rising in areas where the increases had been relatively lower in recent years. Prices were up a record 41.3 per cent y/y in Ibaraki, by 38.8 per cent y/y in Chiba, and 7.6 per cent y/y in Saitama. See 'Land prices in Kanto expected to cool down', *Japan Times*, 13 January 1989.

33. See 'Tokyo land costs levelling off but Kansai prices keep rising', *Japan Times*, 3 October 1989. The survey examined land prices in 1,461 locations in Tokyo as of 1 July, and found that prices had dropped by an annual rate of 2.5 per cent. House prices were down 4.2 per cent y/y, commercial property prices fell by 0.2 per cent.

34. See 'Land prices stable in Tokyo but rising fast in Nara, Osaka', *Japan Times*, 1 April 1989 and 'Tokyo land costs levelling off but Kansai prices keep rising', *Japan Times*, 3 October 1989.

35. See 'Top land prices in prefectural capitals still rising', *Japan Times*, 28 January 1989. See also 'Tokyo's high land prices spreading', *Japan Times*, 8 September 1989.

36. See 'Tokyo residential land boom overshadowed by Osaka rise', *Japan Times*, 10 March 1989.
37. Source: Japan Real Estate Institute. Land prices rose by an annualised rate of 29.7 per cent in the six biggest cities and by 19.7 per cent nationwide. But the rate of increase cooled dramatically during the second quarter of the year. Prices in the six biggest cities rose by an annualised rate of just 10.6 per cent. This was the lowest rate of increase for nearly five years.
38. See 'Land prices ease in buyer's market', *The Japan Economic Journal*, 17 November 1990 and 'Property prices are slipping in Tokyo, Osaka, Nagoya', *Japan Times*, 9 November 1990.
39. See 'Land prices fell up to 10 per cent in some areas in November', *Japan Times*, 14 December 1990.
40. Source: Japan Real Estate Institute. The figures for Q1 1990 were published on 1 July 1990. The last time property prices had fallen in Japan's six major cities was Q4 1974 and Q1 1975, when they dropped by a cumulative 8.6 per cent.
41. Source: Bank of Japan (BoJ). M2+CDs (certificates of deposits) grew at an annualised rate of 15.1 per cent during the three months to December 1989. Over the three months to December 1990, M2+CDs expanded by an annualised rate of 2.0 per cent.
42. The Federation of Bankers Association reported that the growth in bank lending to the leading 13 City banks had fallen to 3.12 per cent during the six months to September, the lowest growth rate since 1980.
43. This concern was compounded by a sudden spike in oil prices following the outbreak of the Gulf war in the summer of 1990. The oil crisis of 1973–74 had left a lasting impression on the Japanese psyche and many feared the potential impact of another surge in energy prices.
44. Source: BoJ. The domestic wholesale price index peaked in March 1991. By November 1991, the annual rate had dropped to –0.2 per cent y/y.
45. Source: Cabinet Office (Japan). The GDP deflator had dropped to 0.3 per cent y/y during the second quarter of 1993.
46. Source: Cabinet Office (Japan). The GDP deflator was falling at an annual rate of 0.2 per cent y/y in the final quarter of 1994, since when it has remained in negative territory, with the exception of the four quarters affected by the rise in the VAT in Q2 1997.
47. See *OECD Economic Surveys, Japan*, 1996, p. 48. Net operating profit for major banks rose from ¥2.4 trillion in FY1991 to ¥3.2 trillion in 1993, ¥3.2 trillion in FY1994, ¥2.8 trillion in FY1995 and then ¥4.8 trillion in 1996.

48. Even when the discount rate was down to 0.5 per cent, there was still scope to bring long term rates down. The yield curve was still comparatively steep at this juncture, with ten-year yields 2.3 per cent higher than the discount rate.
49. Source: BoJ.
50. See *OECD Economic Surveys, Japan*, 1996, p. 47.
51. The velocity of circulation, or the income velocity as it is sometimes referred to, is the rate of turnover per income-generating transaction. A falling velocity of circulation is considered evidence of hoarding.
52. J.K Galbraith, *The Great Crash 1929*, Penguin Books, 1954.
53. Kyowa Corporation, Shuwa Corporation and Yuho Chemical Co. all defaulted in the space of ten days.
54. Source: Ministry of Finance. Total corporate profits fell by 49.1 per cent between Q4 1989 and Q4 1992. Manufacturing profits dropped by 53.1 per cent between the peak of Q3 1989 and Q4 1992.
55. 'Jittery depositors stashing cash in safe-deposit boxes', *Nikkei Weekly*, 8 July 2002.
56. Source: BoJ.
57. Irving Fisher, *Booms and Depression*, Adelphi Company, 1932, pp. 107–8.
58. 'Bad debt problem keeps getting worse', *Nikkei Weekly*, 5 February 2001.

8 Policy Failures in a Liquidity Trap

1. Graham Turner, *Solutions to a Liquidity Trap*, GFC Economics, 2003.
2. Supplementary budgets:

Month	Year	¥ trillion
August	1992	10.7
April	1993	13.2
September	1993	6.2
February	1994	15.3
April	1995	4.6
September	1995	12.8
April	1998	16.7
November	1998	23.9
November	1999	18.0
September	2000	5.0
November	2002	6.2
Total		*132.6*

3. Tax revenue shortfalls were included in supplementary budgets, inflating the fiscal stimulus. For example, the last supplementary budget announced in November 2002 included ¥2.0 trillion to cover a tax revenue shortfall caused by the downturn in the economy.

4. The leading composite index, compiled by the Cabinet Office, peaked in October 1996 at 106.4 and fell to 100.0 by March 1997, a decline of 6.0 per cent. Ministry of Construction data show that housing starts also peaked in October 1996 at 146,670, before dropping 18.5 per cent to 119,600 in March 1997. Construction orders hit a high of ¥2,256.1 billion in October 1996 before sliding 31.2 per cent over the following five months to ¥1,552.5 billion. Cabinet Office data show that private domestic machinery orders fell from a high of ¥1,591.3 billion in October 1996 to ¥1,135.2 billion in March 1997, a drop of 28.7 per cent.

5. Source: Statistics Bureau of the Ministry of Internal Affairs and Communication. The savings ratio started to climb during April 1997, immediately after the collapse of Nissan Mutual Life. It then accelerated when Yamaichi and Hokkaido Takushoku Bank defaulted in November 1997. Using a twelve-month moving average, the savings ratio rose from 12.4 per cent to 15.5 per cent between March 1997 and March 1998.

6. The South East Asian crisis in July 1997 also accelerated the economic downturn.

7. Towards the end of 2002, Prime Minister Koizumi came under concerted pressure to break his pledge to limit the level of new government bond issuance to ¥30 trillion. On 21 November 2002, the government bowed to pressure from within the Liberal Democratic Party and enacted an eleventh supplementary budget, worth ¥6.2 trillion. This brought the total value of supplementary budgets issued since the spring of 1992 to ¥132.6 trillion.

8. J.M. Keynes warned that it may be 'comparatively easy to make capital-goods so abundant that the marginal efficiency of capital is zero' – see J.M. Keynes, *The General Theory of Employment, Interest and Money*, Macmillan Cambridge University Press, 1936, p. 221. 'But I suggest that a more typical, and often the predominant, explanation of the crisis is, not primarily a rise in the rate of interest, but a sudden collapse in the marginal efficiency of capital' (ibid. p. 315).

9. See: 'If – for whatever reason – the rate of interest cannot fall as fast as the marginal efficiency of capital would fall with a rate of accumulation corresponding to what the community would choose to save at a rate of interest equal to the marginal efficiency of capital in conditions of full employment, then even a diversion of

the desire to hold wealth towards assets, which will in fact yield no economic fruits whatever, will increase economic well-being. In so far as millionaires find their satisfaction in building mighty mansions to contain their bodies when alive and pyramids to shelter them after death, or repenting of their sins, erect cathedrals and endow monasteries or foreign missions, the day when the abundance of capital will interfere with abundance of the output may be postponed. "To dig holes in the ground" paid out of savings, will increase, not only employment, but the real dividend of useful goods and services' (Keynes, *The General Theory of Employment, Interest and Money*, pp. 219–20).

10. Bank lending rates were determined by the long term and short term prime rates. The long term prime rate was priced 0.9 per cent above the five-year bank debenture yield, which was in turn influenced by five-year government bond yields.

11. The data for corporate bankruptcies has been constructed by the following formula, where X is corporate defaults in yen, billion: Lag#(Mav#(Ach#(Mav#(Sam#(X),12m),12m),6m),–1Y).

     The data for bond yields have been constructed by the following formula, where Y is ten-year Japanese government bond yields: Mav#((Ach#(Y,12m)),6m).

     Notes: Lag# is a lag. Mav# is a moving average. Ach# is an actual change. Sam# is a moving average. In the case of corporate defaults, the lag is one year.

     Corporate bankruptcies. Source: Tokyo Shoko Research Ltd.

12. See: '... institutional and psychological factors are present which set a limit much above zero to the practicable decline in the rate of interest. In particular, the costs of bringing borrowers and lenders together and uncertainty as to the future of the rate of interest ... set a lower limit' (Keynes, *The General Theory of Employment, Interest and Money*, pp. 218–19).

13. Ibid., p. 202.

14. See: 'In other words, beyond a certain point money's yield from liquidity does not fall in response to an increase in its quantity to anything approaching the extent to which the yield from other types of assets falls when their quantity is comparably increased' (ibid., p. 233).

15. Ibid., p. 219.

16. Ibid., p. 203.

17. See Turner, *Solutions to a Liquidity Trap*.

18. Sources: Bank of Japan (BoJ) and Datastream. The differential between ten-year JGBs and the discount rate rose from 0.95 per cent in March 1992 to a peak of 2.93 per cent in August 1994.

19. Source: BoJ. The impact can also be seen by comparing the discount rate and average lending rates. The differential climbed from a low of 0.93 per cent in August 1990 to a high of 3.08 per cent in September 1993. By the end of 2000, the differential had dropped to 1.61 per cent, but was still well above the low point of 1990 and slightly higher than the differential prevailing at the end of 1989 (1.53 per cent).

20. Source: Organisation for Economic Cooperation and Development (OECD). General government financial liabilities were expected to hit 180.37 per cent of GDP in 2007, up from 68.6 per cent in 1990.

21. See: 'It is invalid, therefore, to transfer the argument to industry as a whole unless we also transfer our assumption that the aggregate effective demand is fixed' (Keynes, *The General Theory of Employment, Interest and Money*, p. 259).

22. See: 'The embarrassment of those indebtors who are heavily indebted may reach the point of insolvency, – with severely adverse effects' (ibid., p. 264).

23. See: '... if labour were to respond to conditions of gradually diminishing employment by offering its services at a gradually diminishing money-wage, this would not, as a rule, have the effect of reducing real wages and might even have the effect of increasing them, through its adverse influence on the volume of output' (ibid., p. 269).

24. Sources: OECD. For example, the proportion of corporate income accruing to companies in the US fell to a low of 18.2 per cent of GDP in 1976 before rising to a peak of 23.4 per cent in 1998.

25. Source: Bureau of Economic Analysis (BEA) and Office for National Statistics. For example, the real investment to GDP ratio hit a low of 5.4 per cent in 1961 in the US and a low of 6.6 per cent in 1966 in the UK.

26. See: 'no one would wish to deny the proposition that a reduction in money-wages accompanied by the same aggregate effective demand as before will be associated with an increase in employment, the precise question at issue is whether the reduction in money wages will or will not be accompanied by the same aggregate effective demand as before measured in money' (Keynes, *The General Theory of Employment, Interest and Money*, p. 259).

27. Sources: Federal Reserve and BEA. Adjusting for core consumption deflator, the Fed funds target fell to a low of –0.3 per cent in July 1992, and by the end of 1993 it was still only 0.7 per cent.

28. Strictly speaking, a liquidity trap had not been reached until long term interest rates had hit a floor too. But the BoJ did not aggressively raise the level of JGB purchases until the spring of 2001, thereby missing the opportunity again to secure any lowering of real borrowing costs.

29. Source: Cabinet Office (Japan). By Q1 2002, real GDP was falling 1.9 per cent y/y.

30. See 'Tough Road for BoJ as Zero Rates Factored In', Dow Jones Newswire, 14 March 2001. BoJ governor Masaru Hayami came under considerable criticism for the theoretical underpinning behind the August rate hike. The BoJ wrongly attributed a 1.7 per cent y/y rise in summer bonuses to the sharp increase in corporate profits, when it actually stemmed from a reshuffling of two-thirds of the data sample. Had the data sample held constant, bonuses would have fallen.

31. See 'Rx for Japan: Back to the future', Milton Friedman, *Wall Street Journal*, 17 December 1997. A similar argument was made by Richard Werner, writing in the *Nikkei Weekly*, 12 July 1999: 'As soon as the BoJ became fully independent – in April last year – printing money suddenly shot up by the highest rate in a quarter century. Since that was all that was needed for a recovery, we can expect to see growth of more than 3 per cent in real gross domestic product in fiscal 1999.' See also 'Why the Bank of Japan is responsible for creating, prolonging the recession', Richard Werner, *Nikkei Weekly*, 7 December 1999.

32. See BoJ press release, 'Change of the Guideline for Money Market Operations', 12 February 1999.

33. See 'Why the BoJ held the line', Kazuo Ueda, *Wall Street Journal*, 22 September 1999.

34. Source: BoJ. The average lending rate for domestically licensed banks was 2.2 per cent at the end of February 2001.

35. Source: BoJ. Total bank holdings of JGBs rose from ¥31.3 trillion in December 1998 to ¥72.2 trillion by the end of 2002.

36. Source: BoJ. Total deposits in the banking industry rose to ¥457.2 trillion in November 2000, while total loans dropped to ¥457.0 trillion. This differential has since widened sharply.

37. Article 5 of the 1947 Finances Law prohibits the BoJ from monetising government debt. See 'BoJ advised to supply cash for bonds', *Nikkei Weekly*, 25 January 1999.

38. 'Limitless purchases of government bonds by the central bank will present a moral hazard to financial policy. It will also negatively affect the rating of government bonds.' See 'BoJ advised to supply cash for bonds', *Nikkei Weekly*, 25 January 1999.

39. The BoJ claimed that buying bonds in the secondary market was not a risk, because it would not be supplying more liquidity than needed. It would not be providing more notes and coins above and beyond that demanded. Therefore, it would not constitute a risk for hyperinflation. See 'BoJ advised to supply cash for bonds', *Nikkei Weekly*, 25 January 1999.

40. See 'Japan: A puzzling analysis', David Malpass, former deputy assistant US Treasury secretary for developing nations in the Reagan Administration, *Wall Street Journal*, 5 October 1999.
41. Source: BoJ.
42. See 'The benefits of a weaker Yen', Jeffrey Sachs, *Financial Times*, 18 April 2001.
43. See 'Why the BoJ held the line', Kazuo Ueda, *Wall Street Journal*, 22 September 1999.
44. When the yen did fall, it failed to lessen the deflation pressures within the economy. The yen fell by 72 per cent against the dollar between late 1995 and early 1998. Import prices rose 12 per cent over this period, but factory gate prices remained stubbornly low.
45. See Keynes, *The General Theory of Employment, Interest and Money*, p. 183.
46. See 'Why I am even more depressed about Japan', Paul Krugman, *Financial Times*, 30 April 1999.
47. Writing in the *Financial Times*, 2 November 1999, the deputy vice minister for international finance, Takatoshi Ito, suggested the 'Bank of Japan could commit to an inflation target of, say, 1 to 3 per cent, to be achieved in two years'.
48. See 'New procedures for money market operators and monetary easing', Bank of Japan, 19 March 2001. See 3(b), CPI guideline for the duration of the new procedures: 'The new procedures for money market operations continue to be in place until the consumer price index (excluding perishables on a nationwide statistics) registers stably a zero percent or an increase year-on-year.'
49. Source: Cabinet Office (Japan). The consumption deflator fell 0.1 per cent y/y in Q4 2007, extending an uninterrupted decline stretching back to Q2 1998.
50. Advocates of inflation targeting also called for yen devaluation as part of the policy.
51. See 'Why I am even more depressed about Japan', Paul Krugman, *Financial Times*, 30 April 1999. Monetary base is the sum of notes and coins in circulation and bank reserves.
52. Source: BoJ.
53. See 'Why the Bank of Japan can't target inflation', Kazuo Ueda, *Wall Street Journal*, 6 March 2000.
54. See 'Why I am even more depressed about Japan', Paul Krugman, *Financial Times*, 14 March 2007.
55. Some were still advocating a more explicit inflation target. See 'Time for a switch to global reflation', by Haruhiko Kuroda and Masahiro Kawai, vice minister and deputy finance minister for international affairs at the Ministry of Finance, Japan. *Financial Times*, 12 December 2002.

56. This point was underlined by his warning that 'It is of the nature of organised investment markets, under the influence of purchasers largely ignorant of what they are buying and of speculators who are more concerned with forecasting the next shift of market sentiment than with a reasonable estimate of the future yield of capital-assets that, when disillusion falls upon an over-optimistic and over-bought market, it should fall with sudden and even catastrophic force' (Keynes, *The General Theory of Employment, Interest and Money*, pp. 315–16).
57. Ibid., p. 322. Keynes described the '"error of pessimism", with the result that the investments, which would in fact yield 2 per cent in conditions of full employment, are expected to yield less than nothing'.
58. See: 'It follows that wage reductions, as a method of securing full employment, are also subject to the same limitations as the method of increasing the quantity of money' (ibid., p. 266).

9 Where Are We Heading?

1. Source: S&P/Case-Shiller. By January 2008, the S&P/Case-Shiller index for 20 cities was falling at a three-month annualised rate of 20.4 per cent, based on seasonally adjusted data.
2. Source: Nationwide Building Society. The March report showed house prices had fallen 0.6 per cent over the previous month, the fifth consecutive monthly decline. The six-month annualised rate was already down to –3.5 per cent, compared with a low of –7.8 per cent in the early 1990s, after the collapse of the Lawson Boom. But, and this is critical, house prices did not bottom out on that occasion until two years after base rates had been cut. And they were slashed in half, from a peak of 15 per cent to 7 per cent. On this occasion, house prices are tumbling, and rates have only been cut twice, by 0.5 per cent.
3. See 'An unforgiving eye: Bankers cry foul over fair value', *Financial Times*, 13 March 2008.
4. Source: Mortgage Bankers Association. The 30-year fixed rate mortgage fell from a high of 10.56 per cent on April 1990 to 6.59 per cent in October 1993. The one-year variable rate dropped from 8.87 per cent in February 1990 to 3.83 per cent in October 1993.
5. See: http://ml-implode.com/.

INDEX

Compiled by Auriol Griffith-Jones

Note: Page numbers in *italics* refer to Figures; those in **bold** refer to Tables

Albania 117, 118
Angola, oil 99
Argentina 53, 89
  balance of payments crisis **127**
  capital flight **125**
  food production 102
  import cover ratio 125–6, **126**
  restrictions on capital inflows
    130–1
Armenia 121
art market, Japanese domination
  136–7
Australia, drought 102
Azerbaijan 54, 99
  current account surplus 120,
    121

Baltic Three 128
  and UK *119*
  see also Estonia; Latvia;
    Lithuania
Bank of England 87, 103, 188
  remit on inflation 44, 56, 106,
    192
  see also Monetary Policy
    Committee
Bank of Japan 84, 153
  assets 178–9, *179*
  and inflation targeting 184–5
  interventions 180–1
  and money supply 173–5,
    178–9
  policy mistakes 140–1, 147,
    148–50, 161, 172

printing of money 175–6, 178
response to stock market crash
  139, 148
bank lending
  alternative simulation 35–7
  effect on economies 37–41
  fear of lending 188–9
  restrictions on 35–6
Bear Stearns 86, 188
Belarus 121
Bernanke, Ben, chairman of
    Federal Reserve 8, 23, 50,
    192
  and foreign investment 55, 56
biofuels 100–1
  ethanol 101–2
Blair, Tony, Prime Minister 48
borrowing *see* debt
Bosnia 117
Boston Consulting Group 86
Brazil 88
  balance of payments crisis **127**
  biofuels 101
  capital flight **125**
  foreign exchange reserves **116**
  import cover ratio 125–6, **126**
  restrictions on capital inflows
    131
  trade surplus 53
Bretton Woods system 23–4, 60
Brown, Gordon, UK Chancellor
    103, 106
  1997 promise 26
  and housing shortage 29

Bulgaria 117, 118
Bush, George W., US President
  and biofuels 101
  and Saudi Arabia 98

Cambodia 110
capital flight
  and financial globalisation
    125–6, **125**, **126**
  South East Asia 124, **124**
capital flows 110, 112–13
  future of 131–2
  IMF view of 122–3
  into Eastern Europe 117
  into US 51, 54–5, 59, 88–9,
    90–1, 128–9
  restrictions on 130–1
carbon emissions
  and food production 102
  from shipping 99
Center for Responsible Lending
  (CRL) 32, 58–9
Central Asia 121
  see also Kazakhstan
central banks 3, 5, 16
  and asset inflation 82
  and capital inflows 128
  and debt deflation 106–7
  intervention policies 123–8,
    129–31
  and money supply 113, 114,
    173–4
  obsession with inflation 140–1
  policy choices 188
  role in monetary policy 50
  South East Asia 114
China 10–11, 44
  as competitive shock 51, 61–2,
    77
  current account surplus 127
  direct investment inflows *61*
  economic policy 79
  exchange rates 79, 90, 130
  foreign exchange reserves
    116–17, **116**, 127

imports 75–7
  labour costs 109
  labour rights 193
  oil production 98
  trade balance *52*, 77–8, *78*,
    131
  trade with UK 64, *65*, 76, 77
  trade with US 75–6, *76*, 77–8
classical economics 168, 186
climate change 102–3
  and Peak Oil 5, 79, 99
  see also carbon emissions
Clinton, Bill, US President 48
Clinton, Hillary 81, 192
Colombia, restrictions on capital
  inflows 131
consumer borrowing *see*
  mortgages; personal debt
consumer goods 14–15
  and consumption deflator
    21–2, *22*
  price falls 93–4
  United States 92–3, *93*
Consumer Price Index 21
consumer prices
  effect on real incomes 104–5
  OECD figures *104*, *105*
consumer spending 55
  overconsumption 14
consumption deflator 21–2, *22*
  Japan *184*
corporate bonds, US 89
corporate power, increased 1, 7,
  11–12, 192–3
Council of Mortgage Lenders
  (UK) 34
credit
  and low inflation 33–5
  trading 3
credit bubble 27, 28, 109–32
  and current account surpluses
    120–2
  Eastern Europe 117–20
  global 70, 73

credit bubble *continued*
  South East Asia 115–16
  unravelling of 82
  see also domestic credit
credit mechanism 189
Czech Republic 63, 64, 118
  trade with UK 66

debt 26–47, 110
  to avoid deflation 40
  and distress selling 154
  government borrowing 1
  and house price inflation 27–9
  and interest rates 69
  restraints on 35–7
  UK servicing costs 34
  US household repayments 34, *34*
  see also credit bubble; mortgages; personal debt
debt deflation 9
  and interest rates 106–7
  Japan 153–4, 158
  risk of 104–5
debt deflation theory 5, 154–5, 157, 158
debt ratio
  under Conservative government 26
  under New Labour 26
deflation 1, 4, 38
  threat of (US) 22–3
  UK retail sales *94, 95*
  see also debt deflation; Japan
deforestation, for biofuels 100–1
deregulation, and incidence of fraud 17–18
developing countries
  domestic credit 114, 116
  excess savings 51–2
  exchange rates 79–80
  foreign exchange reserves 115–16, *115*

free trade and 10–11
imports 74–5, *75*
rise in living standards 110
and trade 110–11
see also emerging markets
dollar
  exchange rates 79, 80
  fall 88, 89–90
  flight from 90–2
  as reserve currency 89–90
dollar standard 23–5
domestic credit **133–4**
  developing countries 114, 116
  Eastern Europe 117–20
  emerging markets 130
  and foreign exchange reserves 123
dotcom bubble 3, 18, 20–1, 28–9
  Federal Reserve response to 46

Earth Policy Institute (EPI) 101
Eastern Europe
  domestic credit 117–20
  emerging markets 53, 62–3
economic crashes
  1929 Wall Street crash 14–15
  1987: 14, 16–17
  1990s housing slump 1, 14, 16, 17–19
  1990s recession 18
  Long Term Capital Management hedge fund (1998) 14
  South East Asia (1997) 14, 18, 44, 52–3, 112–15
economic growth 1, 4, 9, 79
  Japan 141
  South East Asia 123–4
economic policies
  alternative scenarios 41, 44–5
  Federal Reserve 45–7
  gridlock 87–90
  role of central banks 50, 84

education, for skills 51
Egypt, oil 98
emerging markets 10–11, 53,
    62–3
    and capital inflows 110,
        128–9
    and decoupling from West
        131–2
    domestic credit bubbles 130
    trade with each other 74
    see also developing countries;
        Eastern Europe
employment 2
    bubble jobs (UK) 69–73
    manufacturing job losses (UK)
        68–9, **70**
    US manufacturing 74, *74*
    and wages 168
    see also outsourcing;
        unemployment
Enron 20
Ensus, energy firm 102
Estonia 117
    private debt 118, *119*
ethanol 101–2
    subsidies for 101
European Central Bank 87
European Commission, and
    biofuels 102
European single currency 53
European Union
    enlargement 117
    trade imbalances 53
excess savings 51–2, 54–5, 59,
    182–3
exchange rates 10
    China 79, 90, 130
    and crises in Russia and Latin
        America 53
    developing countries 79–80
    effect of devaluations on trade
        181–2
    floating 60

Federal Reserve
    comparison with Bank of
        Japan 85–7, 189
    interest rate cuts 5, 6, 45–7,
        84–5
    interest rate rises 56
    policies 29, 45–7, 106–7, 188
    and Savings and Loan crisis
        190
    view of debt 58, 59
    view of savings 55
    see also Bernanke, Ben;
        Greenspan, Alan
financial markets 2
    historical overview 14–25
    see also stock markets
Financial Services Authority (UK)
    45, 192
Fisher, Irving, *Booms and
    Depressions* 154–5, 157,
    187
food 5, 102
    effect of biofuels on production
        101
food prices, and biofuels 100, 102
foreign exchange reserves 115,
    115, 116–17, **116**, 127
    and domestic credit bubbles
        123
foreign investment
    flight from US 90–2
    and housing bubble 51, 59, 88
    by oil exporters 54–5
    South East Asia 112–13
France 9
fraud 17–18
free trade 111
    backlash in US 81
    critiques of 81–3
    and emerging markets 10
    and pressure on wages 50–1
    unlimited expansion 1, 7, 8–9
    and weak regulation 191–2
Friedman, Milton 173

General Strike (UK) (1926) 168
Georgia, foreign investment
    120–1
Germany 9, 15–16
    trade with UK 68
globalisation 1, 8–9, 92–5
    and credit growth 111
    and distortion of monetary
        policy 88
    effect on inflation mechanism
        104
    effect on prices 40, 59
    financial 125–7
    overinvestment 60, 91–2
    polarisation of debate 81–2
    and trade imbalances 114–15
    unbalanced 7–8
gold standard 23
government bonds
    and interest rates 56–7
    role of bondholders 165–6
    and use of quantitative easing
        189, 190
    yields in Japan 162, 163, 166
Greece 53
Greenspan, Alan, chairman of
        Federal Reserve 20, 31–2,
        45–7, 192
    and asset inflation 106–7
    and foreign investment 55, 56
    and subprime lending 57–8
Greenspan-Guidotti rule 126

Hashimoto, Ryutaro, Prime
        Minister of Japan 161
Hayami, Masaru, governor of
        Bank of Japan 172, 185
homeownership 30–3
    and buy-to-let (UK) 30
    US 31–2, 31
Hong Kong, foreign exchange
        reserves 116, **116**
house price inflation 1, 3–4

and 1987 slump 1, 14, 16,
    17–19
and debt 27–9, 33–4
EU 53–4
and foreign investment 51–2
to fuel economic growth 9
and subprime lending 57
United States 1, 2, 56–7, 59
housing deflation 107–8, 188
    and capital inflows 129
Hubbert, M. King 96
Hungary 63, 64, 128
    trade with UK 66

Iceland 53
import cover ratios 125–6, **126**
import prices 92–3, 93, 94–5
    and wages 63
imports
    China 75–7
    developing countries 74–5, 75
    United Kingdom 64
India 64
    foreign exchange reserves 116,
        116
    restrictions on commercial
        borrowing 131
    trade with UK 67
Indonesia
    1997 crisis 19, 112, 112, 114
    capital flight 124, **124**
    import cover ratio 125–6, **126**
    trade surplus 52
inequality, rising 2, 4, 11
inflation
    1970s 16
    core 104, 106
    easy lending and 33–5
    in emerging markets 130
    fear of 140
    headline 104, 106
    low 33–5, 50
    measurement of 21–2

peak (2001) 22
perceived dangers 5, 44, 56, 87
UK 103
and wages 48, 50, 169
inflation targeting 183–5
interest rates 69, 84–5
    and debt deflation 106–7
    Federal Reserve cuts 5, 6,
        45–7, 84–5
    investors' perception of 164
    Japan 147, 149, 151, 164–6,
        172, 174–5
    Keynes on 163–4
    and property prices 107–8, 188
    rises 17, 56–7
    role of bondholders 165–6
    UK rise (2007) 103
    zero 108
International Energy Agency
    (IEA) 97
International Monetary Fund
    (IMF) 74, 111
    and risks of credit bubble
        122–3
    and South East Asian crisis 124
International Rice Research
    Institute 103
Iraq 54, 99
Ireland 53

Japan 71, 141
    and 1997 crisis 19, 45, 122
    bank assets 176
    bank lending and deposits
        176–7, 177
    bankruptcies 152, 154–5, 163
    battle with deflation 5, 25, 84,
        85–7, 149–50, 183–5
    bear market 135–85
    bond yields 162, 163, 166
    budget deficit monetised
        175–6, 177
    budgets 159–60

consumption deflator 184
corporate restructuring 172
debt burden 158
debt disposals 151–2
and failure of Keynesian
    policies 159–63
foreign exchange reserves 116,
    116
government debt 167
government policy mistakes
    149–50, 151–2
government spending increases
    162
hoarding 152, 156–7
implicit social contract 170–1,
    173
inflation targeting 183–5
interest rates 147, 149, 151,
    164–6, 172, 174–5
karoshi (death from overwork)
    138
and liquidity trap 108, 134–5,
    148–50, 151–3
    causes of 164–6
money supply 153, 153,
    156–7, 172–5
overseas investment 60
personal debt 138, 139, 142,
    155–6
political scandal 138–9
postwar success ('ichi ban')
    135, 136–9, 150
price of yen 147, 147, 179,
    180–2
profits collapse 156–7
property collapse 85–7, 139,
    141–4, 152
property and land prices 28,
    29–30, 137–8, 143, 144,
    145, 160
role of banks 150–1, 152–3
savings ratio 152–3, 161, 180,
    182–3

Japan *continued*
  slump in money supply 144,
    145, 146–7
  speculation frenzy 137–8, 155
  stock market crash (1990)
    139–40, 148
  tax increases 160–1
  trade imbalances 146–7, 180–1
  and US property market 136,
    138
  and US trade deficit 24–5
  wages 172, *173*
  wholesale prices *148*
jobs *see* employment
junk bond market 17

Kazakhstan
  current account surplus 121,
    121
  restrictions on capital inflows
    131
Keynes, John Maynard
  *General Theory of
    Employment, Interest and
    Money* 108, 168
  and interest rates 163
  and liquidity trap 6, 108,
    159–63
  and monetarism 185–7
  and Versailles Peace Treaty 15,
    16
King, Mervyn, governor of Bank
  of England 55, 103
Koizumi, Junichiro, Prime
  Minister of Japan 159, 161
Kuwait 54, 98
Kyzgyz Republic 121

labour costs
  China 77, 78
  drive to cut 109–10
  and trade deficits 60–2, 73
  see also outsourcing

labour rights 9–10, 192
  China 193
laissez faire 16
Laos, wages 110
Latvia 117, 118, *119*
Lawson, Nigel, UK Chancellor
  26, 34
Lebanon 54
liquidity trap 6, 108, 159–88
  causes of 163–6
  and failure of Keynesian
    policies in Japan 159–63
  Japan 108, 134–5, 148–50,
    151–3
  supply-side fallacy 167–70
  and wages 169
  see also money supply
Lithuania 117, 118, *119*
Long Term Capital Management
  hedge fund (1998) 14

Malaysia
  1997 crisis 19, 112, 113, 114
  foreign exchange reserves 116,
    116
  import cover ratio 125–6, **126**
  trade surplus 52
markets
  and debt deflation 5
  housing 6, 12, 17, 27–8
  see also emerging markets;
    stock markets
Mexico 62, 88, 98
  balance of payments crisis **127**
  capital flight 124–5, **125**
  foreign exchange reserves 116,
    116
  import cover ratio 125–6, **126**
  trade balance 53, *63*
Mieno, Yasushi, governor of
  Bank of Japan 146
minimum wage 48

Mohamad, Mahathir, Prime
    Minister of Malaysia 113
Moldova 117, 118
monetarism 16
    alternative policies 41, 44–5
    and distortion of globalisation
        88
    failure in Japan 175–8
    failures of 186–7
    and Keynesian economics
        185–7
    quantitative easing policy 174,
        178, 179, 185, 189, 190
Monetary Policy Committee 6,
    27–8, 44–5
money illusion 3–4
money supply 113, 114, 173–4
    Japan 153, *153*, 156–7, 172–5,
        178–9
moral hazard, principle of 149
mortgages
    buy-to-let 30
    debt servicing costs 33–4, 58–9
    foreign currency 35
    income multiples 34–5
    policy choices on 189–90
    and repossessions (foreclosures
        and delinquencies) 32–3, *32*,
        33, 58–9
    UK approvals 45, *46*
motor industry
    Japan 24–5, 71
    UK 71
Myanmar 110

natural disasters, and food
    production 102
New Labour
    debt burden 26, 44
    and free trade model 192
    GDP growth 3–4
    and job losses 68–9, 70
    trade deficits 71, 73
New Zealand 53

Nigeria 54
Nixon, Richard, US President 24
North American Free Trade
    Agreement 62
Northern Rock 191, 192
Norway 98

oil
    1973 price shock 105
    exploration and discoveries
        96–7
    OPEC cartels 99
    prices 95–6, 99, 104–5
    production 96–7, 98
    see also Peak Oil
oil exporting nations 54
Olympic Games, Beijing (2008)
    79
OPEC, and oil production 99
outsourcing 130, 132, 193
    and import prices 93
    of manufacturing 74–5, 109
overconsumption 14
overinvestment 14–15, 18–19,
    21–2, 59–60
Oxford Economic Forecasting 35

Paulson, Henry, US Treasury
    Secretary 32
Peak Oil 54, 95–7, 98
    and biofuels 100
    and climate change 5, 79, 99
personal debt 1, 26
    Eastern Europe 118, *119*
    Japan 138, 139, 142, 155–6
    United Kingdom 26, 27–8, *36*,
        44
    United States 26–7, *36*
Poland 63, 64, 118, 128
    trade with UK 65
Portugal 53
profits
    ratios 7–8
    and share prices 20

property
  and fall in prices 107–8
  homeownership 30–3
  housing shortages 29–30
  see also house price inflation;
    Japan
public ownership, as policy
  option 191

Qatar, trade surplus 54
quantitative easing 174, 178,
  179, 185, 189, 190

Reaganomics 16, 24
regulation
  and deregulation 17–18
  risk of backlash 191–3
regulators 1–2
Ricardo, David, *On the
  Principles of Political
  Economy and Taxation* 168
rice, yields and prices 102–3
Rumania 117, 118
Russia 88
  balance of payments crisis **127**
  capital flight **125**
  current account surplus 120,
    121
  domestic credit 120
  foreign exchange reserves 116,
    116
  oil 99, 120
  trade surplus 53, 54

Samuelson, Paul 81
Saudi Arabia
  fall in oil production 97–8
  trade surplus 54
savings
  excess 51–2, 54–5, 59, 182–3
  low level of 55–6
Savings & Loan Institutions (US)
  17, 190–1

Say, J.B., 'Say's Law' 168
Second World War, economic
  causes 15–16
Serbia 117
service industries
  export earnings 71
  UK 69–70, 71, *71*
share prices, and profits 20
Simmons, Matthew 97, 98
Singapore, foreign exchange
  reserves 116, **116**
skills, and retraining 51
Slovakia 63, 64, 118
Slovenia 117
social contract, implicit in Japan
  170–1
South Africa 53
  balance of payments **119**, 120
South East Asia
  capital flight 124, **124**
  economic crisis (1997) 14, 18,
    44, 52–3, 112–15
  economic growth 123–4
  foreign exchange reserves
    115–16, *115*
  see also Indonesia; Malaysia;
    South Korea; Thailand
South Korea
  1997 crisis 19, 112, *112*, 114
  capital flight 124, **124**
  foreign exchange reserves 116,
    116
  restrictions on capital inflows
    131
  trade surplus 52
Spain 9, 30, 53
stagflation 105
stock markets
  1987 crash 14, 16–17
  rise (from 1995) 20, 22
  US 89, 95
  and US housing market 87
subprime lending, US 31, 57–9

Sumita, Satoshi, governor of
    Bank of Japan 140
supply-side fallacy 167–70

Taiwan, foreign exchange
    reserves 116, **116**
Tajikistan, capitalism 121
Takeshita, Noboru, Prime
    Minister of Japan 138
technology 82
    and pressure on wages 50–1
Thailand
    1997 crisis 18–19, 88, 112,
        112, 113, 114
    capital flight 124, **124**
    foreign exchange reserves 116,
        116
    import cover ratio 125–6, **126**
    restrictions on capital inflows
        131
    trade surplus 52
Thatcherism 16
Tokyo, and property crash 142–3
trade
    and comparative advantage 81
    see also free trade
trade deficits 40–1
    Eastern Europe 117
    and economic growth 79
    and labour costs 60–2, 80
    UK 63, 71
    US 24, *24*, 62
trade flows 11, 110
    and exchange rates 80
trade surpluses
    in Asia 52, 113
    oil exporters 54
trade unions 10
    restrictions on 16
    see also labour rights
transnational corporations 8–9,
    10
    and cheap labour costs 60–2,
        73, 84

Japanese 137
power of 1, 7, 11–12, 192–3
Turkey 64, 89
    balance of payments 119, **119**,
        127
    capital flight **125**
    emerging market 53
    import cover ratio 125–6, **126**
    trade with UK 67

Ueda, Kazuo, member of Bank of
    Japan board 181, 185
Ukraine 102
unemployment
    Eastern Europe 117
    prospect of 191
    USA 6–7
    see also employment
United Arab Emirates 54, 98
United Kingdom 4, 64, 102
    average earnings 40, *40*, 49
    and Baltic Three *119*
    current account balance *72*, 73
    debt burden 110–11
    and Eastern Europe 63, 118,
        118
    economic trends 70–1
    government borrowing 1, 26
    house prices *43*, 188
    housing market 6, 12, 27–8
    inflation *39*
    manufacturing job losses 68–9,
        70
    mortgage approvals 45, *46*
    net external assets *72*, 73
    oil production 98
    personal debt 26, 27–8, *36*
    retail sales deflation *94*, *95*
    savings levels 55–6
    service sector jobs *71*
    trade balance *42*, 64
        China 64, *65*
        Czech Republic 66

UK, trade balance *continued*
  Hungary 66
  India 67
  Poland 65
  Turkey 67
  trade deficit 63–4, 88
  see also Bank of England;
    Monetary Policy Committee;
    New Labour
United States
  asset-backed securities 91, *91*
  average earnings 40, *41*
  compared with Japan's
    downturn 85–7
  consumer goods 92–3, *93*
  current account/GDP 24, *24*
  danger of liquidity trap 189
  debt burden 110–11
  debt trap 5–7, 12
  and dollar standard 23–5
  economic trends 59–60
  foreclosures and delinquencies
    32–3, *32*, *33*, 85
  foreign investment in 51, 54–5,
    59, 88–9, 90–1, 128–9
  government borrowing 26
  homeownership 31–2, *31*
  house prices *43*, 85, 188
    inflation 1, 2, 56–7, 59
  housing crisis 1, 2, 5, 85–7
  housing market 17, 27
  inflation *39*
  manufacturing employment 74,
    74
  median wage 48, *49*
  oil production 98
  overinvestment 14–15, 20, *21*
  overseas investments 64–5
  personal debt 26–7, 34, *34*, 36
  policy choices for 188–9
  protectionism 81
  rise in capital spending 20

  savings levels 55, 56
  supply-side policies 169–70,
    171
  trade balance 42
  trade with China 75–6, 76,
    77–8
  trade deficit 88, 89
  see also Bernanke, Ben; Federal
    Reserve; Greenspan, Alan
Uzbekistan 54

Venezuela 54, 98
Vietnam, wages 109–10
Vietnam War 23
Vogel, Ezra, *Japan as Number
  One* 136
Volcker, Paul, chairman of
  Federal Reserve 140

wages
  and cheap imports 63
  debt as compensation for low
    48
  and employment 168
  and liquidity trap 169
  and oil price rise 103
  pressure on 27, 40, *40*, *41*, 44,
    48, 105–6
Wal-Mart 10, 73–4
  Chinese goods 93
Wall Street crash (1929) 14–15
wealth, net 27–9
wheat, surpluses 102
workers, labour rights 9–10,
  192–3
World Trade Organisation 11, 92
  China as member 61, 76, 109
  Doha round 82

Yamaichi Securities, bankruptcy
  19
Yemen, oil 98